365 Ways to Cook Fish & Shellfish

Charles Pierce

A JOHN BOSWELL ASSOCIATES BOOK

 HarperCollins*Publishers*

HarperCollins books may be
purchased for educational, business,
or sales promotional use. For
information, please write:
Special Markets Department,
HarperCollins Publishers, Inc.,
10 East 53rd Street, New York, NY
10022.

FIRST EDITION

Series Editor: Susan Wyler
Design: Nigel Rollings
Index: Maro Riofrancos

LIBRARY OF CONGRESS CATALOG CARD NUMBER
92-54737
ISBN 0-06-016841-2

93 94 95 96 97 HC 10 9 8 7 6 5 4 3 2 1

Dear Reader:

We welcome your recommendations for future 365 Ways books. Send your suggestions and a recipe, if you'd like, to Cookbook Editor, HarperCollins Publishers, 10 East 53rd Street, New York, NY 10022. If we choose your title suggestion or your recipe we will acknowledge you in the book and send you a free copy.

Thank you for your support.

Sincerely yours,
The Editor

Acknowledgments

Many thanks to Trish Allen, whose participation in the creation of this book was invaluable. I couldn't have done it without her. Thanks also to Wes Albinger, who was as good a sport as any test taster could ever be; to Susan Wyler, who made the whole thing possible; to Tina Ujlaki and Richard Marmet, Mauny Kaseberg and all others who so readily gave me advice and consent.

I'd like to acknowledge the following concerns for their contributions of materials and information: The Catfish Institute; Raymond A. Dackerman from Ralboray, Inc.; Anthony Pettegrow from Trenton Bridge Lobster Pound in Maine; Handy Soft Shell Crab Co.; National Fisheries Institute, Inc.; South Carolina Wildlife and Marine Resources Department; Jake's Fish Market in New York City; Tammi Ratliss from Sea Farm Washington, Inc.; Seafest/Jac Creative Foods

About the Author

Charles Pierce is a New York City–based food writer and editor who was born and raised in Georgia. His love of food and gastronomy blossomed while working in the French cooking school La Varenne, where he earned the Grand Diplôme. He is a freelance writer and recipe developer for food magazines and cookbooks. He recently revised and updated an American classic, the *New Settlement Cookbook*.

Contents

1 Seafood Salads, Starters, and Appetizers

Everything to begin a meal, star at a light lunch, pass around at a cocktail party. Ideas range from Garlic Baked Clams and Crab-Stuffed Mushrooms to Fresh Tuna Salad with Olives and Chick-Peas and Salmon and Leek Tart.

2 Fish Soups, Stews, and Chowders

The best of the sea ladled into a bowl includes staples, such as New England Clam Chowder and Seafood Gumbo, as well as some new flavor combinations, such as Gingered Cream of Shrimp Soup and Seafood Gazpacho.

3 Fish in the Oven

Baked, stuffed and baked, and braised fish are all covered in this chapter. Mustardy Baked Bluefish with Capers and Olives, Flounder with Shiitake Mushrooms in Fresh Tomato Sauce, Halibut Parmesan, and Citrus Baked Sole with Orange are just several of the simple but savory selections.

4 Fish in the Pan

Blackened Catfish Fillets, Fried Clams, Flounder Piccata, Shrimp Tempura, and Tuna Hawaiian are some of the ways seafood in this chapter is stir-fried, pan-fried, sautéed, and deep-fried.

5 Flaming Fish

Quick and easy Broiled Snapper with Cilantro-Lime Butter, Grilled Mako Shark with Black Bean Salsa, Sizzling Skewered Shrimp, and Whiting Broiled with Soy Sauce and Sesame will send you running to light your grill or preheat your broiler.

6 On the Light Side

Steaming and poaching require no fat. Some of these recipes are completely lean; others have enriched sauces. Suggestions include Spicy Steamed Blue Crabs, Chilled Poached Salmon Steaks with Dilled Yogurt Sauce, Steamed Sea Bass with Beet Relish, and Steamed Scallops with Wilted Spinach and Lemon Cream Sauce.

Introduction

Like many Americans who grew up outside large urban communities, I didn't have a great variety of fish prepared in my home in inland Georgia. I mostly recollect the large fish fries where wide black skillets contained golden nuggets of catfish and egg-shaped hushpuppies submerged in bubbling, spattering fat. There were the somewhat steamy fish houses that sold the same kind of fare with lots of ketchup and paper cupfuls of tartar sauce. My parents liked to go fishing, so we occasionally had fresh bream, trout, or bass for dinner. Mackerel came up from warm Florida waters in the form of kingfish, a variety I'm partial to even today. Pompano was a special treat at the fancy restaurant in town. Waiters brought it out broiled on a plank, crisp and meaty, delightfully exotic to a budding eight-year-old gourmet. Shrimp was seen mostly at wedding receptions, sent down from the large Atlanta caterers, who mounded it in big bowls with cocktail sauce for dipping. We did have good oysters, though. They were the large, oily ones from Apalachicola which were perfect for frying and always seen, scalloped, at Thanksgiving. Food from the sea was exotica, not shunned by any means but not understood or treated with the same respect that we had for beef, pork, or chicken.

It was when as a young adult I studied cooking in France that I learned the subtleties of fish and seafood. Markets were full of an incredible array of gleaming, colorful fish set on beds of carefully raked or shaved ice. Oysters were piled high with all sorts of gradations and geographic designations; some opened to show off the plump flesh nestled in a briny shell of pearl-white perfection. Crabs, lobsters, langoustines, and crayfish were invitingly displayed, all pink and orange with strange appendages, begging to be bought. I was particularly impressed by the respect fishmongers gave their products. Handling was expert, attentive, and careful—a far cry from the dark, smelly fish stores I'd known at home. In the Paris cooking school I attended, the head chef was known for his affinity for seafood. There wasn't much delicacy in the nature of this rotund, fat-fingered fellow who could raise the ire of most of us who worked with him. To see him work so deftly with fish and shellfish made a deep and lasting impression that endures today. I was lucky enough to accompany him often to the large wholesale market just outside the city where, thanks to him, I came to understand fish. He taught me what to look for, how to appreciate seasonal bounties, and most important, how to cook what we found at the market in the most simple way.

My goal in *365 Ways to Cook Fish and Shellfish* is to help people overcome their fear of buying and preparing seafood and to offer easy, tasty ways to enjoy the great bounty of the sea. According to the National Fisheries Institute, U.S. per capita consumption of seafood has risen sharply in the last thirty years. In 1990, Americans consumed an average of 15.5 pounds per person of fish and shellfish compared with about 10 pounds in 1954. The trend is increasing and most industry experts believe the per capita consumption rate will increase to 20 pounds by the year 2000. At the same time, it is interesting to note that we eat less fish and seafood than people in many other countries of the world. Japan consumes more than 63 pounds of seafood per capita annually, for example.

Convenient and versatile, most fish and seafood take a comparatively short time to cook. Fillets and steaks are done in a matter of minutes, as are most kinds of shellfish. Even whole fish take a lot less time to prepare and cook than most meat and poultry dishes. And there are some good health considerations to keep in mind when choosing to cook fish.

Low in saturated fat, high in protein, providing all essential amino acids, full of vitamin B and minerals like iron, calcium, and potassium, and low in sodium, fish and shellfish are natural choices for the health-conscious consumer. And there is a new health factor to consider. By observing Eskimos in Greenland, scientists have discovered that a diet high in fish containing the polyunsaturated fatty acids called omega-3s can reduce the rate of heart disease. In areas where fish consumption is especially high, like Scandinavia, Holland, and Japan, the rate of heart disease is low. The link found by researchers has been the omega-3 oils that are almost exclusively found in fish and shellfish. Oily fish like mackerel, anchovies, herring, salmon, sardines, and tuna have the highest amount of these acids. Moderate amounts of omega-3s are found in bluefish, bass, shark, swordfish, and trout. Crab, lobster, shrimp, mussels, and squid have fair amounts as well.

Shellfish has a reputation for being high in cholesterol. This is misleading, according to Anne M. Fletcher, who writes for the National Fisheries Institute. Fletcher says that shellfish got their unfair reputation because of outdated scientific methods that detected cholesterol-like substances called noncholesterol sterols as well as real cholesterol in shellfish. The result was that cholesterol readings for many shellfish were falsely high. It turns out that cholesterol accounts for only 30 to 40 percent of the total sterols in mollusks like clams, mussels, oysters, and scallops, which we now know to be very low in cholesterol. It's true that crustaceans, such as shrimp, lobster, and crab, do have certain relatively high amounts of cholesterol, but they are low in total saturated fat. The bottom line according to most experts is that because most shellfish *are* low in saturated fat, eating moderate amounts does not raise the blood cholesterol level. Even lobster and shrimp, which have a relatively high amount of cholesterol, are so low in saturated fat that they turn out to be a healthier choice than most cuts of red meat.

Buying fish need not be an overwhelming chore. There are over 200 species of fish that are known for good eating in the U.S. Some lesser-known fish are also less expensive and just as tasty as traditional favorites. In addition to our abundant supplies of fish from the wild, aquaculture has become a successful business. To keep up with increased demand, catfish, tilapia, sturgeon, salmon, oysters, shrimp, mussels, and trout are farm-raised in carefully monitored, clean growing waters. The chances of finding a source for some of these local, seasonal fish and shellfish as well as some of the farm-raised specialties are increasing. Look for more fresh fish in large supermarkets, in expanded sections of specialty food stores, and in local fish markets. And if you're lucky enough to have a sporting enthusiast who brings home a basketful of fish he or she has caught, so much the better!

No matter what kind of fish or shellfish is on the menu, there are some generalities to keep in mind when making your selection. If you live in a large urban center where there are several fish stores at your disposal, the most important rule is to know and trust your fishmonger. Just as the proprietor of a good wine store can make the right suggestion for a special meal, a trustworthy fish store clerk or owner can provide information on what is good on a particular day, what method is best for cooking which fish, and what to avoid. Most of us aren't lucky enough to have this sort of knowledgeable person on hand and are therefore left to our own devices. Selecting fare from the sea is pretty simple. Look for a gleaming, firm-fleshed fish with bright eyes. Avoid dull-looking fish with sunken, milky eyes. If possible, touch the fish. The flesh should spring back slightly and not be mushy. Odor is important. The fish should smell clean, oceanlike, and delicate. Scales should be tight and shiny. If there are gills, they should be a vibrant bright red. Fish fillets and steaks should be firm, moist, and translucent, not dry, listless, or discolored around the edges. Avoid cut fish that sits in trays of excess liquid. Many fish stores will fillet selected whole fish on the spot—always a better choice. Shellfish should be well cared for and set on beds of ice. Bivalves should be tightly closed but alive. Lobsters and crab should be kept in clean, deep tanks. Look for shrimp that glisten and are firm, not mushy and limp.

Thanks to modern methods of fishing, many catches are processed on board ship and frozen with surprisingly good results. A flash-frozen fish just out of the ocean is sometimes better than one that has been sitting in boxes and languidly taken to shore to be cleaned, gutted, and cut into fillets two days later. Most frozen fish is boxed, making careful inspection difficult to achieve. Avoid boxes that have been torn, are crushed, or have ice around the edges. This could mean that the fish has been defrosted and frozen again, which could result in spoilage or at best a dry and tasteless product. Most frozen fish comes in blocks of ice and likes to be defrosted slowly, overnight in the refrigerator if possible. The process can be speeded along by setting it under cold running water or by using the microwave to at least melt away the surrounding ice. Shrimp freezes well, and most of what we see in the marketplace has been frozen somewhere along the way. Crab is sometimes found frozen, but because it tends to deteriorate relatively quickly, it is more likely to be preserved in cans. Imported lobster tails are sold frozen and need to be defrosted slowly in the refrigerator.

Once purchased, whole fish should be wrapped in plastic and kept on ice until ready to use. If it is fresh and has been properly handled, gutted whole fish can be kept for up to five days in the coldest part of the refrigerator. Fillets and steaks are perishable and should be consumed within a day or two of purchasing. Wrap them well in plastic wrap and keep as cold as possible. Keep shrimp, crabs, mussels, and clams on ice in the refrigerator if possible and drain off melting liquid as often as possible. Lobsters can last a day or two refrigerated before cooking but are best when prepared right away.

Size, fat content, and texture are the most important characteristics when cooking fish. Certain techniques work better for some kinds of fish than for others. Oily fish like salmon, bluefish, mackerel, herring, and mullet have relatively dark flesh and pronounced flavor. Their natural juices prevent their drying out when baked or broiled with a minimum amount of moisture. Fish with a low fat content like cod, halibut, monkfish, snapper, sole, bass, trout, and tilefish need moisture and do well poached, steamed, or broiled if brushed lightly with oil or butter. Lean fish like catfish, flounder, cod, or whiting do well deep-fried. In the same vein, haddock, halibut, perch, pike, snapper, sole, tuna, swordfish, trout, and whitefish are good candidates for pan-frying with a bit of fat to prevent drying out. Almost any fish can be cooked in foil or parchment paper as described in Chapter 8, Seafood Under Wraps.

The amount of fish to buy depends on several factors. The method of cooking used, what other dishes are to be served, and the appetites of those at the table are important considerations. As a general rule, count on ¾ pound of whole fish with bone and head intact per person. For dressed or pan-dressed fish, count on ½ pound per person. For fillets or steaks, 4 to 6 ounces is the right amount. Count on 8 clams per person per serving, ¼ pound of crabmeat per person, and 1 whole small or medium live lobster per serving. One serving of oysters in the shell is 6; as for shucked oysters, count on ½ pint per serving. When buying shrimp, allow ⅓ to ½ pound headless shrimp per person, ¼ to ⅓ pound shelled and deveined shrimp per person, and ¼ to ⅓ pound cooked fish per person. The recipes in this book use these guidelines for serving portions.

I hope this book will encourage home cooks to enjoy the world of fish and shellfish. I've tried to keep the recipes simple and direct, not intimidating or overdone. Nothing is more fulfilling than preparing healthy, flavorful fare for friends and family. Let seafood become a part of this process.

Chapter 1

Seafood Salads, Starters, and Appetizers

A little of something good is always a great place to start. When it comes to a meal, fish and shellfish are always a harbinger of great things to come. Easy seafood salads, quick and delicious hors d'oeuvres, cold shrimp or crab with a spicy sauce are the kinds of starters that strike a balance when followed by a heavier main course. Susy's Fish Soufflé with Raw Tomato Sauce, hot, garlicky Snappy Snails, or a slice of quick Quiche from the Deep can be followed by a lighter main course for the same sort of evenly weighted menu planning.

Gravlax as well as Simca's Smoked Salmon Spread and the Sole Terrine with Broccoli and Cauliflower can be made in advance for a first course or a party. The Ponte Vedra Pizza can be a fun group-cooking project for a small gathering of friends or family.

Combining fish and seafoods with greens, vegetables, breading, pastry, eggs, and sauces, the recipes in this chapter make an excellent starting place for enjoying nature's bounty from the sea.

---

1 SMOKED SALMON CANAPÉS
Prep: 10 minutes   Cook: none   Serves: 10 to 12

4 ounces cream cheese, softened
1 teaspoon finely grated lemon zest
¼ teaspoon salt
⅛ teaspoon pepper
6 very thin slices of white, pumpernickel, or whole wheat bread

½ pound smoked salmon, thinly sliced
1 small red onion, finely diced
Sprigs of fresh dill

1. In a small bowl, combine cream cheese, lemon zest, salt, and pepper. Mix to blend well.

2. Remove crusts from bread and cut each piece into 4 squares. Cut salmon slices into pieces to cover squares.

3. To assemble canapés, spread a small amount of cream cheese mixture evenly over each square. Top with salmon. Garnish each piece with a sprinkling of diced onion and a tiny sprig of dill.

2   AVOCADO COASTAL DELIGHT
Prep: 10 minutes   Cook: 2 minutes   Chill: 2 hours   Serves: 4

1 pound bay scallops or	½ cup olive oil
halved sea scallops	1 tablespoon minced fresh
¼ cup white wine vinegar	oregano or ½ teaspoon
3 lemons	dried
1 teaspoon Dijon mustard	2 medium avocados
¼ teaspoon salt	1 head of leafy lettuce
⅛ teaspoon pepper	

1. Rinse scallops in water; drain well. In a large nonreactive skillet, combine scallops, vinegar, and ¾ cup water. Bring to a boil over high heat. Reduce heat to low and cook until scallops are opaque throughout, about 2 minutes. Drain and spread on paper towels to absorb moisture.

2. Squeeze 1 to 1½ lemons to yield ¼ cup juice. Reserve remaining lemons. In a small mixing bowl, combine mustard, salt, and pepper. Add lemon juice and whisk until salt is dissolved. Gradually whisk in olive oil until smooth and blended. Add oregano and scallops. Stir gently to coat. Cover and refrigerate until chilled, at least 2 hours or overnight, stirring occasionally.

3. Just before serving, cut avocados in half. Remove and discard pits. Arrange avocado halves on large plates lined with lettuce leaves. Divide scallop mixture evenly among avocado halves, allowing some to spill over onto lettuce. Cut reserved lemons into wedges and use as garnish.

3   SIMCA'S SMOKED SALMON SPREAD
Prep: 10 minutes   Cook: none   Serves: 10 to 12

This is closely adapted from one of my favorite recipes of Simone Beck, affectionately known as Simca, who was a teacher and cookbook writer from France. She inspired many food enthusiasts and mixed extraordinary taste with a penchant for simplicity. Serve her smoked salmon spread with toasts, bread rounds, or crackers.

1 (8-ounce) can salmon	½ teaspoon salt
8 ounces smoked salmon,	¼ teaspoon pepper
cut into ½-inch pieces	Dash of cayenne
2 sticks (8 ounces) butter,	¼ cup vodka
slightly softened	Sprigs of fresh dill or
2 tablespoons chopped fresh	parsley
dill or 2 teaspoons dried	

1. Pick through canned salmon to remove any skin and bones and drain on paper towels. In a food processor, combine canned salmon with smoked salmon and puree until smooth.

2. Add butter, dill, salt, pepper, cayenne, and vodka and process again until very smooth. Garnish with sprigs of dill.

4   CRAB CAKES

Prep: 5 minutes   Cook: 6 minutes   Serves: 4

4 tablespoons unsalted butter	1 teaspoon grated lemon zest
1 small onion, finely chopped	1 tablespoon fresh lemon
1 celery rib, finely chopped	juice
½ garlic clove, minced	½ teaspoon salt
1 pound fresh lump crabmeat	¼ teaspoon pepper
1 cup fresh bread crumbs	1 cup cornmeal
1 tablespoon chopped parsley	2 tablespoons vegetable oil

1. Melt 2 tablespoons butter in a medium skillet. Add onion, celery, and garlic. Cook over medium-high heat until softened but not browned, about 3 minutes.

2. In a large mixing bowl, combine crabmeat, bread crumbs, parsley, lemon zest, lemon juice, salt, pepper, and cooked onion, celery, and garlic. Stir gently to blend. Using wet hands, form into 8 small cakes about 2 inches in diameter. Place cornmeal in a shallow bowl and dredge each crab cake in cornmeal to coat.

3. In a large skillet, melt remaining 2 tablespoons butter in oil over high heat. Add crab cakes and cook, turning once, until golden brown, about 1½ minutes per side.

5   SALMON CAVIAR POTATO BOATS

Prep: 10 minutes   Cook: 55 to 75 minutes   Serves: 4

This first course can be prepared ahead through step 2. Set aside at room temperature for up to two hours or cover and refrigerate for up to a day.

2 large baking potatoes,	½ teaspoon salt
scrubbed and dried	¼ teaspoon freshly ground
1 teaspoon olive oil	pepper
2 tablespoons butter	4 ounces salmon caviar
½ cup milk	Sour cream
2 tablespoons chopped chives	

1. Preheat oven to 375°F. Grease each potato lightly with ½ teaspoon olive oil. Place on a small baking sheet and bake until soft, 45 minutes to 1 hour. Cut potatoes in half lengthwise and let cool slightly. Leave oven on.

2. Use a spoon to scoop out pulp, leaving a ¼-inch-thick shell. In a medium bowl, combine potato, butter, milk, chives, salt, and pepper. Mix with a fork until well blended. Refill shells with potato mixture and return to baking sheet.

3. Bake until warmed through and lightly browned on top, 10 to 15 minutes. Remove from oven and, while hot, top with equal portions of salmon caviar. Serve with a heaping bowl of sour cream on the side.

6   OYSTERS ROCKEFELLER

Prep: 15 minutes   Cook: 7 to 8 minutes   Serves: 6

Rock salt or kosher salt
6 tablespoons unsalted butter, softened
1 tablespoon lemon juice
1 tablespoon chopped parsley
¼ teaspoon salt
⅛ teaspoon cayenne
24 oysters, opened, bottom shells reserved

½ cup cooked fresh or frozen spinach, squeezed dry and finely chopped
6 slices of crisply cooked bacon, crumbled
1 cup fresh bread crumbs

1. Preheat oven to 375°F. Spread ½ inch of rock salt or kosher salt over bottom of a large baking dish. Place in oven and heat for 10 minutes.

2. In a small bowl, combine 4 tablespoons softened butter with lemon juice, parsley, salt, and cayenne. Mix to blend well.

3. Arrange oyster shells on top of hot salt, pushing them down to prevent tipping. Place 1 oyster in each shell and top with a spoonful of flavored butter. Add a scant teaspoon of spinach and a sprinkling of bacon to each.

4. In a medium skillet, melt remaining 2 tablespoons butter over medium heat. Add bread crumbs and cook, stirring, until lightly browned, 2 to 3 minutes. Sprinkle over oysters.

5. Bake in 375° oven until oysters curl around edges, about 5 minutes. Serve hot.

7   PIGGYBACK SCALLOPS

Prep: 5 minutes   Cook: 10 to 12 minutes   Serves: 4

This recipe can be doubled or tripled easily to serve at a cocktail party. If you do serve these scallops as a hot hors d'oeuvre, skewer them on toothpicks and pass on a platter.

1 pound sea scallops
¼ teaspoon freshly ground pepper
½ pound sliced bacon

Sprigs of parsley
1 small lemon, very thinly sliced

1. Rinse scallops and drain on paper towels. Season with pepper.

2. Preheat broiler. Cut each bacon slice in half crosswise. Wrap each scallop in a piece of bacon. Place on a broiling pan and broil about 6 inches from heat, turning, 10 to 12 minutes, until bacon is crisp and scallops are opaque throughout. Remove to drain on paper towels.

3. Divide among 4 individual serving plates and garnish with sprigs of parsley and thin slices of lemon.

8 CRAB CRESCENTS

Prep: 15 minutes   Cook: 10 to 12 minutes   Serves: 8

½ pound crabmeat
1 celery rib, finely chopped
2 scallions, thinly sliced
3 tablespoons melted butter
½ teaspoon salt
¼ teaspoon pepper

1 (8-ounce) package
    refrigerated crescent
    dinner roll dough
2 lemons, cut into wedges
    Sauce Gribiche (recipe
    follows)

1. Preheat oven to 375°F. In a medium mixing bowl, combine crabmeat, celery, scallions, melted butter, salt, and pepper. Stir to mix well.

2. Remove dough from package. Separate into 8 pieces and lay flat on a floured work surface. Use fingertips to form into rough triangles. Place 2 tablespoons of crab mixture in center of each. Beginning at short end, roll into crescent shapes. Crimp edges to seal in filling. Transfer to a large baking sheet.

3. Bake crescents 10 to 12 minutes, until golden brown. Transfer to individual serving places and garnish with lemon wedges. Serve with Sauce Gribiche on the side.

SAUCE GRIBICHE

Makes about 1½ cups

2 hard-boiled eggs, finely
    chopped
½ cup chopped red onion
¼ cup chopped dill pickles
2 tablespoons capers
1 tablespoon chopped fresh
    tarragon or 1 teaspoon
    dried

2 teaspoons lemon juice
½ teaspoon salt
¼ teaspoon pepper
1 cup mayonnaise

In a small bowl, combine eggs, red onion, pickles, capers, tarragon, lemon juice, salt, and pepper. Toss to mix. Stir in mayonnaise and blend well. Serve at once or cover and refrigerate until ready to serve.

9 PONTE VEDRA PIZZA
Prep: 12 minutes   Cook: 25 to 28 minutes   Serves: 4 to 6

1 recipe Pizza Dough (recipe
   follows) or 1 (10- to
   12-inch) store-bought
   pizza crust
1 small onion, thinly sliced
1 garlic clove, minced
2 tablespoons olive oil
2 ripe tomatoes, peeled,
   seeded, and chopped
¼ teaspoon crushed hot red
   pepper

½ teaspoon salt
¼ cup shredded fresh basil or 1
   teaspoon dried
½ cup shredded mozzarella
   cheese
½ pound medium shrimp,
   shelled and deveined
½ pound bay scallops or
   halved sea scallops
2 tablespoons grated
   Parmesan cheese

1. Roll out dough evenly into a 12-inch circle. Place on an oiled baking sheet or round pizza pan. (If using store-bought crust, follow package instructions.)

2. In a medium saucepan, cook the onion and garlic in olive oil over medium-high heat until softened, about 3 minutes. Add tomatoes, hot pepper, salt, and basil. Reduce heat to medium-low and simmer, stirring occasionally, until thickened, about 10 minutes.

3. Preheat oven to 425°F. Spread tomato mixture evenly over dough. Top with mozzarella, shrimp, and scallops. Sprinkle Parmesan cheese over top of pizza.

4. Bake until crust is brown and cheese is bubbly, 12 to 15 minutes. Cut into wedges and serve hot.

PIZZA DOUGH

1 (¼-ounce) envelope active
   dry yeast
¾ cup warm water (105° to
   115°F)

2 cups flour
1 teaspoon salt
2 tablespoons olive oil

1. In a small bowl, sprinkle yeast over warm water. Let stand until dissolved, about 5 minutes.

2. In a food processor, combine flour and salt. Pulse briefly to mix. With machine on, add dissolved yeast and process briefly to blend. Add olive oil and process until mixture forms a ball around blades. Continue to process for 30 seconds to knead dough.

3. Place dough in an oiled mixing bowl; turn to coat. Cover and let rise in a warm spot until doubled in bulk, 1 to 1½ hours. Turn dough out onto a floured work surface and knead a few times until smooth. The dough is now ready to use as called for in recipe.

10 HOT DIGGITY CLAM FRITTERS

Prep: 7 minutes   Cook: 2 minutes per batch   Serves: 4 to 6

1½ cups flour
2 teaspoons baking powder
½ teaspoon salt
¼ teaspoon pepper
1 egg
¾ cup milk
Vegetable oil, for frying
½ pound shucked fresh clams
or 1 (8-ounce) can whole
clams, drained and
chopped

2 tablespoons minced onion
2 teaspoons fresh thyme
leaves or ½ teaspoon
dried
Lemon or lime wedges

1. In a medium mixing bowl, combine flour, baking powder, salt, and pepper. In a small bowl, beat egg with milk until blended. Pour into flour mixture and stir quickly to blend. Do not overwork batter.

2. Pour enough oil into a deep-fat fryer or large heavy saucepan to measure 2 inches deep. Heat oil to 375°F over medium-high heat.

3. Add clams, onion, and thyme to batter. Drop fritter batter by tablespoons into hot oil without crowding and fry in batches until golden brown, about 2 minutes. Drain on paper towels and serve on a large platter with lemon or lime wedges.

11 SHRIMP COCKTAIL

Prep: 7 minutes   Cook: 3 to 4 minutes   Chill: 2 hours   Serves 4

Shrimp cocktail is an old-fashioned standby that is hard to beat. The same formula applies to oysters, crabmeat, and clams. Count on 2 to 3 oysters or clams or ¼ to ⅓ pound of lump crabmeat per person. For a more elegant sauce, try using 3 or 4 very ripe peeled, seeded, and diced tomatoes in place of the ketchup.

1 pound large or jumbo
shrimp
1 cup ketchup
2 tablespoons prepared white
horseradish

1 tablespoon Worcestershire
sauce
1 teaspoon lemon juice
Salt and pepper

1. Rinse and drain shrimp. Bring a large saucepan of salted water to boil over high heat. Add shrimp, return to a boil, and cook until pink and curled, 3 to 4 minutes. Drain into a colander and let stand until cool enough to handle. Shell and devein shrimp. Refrigerate until chilled, 2 to 3 hours.

2. In a small bowl, combine ketchup, horseradish, Worcestershire sauce, and lemon juice. Mix well and season to taste with salt and pepper. Divide cocktail sauce among 4 small ramekins or serving bowls. Surround with chilled shrimp.

12 CLAMS CASINO
Prep: 10 minutes   Cook: 12 to 16 minutes   Serves: 4 to 6

3 dozen littleneck clams,
    shucked, on the half shell
½ pound bacon, cut into
    ½-inch pieces
1 small onion, finely chopped
½ red bell pepper, seeded and
    finely chopped
½ green bell pepper, seeded
    and finely chopped

2 sticks (½ pound) butter,
    softened
2 teaspoons grated lemon zest
½ teaspoon salt
¼ teaspoon pepper
1 cup fresh bread crumbs

1. Preheat oven to 425°F. Arrange clams flat on one or two baking sheets.

2. In a medium skillet, cook bacon over medium-high heat until crisp, 2 to 3 minutes. Remove to drain on paper towels. Pour off all but 2 tablespoons fat.

3. Reduce heat to medium, add onion and bell peppers to bacon fat, and cook, stirring often, until softened, about 3 minutes. Remove to a small bowl and let cool.

4. In a medium mixing bowl, combine softened butter, cooked onion and peppers, lemon zest, salt, and pepper. Blend well.

5. Top each clam with 1 teaspoon of butter mixture. Sprinkle bread crumbs on top. Bake 7 to 10 minutes, until browned and bubbly.

13 CRAB-STUFFED MUSHROOMS
Prep: 10 minutes   Cook: 12 to 15 minutes   Serves: 6 to 8

1 (6-ounce) can crabmeat,
    drained
½ cup fresh bread crumbs
1 medium tomato, peeled,
    seeded, and finely
    chopped
1 tablespoon chopped parsley

1 garlic clove, finely minced
½ teaspoon salt
¼ teaspoon cayenne
24 large mushrooms, stems
    removed
¼ cup grated Parmesan cheese

1. Pick crab over to remove any cartilage or bits of shell. In a medium bowl, combine crab, bread crumbs, tomato, parsley, garlic, salt, and cayenne.

2. Preheat oven to 400°F. Fill each mushroom cap with about 1 tablespoon of crabmeat mixture. Place filled caps in a lightly oiled baking dish. Sprinkle ½ teaspoon Parmesan cheese over each. Bake until piping hot and lightly browned on top, 12 to 15 minutes. Serve warm.

14   SAUCY SHRIMP WITH FRESH SALSA

Prep: 10 minutes   Cook: 3 to 5 minutes   Stand: 1 hour
Chill: 1 hour   Serves: 4 to 6

4 medium tomatoes, finely
   chopped
1 small onion, finely chopped
1 medium green bell pepper,
   finely chopped
2 tablespoons chopped
   parsley

1 tablespoon lemon juice
½ teaspoon salt
2 pounds medium shrimp,
   shelled and deveined

1. In a medium bowl, combine chopped tomatoes, onion, and bell pepper with parsley, lemon juice, and salt. Stir to blend well. Let salsa stand at room temperature for 1 to 2 hours before serving.

2. Meanwhile, bring a large pot of water to a boil over high heat. Add shrimp and return to a boil. Let cook until bright pink and curled, 3 to 5 minutes; drain. Pat dry with paper towels. Refrigerate shrimp until chilled, 1 to 2 hours. Serve with tomato salsa for dipping.

15   JALAPEÑO SHRIMPIES

Prep: 10 minutes   Cook: 2 to 4 minutes   Serves: 4 to 6

Chili peppers are hard on sensitive skin. For ease and comfort, use rubber gloves for protection in this recipe.

12 jalapeño peppers
¼ pound goat cheese,
   softened
24 cilantro leaves
12 medium shrimp, shelled
   and deveined, tails intact

½ teaspoon salt
   Vegetable oil, for deep-
   frying
2 eggs
1 cup cornmeal

1. Remove stem end of jalapeño and hollow out inside with a small paring knife to remove seeds and whitish ribs. Using fingers, stuff each pepper with 1 teaspoonful of goat cheese and 2 cilantro leaves.

2. In a medium bowl, toss shrimp with salt. Force a shrimp deep into each pepper—work carefully to avoid splitting. Tail should extend slightly from end of pepper.

3. In an electric frying pan or large deep skillet, pour in enough oil to measure 2 inches deep. Heat to 375°F over medium-high heat. In a medium bowl, beat eggs with a fork until well blended. Cover bottom of a small baking pan with cornmeal. Dip each stuffed pepper into the beaten egg, then dredge in cornmeal. Fry in hot oil until lightly browned, 2 to 4 minutes. Drain briefly on paper towels and serve at once.

16   TABBOULEH TITANIC
Prep: 20 minutes   Soak: 20 minutes   Cook: 6 to 9 minutes
Serves: 4 to 6

Serve tabbouleh on a large platter lined with lettuce. Garnish with lemon wedges, tomatoes, and rings of green and red pepper.

1½ cups fine-grained bulgur
    (cracked wheat)
5 scallions (white part only),
    thinly sliced
2 cups chopped parsley
½ cup chopped fresh mint
2 ripe medium tomatoes,
    peeled, seeded, and diced
½ cup olive oil
2 tablespoons lemon juice
2 tablespoons red wine
    vinegar

1 teaspoon salt
½ teaspoon freshly ground
    pepper
1 dozen medium mussels,
    scrubbed and debearded
½ cup dry white wine
1 small onion, thinly sliced
½ pound small shrimp,
    shelled and deveined
½ pound bay scallops or
    halved sea scallops

1. Soak bulgur in cold water to cover until softened, about 20 minutes. Use hands to squeeze out excess moisture; place bulgur in a large bowl. Add scallions, parsley, mint, and tomatoes. In a small bowl, whisk together olive oil, lemon juice, vinegar, salt, and pepper. Pour over bulgur and stir well. Cover and set tabbouleh aside.

2. In a large nonreactive saucepan, combine mussels, wine, and onion. Cover and bring to a boil over medium-high heat. Steam mussels until shells open and meat pulls away, 3 to 5 minutes. Remove with a slotted spoon and let cool slightly. Discard any mussels that do not open. Strain cooking liquid through a fine-mesh sieve lined with a double thickness of dampened cheesecloth and reserve. Remove mussels from shells and set aside.

3. Pour mussel liquid into a medium skillet and bring to a simmer over medium-high heat. Add shrimp and cook until pink, about 2 minutes. Add scallops and cook until firm and opaque throughout, 1 to 2 minutes longer.

4. Add mussels, shrimp, and scallops with cooking liquid to tabbouleh and mix well. Serve at room temperature.

17   MINTED SHRIMP SALAD

Prep: 5 minutes   Cook: 6 to 10 minutes   Serves: 4

1 pound medium shrimp, shelled and deveined
1 pound fresh green peas, shelled, or 1 (10-ounce) package frozen green peas
1 teaspoon Dijon mustard
1 teaspoon white wine vinegar
1 teaspoon lemon juice
¼ teaspoon salt
⅛ teaspoon pepper
2 tablespoons olive oil
¼ cup mayonnaise
6 scallions (white part only), thinly sliced
2 celery ribs, finely chopped
2 tablespoons chopped fresh mint plus several mint sprigs

1. In a large saucepan of boiling water, cook shrimp until pink and opaque throughout, 3 to 5 minutes. Drain, let cool, and then cut into ¼-inch dice.

2. In a large pan of boiling salted water, cook peas over high heat until tender, 3 to 5 minutes. Drain and rinse under cold running water; drain again. Spread out on paper towels to dry.

3. In a large bowl, combine mustard, vinegar, lemon juice, salt, and pepper. Whisk to blend well. Whisk in olive oil. Add mayonnaise and whisk until smooth and creamy. Fold in peas, scallions, celery, and shrimp until coated with sauce.

4. Just before serving, gently stir in chopped mint. Serve slightly chilled or at room temperature, garnished with sprigs of fresh mint. Cover and refrigerate if made ahead.

18   GARLIC BAKED CLAMS

Prep: 7 minutes   Cook: 7 to 10 minutes   Serves: 4

Unless you are an expert at opening shellfish, ask your fishmonger to shuck for you, leaving the clams on the half shell. Baked clams are usually served as an appetizer. For a main dish, double quantities and serve with a green salad and bread.

2 dozen littleneck clams, on the half shell
1 stick (4 ounces) butter
2 garlic cloves, minced
2 tablespoons chopped parsley

1. Preheat oven to 425°F. Arrange clams flat on a baking sheet.

2. In a small saucepan, melt butter over low heat. Stir in garlic and parsley. Distribute this mixture over clams.

3. Bake 7 to 10 minutes, or until garlic butter is bubbly and clams are firm. Transfer to plates and serve hot.

19 HOT CRAB AND ARTICHOKE DIP

Prep: 3 minutes   Cook: 20 to 30 minutes   Serves: 6 to 8

Serve dip hot, right from the casserole, with crackers or toasts.

2 (6-ounce) cans crabmeat,
  drained and flaked
1 (14-ounce) can artichokes in
  water, drained and
  chopped

1 cup grated Parmesan cheese
⅔ cup mayonnaise
½ teaspoon pepper
½ teaspoon garlic powder

1. Preheat oven to 350°F. In a medium bowl, combine crabmeat, artichokes, Parmesan cheese, mayonnaise, pepper, and garlic powder. Stir well to blend.

2. Spread in a medium casserole and bake 20 to 30 minutes, until golden brown on top.

20 SNAPPY SNAILS

Prep: 5 minutes   Cook: 27 minutes   Serves: 4

There are special pans that hold snail shells in just the right position for cooking. If you're a real snail enthusiast, you might want to invest in such an implement. Serve snails with lightly buttered toasts or thickly sliced French bread for sopping up buttery juices.

2 sticks (½ pound) butter
4 garlic cloves, minced
4 shallots, finely chopped
1 teaspoon salt
½ teaspoon freshly ground
  pepper

¼ cup chopped parsley
½ cup dry white wine
2 (8-ounce) cans large snails
  with shells

1. In a small saucepan, combine butter, garlic, shallots, salt, and pepper and cook over very low heat until garlic and shallots are softened and flavors are blended, about 10 minutes. Add parsley and wine, increase heat to medium, and simmer for 5 minutes.

2. Preheat oven to 350°F. Rinse snails under cold running water and drain on paper towels. Place about ½ teaspoon of butter mixture in bottom of each shell. Place 1 snail in each shell and top with 1 teaspoon flavored butter. Arrange wide side up in a snail pan made especially for cooking snails. Alternatively, arrange snugly in the bottom of a 9 x 13-inch baking dish. Bake about 12 minutes, until hot and bubbly.

21 WARM COD AND WATERCRESS SALAD WITH WALNUT VINAIGRETTE

Prep: 7 minutes   Cook: 5 minutes   Serves: 4

2 bunches of watercress
1 pound cod fillets,
    cut into 4 equal pieces
½ teaspoon salt
¼ teaspoon freshly ground
    pepper
½ cup plus 1 tablespoon
    walnut oil or extra virgin
    olive oil

3 tablespoons white wine
    vinegar
2 tablespoons chopped
    cilantro or parsley

1. Remove tough stems from watercress. Rinse well and dry in a salad spinner. Spread out on a large serving platter.

2. Season cod fillets with half of salt and pepper. Pour ½ inch of water into a large skillet. Bring to a simmer over medium heat. Reduce heat to low, add fish, cover, and gently poach fillets until firm to the touch and opaque throughout, about 5 minutes. Lift carefully with a slotted spatula and drain off liquid. Gently place the hot fillets on top of watercress.

3. In a small bowl, whisk together oil, vinegar, and remaining salt and pepper. Spoon a small amount of vinaigrette over each fillet and sprinkle with chopped cilantro. Serve remaining vinaigrette on the side.

22 CRAB AND BRIE STUFFED MUSHROOMS

Prep: 10 minutes   Cook: 10 minutes   Serves: 10 to 12

1 tablespoon olive oil
1 pound mushrooms
½ teaspoon salt
¼ teaspoon black pepper

½ pound crabmeat
½ pound Brie
2 tablespoons chopped
    parsley

1. Preheat oven to 375°F. Brush a large baking dish with olive oil. Remove stems from mushrooms and reserve for another use. Wipe caps clean with a damp cloth. Season cavities with salt and pepper.

2. Separate crab into ½-inch morsels, discarding any cartilage. Cut Brie into ½-inch pieces. Fill each mushroom cap halfway with crab and top with a piece of Brie. Place in greased baking dish.

3. Bake until cheese is bubbly and lightly browned, about 10 minutes. Garnish stuffed mushroom caps with chopped parsley and serve while hot.

23   FRESH TUNA SALAD WITH OLIVES AND CHICK-PEAS

Prep: 10 minutes   Cook: 10 minutes   Serves: 8

Vegetable cooking spray
1 pound fresh tuna steaks, cut about 1 inch thick
1 tablespoon Dijon mustard
¼ teaspoon ground cumin
¼ teaspoon salt
⅛ teaspoon pepper
1 tablespoon red wine vinegar
1 teaspoon lemon juice
½ cup olive oil
1 cup oil-cured black olives, pitted and coarsely chopped

1 cup canned chick-peas (garbanzo beans), rinsed and drained
10 small cherry tomatoes, halved
2 tablespoons chopped parsley
2 teaspoons chopped fresh rosemary or 1 teaspoon dried

1. Coat a large heavy skillet with vegetable cooking spray. Add tuna and cook over medium-high heat, turning once, until lightly browned outside and just done in center but still moist, about 5 minutes on each side. Remove to a plate and let cool. When cool enough to handle, use your fingers to break into 1-inch pieces.

2. In a large bowl, combine mustard, cumin, salt, and pepper. Add vinegar and lemon juice. Stir to dissolve salt. Gradually whisk in olive oil until sauce is smooth and blended. Add tuna, olives, chick-peas, tomatoes, parsley, and rosemary. Gently stir to coat ingredients with sauce. Serve at room temperature.

24   BAHAMIAN CONCH FRITTERS

Prep: 7 minutes   Cook: 2 minutes per batch   Serves: 4 to 6

1½ cups flour
2 teaspoons baking powder
½ teaspoon salt
¼ teaspoon freshly ground pepper
1 egg
¾ cup milk
Vegetable oil, for frying

1 pound conch, cut into ¼-inch dice
2 tablespoons minced onion
½ teaspoon dried thyme leaves
Lemon and lime wedges

1. In a medium mixing bowl, combine flour, baking powder, salt, and pepper. Whisk gently to blend. In a separate bowl, beat egg with milk. Pour into flour mixture and stir quickly to mix evenly. Do not overwork batter.

2. Pour enough oil into a deep-fat fryer or large saucepan to measure 2 inches deep. Heat to 375°F over medium-high heat.

3. Add conch, onion, and thyme to batter; stir to mix. Drop tablespoons of fritter batter into hot oil in batches without crowding. Fry, turning once, until golden brown, about 2 minutes. Drain on paper towels and serve on a large platter with lemon and lime wedges.

---

25 SALMON AND LEEK TART

Prep: 25 minutes   Chill: 30 minutes   Cook: 35 to 45 minutes
Cool: 30 minutes   Serves: 6 to 8

1 (10-ounce) package frozen puff pastry, thawed according to package directions
2 tablespoons butter
3 medium leeks (white part only), rinsed well and cut into ¼-inch slices
½ cup heavy cream
¼ teaspoon salt
¼ teaspoon pepper
¾ pound fresh salmon fillet, preferably center cut
1 egg white, beaten with 1 teaspoon water
2 tablespoons grated Parmesan cheese

1. On a lightly floured surface, roll dough out to ⅛-inch thickness and use it to line a 9-inch tart mold with removable bottom. (Save trimmings for another use.) Prick bottom all over with a fork. Refrigerate for 30 minutes.

2. In a large saucepan, melt butter over medium-high heat. Add leeks and stir well. Reduce heat to low, cover, and cook, stirring occasionally, until softened, 5 to 7 minutes. Add cream and continue cooking until liquid is mostly absorbed, about 5 minutes. Season with salt and pepper, remove from heat, and set aside.

3. Lay salmon flat on a work surface, skin side down. With a sharp knife, cut crosswise on the bias into ¼-inch slices, detaching fish from skin as you cut. Keep refrigerated until ready to assemble tart.

4. Preheat oven to 425°F. Remove tart shall from refrigerator, prick again, and line with foil. Fill with pie weights or dried beans. Place in oven and bake until edges are browned, 12 to 15 minutes. Carefully lift out foil with weights and prick again. Brush lightly with egg white wash, return to oven, and bake until bottom is lightly browned, about 3 minutes. Remove from oven and let cool slightly. Reduce oven temperature to 375°.

5. Spoon half of leek mixture over bottom of shell. Arrange salmon slices over leeks, slightly overlapping if necessary. Spread remaining leek mixture over fish. Sprinkle with cheese.

6. Bake until cheese is melted and lightly browned on top, 10 to 15 minutes. Let cool on a wire rack for at least 30 minutes before serving. Serve at room temperature.

26 GRAVLAX

Prep: 30 minutes   Cook: none   Cure: 2 days   Serves: 10 to 15

Scaling salmon at home can be a messy job. To save time and trouble, ask your fishmonger to prepare the fish for curing. Serve gravlax with black bread and honey mustard as an appetizer.

A word of warning for the cautious: Curing is not as effective as cooking when it comes to killing parasites and bacteria. If you consider the consumption of uncooked fish undesirable, gravlax is a recipe you might want to avoid.

2 (1¼-pound) fillets of center-
   cut salmon, scaled
½ cup salt
½ cup sugar

1 teaspoon coarsely cracked
   black pepper
2 cups chopped fresh dill

1. Remove small bones from salmon with tweezers and pat fish dry. In a small bowl, combine salt, sugar, and pepper. Stir to mix well.

2. Sprinkle ⅓ cup of seasoning mixture over bottom of a glass baking dish large enough to hold 1 fillet flat. Place 1 salmon fillet skin side down in dish. Sprinkle 1 cup dill and another ⅓ cup seasoning mixture over fish. Top with second piece of salmon skin side up. Cover with remaining dill and remaining ⅓ cup seasoning mixture. Cover dish tightly with plastic wrap.

3. Place a small chopping board, a flat platter, or a large plate on top of salmon and weight down with heavy cans, bottles, pie weights, large stones, or a brick. Refrigerate for at least 2 days and up to 2 weeks, turning fillets over (the two pieces still flesh to flesh) and basting with accumulated juices daily.

4. To serve, carve into very thin slices, cutting against the grain with a very sharp knife.

27   SUSY'S FISH SOUFFLÉ WITH RAW TOMATO SAUCE

Prep: 15 minutes   Cook: 45 to 58 minutes   Serves: 4

3 medium tomatoes
2 tablespoons balsamic vinegar
2 tablespoons olive oil
½ teaspoon fresh thyme leaves or ¼ teaspoon dried
½ teaspoon salt
¼ teaspoon pepper

1½ pounds cod fillet
½ small onion, sliced
2 cups milk
3 tablespoons unsalted butter
3 tablespoons flour
4 whole eggs, separated
1 egg white

1. Core tomatoes, cut in half, and squeeze gently to remove seeds. Coarsely chop and place in a mixing bowl. Stir in vinegar and olive oil. Season with thyme, ¼ teaspoon salt, and ⅛ teaspoon pepper. Set raw tomato sauce aside at room temperature; do not refrigerate.

2. Lay fish flat in a large skillet. Add onion and pour in milk. Bring to a boil over medium-high heat. Immediately reduce heat to low and simmer 5 minutes. Use 2 spatulas to turn fish over and simmer until firm and opaque throughout, 5 to 7 minutes longer. Remove with a slotted spatula and drain on paper towels. Reserve cooking liquid.

3. Preheat oven to 375°F. Butter a ½-quart soufflé dish and set aside. In a medium saucepan, melt butter over medium-high heat. Add flour and cook, whisking, 1 minute. Strain in reserved cooking liquid. Bring to a boil, whisking until smooth and thickened, 1 to 2 minutes. Reduce heat to low and simmer for 3 minutes, stirring often. Season with remaining salt and pepper. Remove from heat and beat in egg yolks, one at a time. Using your fingers, break fish into small pieces, discarding any bones. Stir fish into sauce.

4. In a large mixing bowl, beat 5 egg whites until stiff but not dry. Stir about ¼ of beaten egg whites into sauce with fish to lighten mixture. Gently fold in remaining whites, being careful not to overmix. Pour into prepared soufflé dish.

5. Place in center of preheated oven and bake 30 to 40 minutes, or until puffed and golden brown on top and set in the middle. Serve with tomato sauce on the side.

28 QUICHE FROM THE DEEP

Prep: 20 minutes   Chill: 1 hour   Cook: 53 to 60 minutes
Serves: 6 to 8

Food Processor Flaky Pastry
  (recipe follows)
1 pound mussels
¼ cup Fish Stock (page 33), dry
  white wine, bottled clam
  juice, or water

1 pound medium shrimp,
  shelled and deveined
1 pound scallops
3 eggs
1 cup half-and-half
⅛ teaspoon grated nutmeg

1. On a floured surface, roll out chilled pastry into a circle that is less than ¼ inch thick and measures 12 to 13 inches in diameter. Line a 10-inch pie plate with dough. Trim away all but ½ inch excess. Fold extra dough under edge and use two fingers or a fork to crimp edge, forming a decorative rim. Refrigerate for 30 minutes.

2. Meanwhile, preheat oven to 350°F. Scrub mussels with a brush and cut off hairy brown beard that protrudes from shells. In a large flameproof casserole or soup kettle, bring fish stock to a boil over medium-high heat. Add mussels and cover. Reduce heat to medium and cook, shaking pan frequently and stirring several times, until shells open, 5 to 10 minutes. Line a colander or sieve with a double layer of cheesecloth. Pour in mussels and all their liquid. Allow to strain through cloth. Remove mussels from shells and drain on paper towels. Discard shells and any mussels that do not open.

3. Rinse out mussel pot and return strained liquid to pan. Add shrimp and scallops. Cook over medium-low heat until shrimp are bright pink and curled and scallops are firm, 3 to 5 minutes. Remove with a slotted spoon and drain on paper towels.

4. Coarsely chop mussels, shrimp, and scallops. Pay dry with paper towels, then spread out over bottom of pastry shell. In a medium bowl, beat together eggs, half-and-half, and nutmeg until blended. Pour over seafood.

5. Bake 45 minutes, or until filling is set and firm. Insert tip of a sharp knife blade into center to test for doneness: it should come out clean. Let cool on a wire rack. Serve at room temperature.

FOOD PROCESSOR FLAKY PASTRY
Makes a 10-inch single crust

1½ cups all-purpose flour
1 teaspoon salt
4 tablespoons butter, cut into
  small pieces

3 tablespoons solid vegetable
  shortening, chilled
3 tablespoons ice water

1. In a food processor, combine flour and salt. Pulse briefly to mix. Add butter and shortening. Process in several quick, short pulses until mixture is crumbly and resembles texture of coarse meal. With machine on, add ice water all at once. Process just until dough begins to form in a ball around blade.

2. Empty dough onto a floured work surface. Knead gently into a round, smooth ball. Wrap in plastic and refrigerate for at least 30 minutes before rolling out.

29 SUMMER FISH SALAD

Prep: 10 minutes   Cook: 17 to 20 minutes   Chill: 4 hours   Serves: 4

This delicate salad is best served with thin buttered toasts or good-quality crackers. Ripe tomatoes in season make all the difference in the world!

2 pounds firm white fish
   fillets (mahi-mahi, cod,
   halibut, scrod, monkfish,
   or orange roughy)
1 cup dry white wine
2 tablespoons olive oil
1 tablespoon lemon juice
2 tablespoons chopped capers
1 tablespoon chopped fresh
   tarragon or 1 teaspoon
   dried

¼ teaspoon salt
⅛ teaspoon pepper
⅛ teaspoon cayenne
4 hard-boiled eggs, quartered
2 large tomatoes, quartered
   Sprigs of parsley and thin
   slices of lemon

1. In a large nonreactive skillet, combine fish, wine, and 1 cup water. Bring to a simmer over medium-high heat. Reduce heat to medium and poach, turning once, until fish is firm to the touch and opaque throughout, 7 to 10 minutes. Remove with a slotted spoon and drain on paper towels.

2. Boil poaching liquid in skillet over high heat until reduced to ¼ cup and syrupy, about 10 minutes. Remove from heat and let cool completely.

3. In a medium bowl, combine reduced poaching liquid with olive oil, lemon juice, capers, tarragon, salt, pepper, and cayenne. Whisk to blend well.

4. Cut fish into large chunks. Add to bowl and toss gently. Cover and refrigerate until well chilled, 4 to 6 hours, gently stirring from time to time.

5. Mound fish salad in center of a large platter. Surround with alternating pieces of egg and tomato. Garnish with parsley and lemon slices. Serve chilled or at room temperature.

30 DILLED SALMON SALAD

Prep: 10 minutes   Chill: 1 hour   Cook: 8 to 10 minutes
Serves: 4 to 6

2 pounds salmon fillets,
skin attached
1 cup dry white wine
½ teaspoon salt
1 cup plain yogurt
2 tablespoons finely chopped
fresh dill or 1 tablespoon
dried, plus additional for
garnish, if desired
1 tablespoon red wine vinegar

Freshly ground pepper
4 scallions
1 medium cucumber
Curly or red-leaf lettuce
2 hard-boiled eggs, cut into
wedges
2 medium tomatoes,
quartered
1 lemon, halved lengthwise,
thinly sliced

1. Place fillets skin side down in a large skillet. Pour in wine and 1 cup water. Season with salt. Bring to a boil over medium-high heat; reduce heat to medium-low and cover. Cook until light pink and firm, 8 to 10 minutes. With a spatula, remove to paper towels to drain and let cool. Wrap in plastic wrap and refrigerate until well chilled, 1 to 2 hours. Then use fingers to remove skin and gently break fish into thin flakes, discarding any bones.

2. In a large mixing bowl, combine salmon, yogurt, dill, and vinegar. Carefully fold to blend. Season with additional salt and pepper. Cover and refrigerate.

3. Trim root ends of scallions and cut off all but 1 inch of green tops. Using a small paring knife, quarter scallion lengthwise about 1 inch from the end, leaving bottom white part uncut. Place in a bowl of cold water with ice cubes. Scallions will form curly frills in about 30 minutes. Remove from water and shake just before garnishing.

4. Just before serving, peel cucumber and cut in half lengthwise. Using a small spoon, scrape down the center to remove seeds. Thinly slice.

5. Mound salmon mixture in the center of a large platter lined with lettuce leaves. Surround with cucumber, eggs, tomatoes, scallions, and lemon slices. Garnish with dill.

31 SOLE TERRINE WITH BROCCOLI AND CAULIFLOWER

Prep: 18 minutes   Cook: 35 to 37 minutes   Serves: 4 to 6

The creative cook can make this a versatile recipe. Carrots, green beans, mushrooms, or even spinach could be used for a colorful variation. Another trick is to alternate sole and thin strips of salmon from center-cut fillets. The results are visually and flavorfully dramatic. A fresh tomato sauce is the perfect accompaniment.

1 small head of broccoli	½ head of cauliflower
2 eggs	¼ cup dried bread crumbs
1 teaspoon salt	4 gray sole fillets, about
½ teaspoon black pepper	7 ounces each

1. Preheat oven to 350°F. Butter an 8½ x 4½ x 2½-inch glass loaf pan.

2. Trim broccoli into 1-inch florets; discard stems. In a large pot of rapidly boiling salted water, cook broccoli until tender, about 2 minutes. Drain and rinse under cold running water. Drain again. Transfer to a food processor and puree until very smooth. (There should be about 1 cup puree; if you have more than this amount, reserve for another use.) Add 1 egg and pulse briefly to blend. Season with ½ teaspoon salt and ¼ teaspoon pepper. Transfer to a bowl and rinse and dry processor.

3. Trim cauliflower into small pieces, discarding tough stem. Cook in a large pot of boiling water until tender, 3 to 5 minutes. Drain and puree in a food processor. (There should be about 2 cups puree; save any excess for another use.) Add the remaining 1 egg and the bread crumbs, and season with remaining ½ teaspoon salt and ¼ teaspoon pepper. Set aside.

4. Cut all but one sole fillet in half lengthwise. Line buttered loaf pan with fish, shiny side up, ends overhanging. Overlap slightly if necessary; entire bottom surface should be covered with fish. Reserve any scraps and remaining fillet for top of terrine.

5. Spoon the broccoli puree into bottom of fish-lined pan; spread to cover evenly. Top with cauliflower puree and spread evenly. Fold over any overhanging ends of fish to cover puree. Cover the top with the remaining fillet and fill in with any scraps. Cover top with buttered piece of aluminum foil.

6. Set loaf pan in a larger baking dish. Pour enough boiling water into larger pan to reach halfway up sides of the terrine. Place in oven and bake 30 minutes, or until firm to the touch and cooked through. Remove loaf pan from baking dish. Carefully tilt loaf pan and drain off excess liquid. Turn out terrine onto a cutting board. Gently cut into thick slices and transfer to individual serving plates. Serve at once.

Chapter 2

Fish Soups, Stews, and Chowders

Fish soups, stews, and chowders are noble preparations that make good use of our bounty from the sea. A trip to a local fish market can become the inspiration for a delicious concoction made from what is available that day.

Fish soups can be either a first course or a main course, depending on how rich they are or the amount to be served. The base for many a good soup is fish stock (see recipe page 33). In most cases, an equal amount of bottled clam juice is a perfectly acceptable substitute, diluted with water or not as desired. A fish soup can be chunky with bits of seafood and vegetables, as in the Early Fall Fish Soup and the Portuguese Fish Soup, or it can be silky smooth and creamy like the Gingered Cream of Shrimp Soup or the Seafood Vichyssoise. Either way, the essence of fish and shellfish is subtle but intensely flavorful, a perfect combination for good soup.

The word chowder comes from the French *chaudière*, a large pot traditionally used for making stews. Fish chowders contain chunks of fresh fish in a flavorful base of broth and aromatic vegetables. Clam chowders are a special category. There are two kinds, each with its own devoted following. Manhattan Clam Chowder is tomato based and New England Clam Chowder is milk or cream based. There is nothing more satisfying than a simple chowder filled with chewy bits of tasty clams to ward off the cold winds of winter.

Fish stews like Bouillabaisse and Cioppino are hearty, earthy mixtures. The exception is Oyster Stew (a real misnomer), which is nothing more than plump oysters floating in a base of milk with a touch of butter.

Frozen, canned, and bottled convenience foods require little preparation and can be used to put together a fine soup with a moment's notice. Add thawed frozen fish fillets cut into chunks in place of some of the fresh fish called for herein when in a hurry. Substitute canned crab, shrimp, or clams for a quick shortcut.

Stir a tablespoonful of tomato concentrate into some of the soups, stews, and chowders in this chapter for color and enrichment. A spoonful of sherry will add depth to almost any soup. Remember that chopped fresh herbs are always welcome. A handful of this and a pinch of that make this sort of cooking a work of art. Use your imagination!

32   NEW ENGLAND CLAM CHOWDER

Prep: 15 minutes   Refrigerate: overnight   Cook: 30 minutes
Serves: 4 to 6

I borrowed the technique of using steamers rather than large quahogs and separating their soft and firmer parts from Judith and Evan Jones' Clam Chowder in *The L. L. Bean Book of New England Cookery*. This procedure is a bit time-consuming, but the results are authentic and worth the effort. Serve the chowder with saltines or oyster crackers.

4 dozen soft-shell clams, or "steamers," scrubbed clean	½ teaspoon chopped fresh sage or ¼ teaspoon dried
¼ pound salt pork, finely diced	1 bay leaf
1 medium onion, finely chopped	1 whole clove
1 medium celery rib, chopped	2 cups boiling water
2 large all-purpose potatoes, peeled and cut into ½-inch dice	4 cups milk
	2 tablespoons butter
	½ teaspoon salt
	¼ teaspoon pepper
	2 tablespoons chopped parsley

1. In a large soup pot or kettle, combine clams and 1 cup water. Bring to a boil over high heat, cover, reduce heat to medium, and steam until clams open, about 10 minutes. Let clams cool slightly, discarding any that have not opened. Remove clams from shells, holding them over pot as you work to catch juices. Separate soft part from hard part of clams and finely chop hard part. Set aside. Strain cooking liquid though a sieve lined with a double layer of dampened cheesecloth set over a bowl; refrigerate and reserve.

2. In a large heavy saucepan, cook salt pork over medium-high heat, stirring often, until fat is partially rendered, about 2 minutes. Add onion and celery and cook until softened, about 3 minutes. Add potatoes, sage, bay leaf, clove, reserved chopped hard part of clams, and boiling water. Reduce heat to medium and cook until potatoes are tender, about 15 minutes. Remove and discard bay leaf and clove. Add soft part of clams and set aside to cool at room temperature. Cover and refrigerate overnight.

3. The next day, stir in reserved clam juice and milk. Bring to a simmer over medium heat. Float butter on top and season with salt and pepper. Serve hot, sprinkled with parsley.

33   MANHATTAN CLAM CHOWDER

Prep: 12 minutes   Cook: 35 minutes   Serves: 6 to 8

3 dozen littleneck or
  cherrystone clams,
  scrubbed clean
1 cup dry white wine
¼ pound salt pork or bacon,
  finely chopped
1 medium onion, finely
  chopped
2 celery ribs, finely chopped
1 teaspoon chopped fresh
  thyme leaves or
  ½ teaspoon dried

1 (28-ounce) can Italian peeled
  tomatoes, drained and
  chopped
2 large all-purpose potatoes,
  cut into ½-inch dice
¾ teaspoon salt
¼ teaspoon pepper
2 tablespoons chopped fresh
  parsley

1. In a large soup pot or kettle, combine clams and wine with 2 cups water. Bring to a boil over high heat, cover, reduce heat to medium and steam until clams open, about 10 minutes. Let clams cool slightly, discarding any that don't open. Remove clams from shells, holding them over pot as you work to catch juices. Finely chop. Set aside. Strain cooking liquid through a sieve lined with a double layer of dampened cheesecloth set over a bowl and reserve.

2. In a large heavy kettle, cook salt pork over medium-high heat, stirring, until fat is rendered, about 2 minutes. Add onion and celery and cook, stirring occasionally, until softened, about 3 minutes. Add thyme and tomatoes. Pour in reserved clam broth and bring to a boil. Reduce heat to medium and simmer for 20 minutes.

3. Meanwhile, place potatoes in a large pot and cover with cold water. Add ½ teaspoon salt and bring to a boil over high heat. Reduce heat to medium and simmer until tender, about 20 minutes. Drain well.

4. Just before serving, add potatoes and reserved clams to soup. Gently heat over low heat but do not boil. Season with remaining ¼ teaspoon salt and pepper, stir in chopped parsley, and serve at once.

34   NEW ENGLAND FISH CHOWDER

Prep: 5 minutes   Cook: 20 to 23 minutes   Serves: 4

½ pound bacon, cut into 1-inch
   pieces
1 small onion, finely chopped
2 medium all-purpose
   potatoes, peeled and cut
   into ½-inch dice
2 cups bottled clam juice

2 cups milk
2 pounds cod fillets, cut into
   2-inch chunks
½ teaspoon salt
¼ teaspoon freshly ground
   pepper

1. In a large saucepan, cook bacon over medium-high heat, stirring, until browned and crisp, about 3 minutes. Remove with a slotted spoon to drain on paper towels. Pour off all but 2 tablespoons fat.

2. Add onion to bacon fat and cook over medium heat, stirring occasionally, until softened, 2 to 3 minutes. Add potatoes, clam juice, and milk. Bring to a simmer over medium-high heat, lower heat to medium, and cook 5 minutes.

3. Add fish and cook 10 to 12 minutes, or until potatoes are tender and fish is opaque throughout. Add cooked bacon and season chowder with salt and pepper. Serve at once.

35   SEAFOOD VICHYSSOISE

Prep: 1 minute   Cook: 5 minutes   Serves: 4

This soup is good chilled, too. After heating, transfer to a bowl and let cool to room temperature. Cover with plastic wrap and refrigerate until completely cold, at least 3 to 4 hours. Thin out with a small amount of additional cream if cold soup is too thick.

2 (10¾-ounce) cans
   vichyssoise soup
1 cup heavy cream
1 pound bay scallops or
   halved sea scallops

⅛ teaspoon grated nutmeg
¼ teaspoon freshly ground
   pepper
2 tablespoons minced chives

In a medium saucepan, bring the soup and heavy cream to a simmer over medium heat. Add scallops, nutmeg, and pepper. Cook until scallops are opaque and firm to the touch, about 5 minutes. Serve in warmed bowls and garnish each with chives.

36   BAHAMIAN FISH CHOWDER
Prep: 10 minutes   Cook: 38 to 43 minutes   Serves: 4

½ pound salt pork, cut into
    ¼-inch dice
1 small onion, finely chopped
1 medium green bell pepper,
    finely chopped
3 to 4 medium tomatoes,
    peeled, seeded, and
    chopped
2 all-purpose potatoes, peeled
    and cut into ½-inch cubes
    About 4 cups Fish Stock
    (recipe follows) or water

½ teaspoon salt
¼ teaspoon freshly ground
    pepper
2 pounds skinless grouper
    fillets, cut into 1-inch
    pieces
1 pound mackerel, cut into
    1-inch pieces
    Chopped parsley

1. In a large skillet, cook salt pork over medium-high heat, stirring frequently, until lightly browned and fat is rendered, about 5 minutes. Add onion and bell pepper. Cook, stirring occasionally, until softened, about 3 minutes. Add tomatoes and cook until slightly thickened, about 5 minutes. Add potatoes and enough stock to cover. Season with salt and pepper. Partially cover, reduce heat to medium-low, and cook until potatoes are tender, 15 to 20 minutes.

2. Add grouper and mackerel to stew. Simmer over medium heat until fish is opaque throughout, about 10 minutes. Season with additional salt and pepper to taste. Garnish with chopped parsley.

37   FISH STOCK
Prep: 5 minutes   Cook: 25 minutes   Makes: 1 quart

Lean white fish like sole, flounder, whiting, and sea bass have bones that make the best stock. Use head and tail for full effect. Rinse fish under cold running water before making stock. Do not cook for more than 20 minutes as bones can turn stock bitter.

2 tablespoons butter or olive
    oil
1 medium onion, finely
    chopped

1½ to 2 pounds fish bones (cut
     into 2-inch pieces)
½ teaspoon salt
¼ teaspoon pepper

1. In a large saucepan or soup kettle, heat butter or olive oil over medium-high heat. Add onion and cook, stirring frequently, until softened, about 3 minutes. Add fish bones and cook, stirring, 2 minutes longer.

2. Pour in 4 cups water and season with salt and pepper. Raise heat to high and bring to a boil. Reduce heat to medium and simmer, partially covered, for 20 minutes. Strain and let cool to room temperature if not to be used right away. Cover and refrigerate for up to 3 days or freeze for up to 2 months until ready to use.

38 BOUILLABAISSE

Prep: 10 minutes   Cook: 1 hour 35 minutes
Serves: 6 to 8

3½ pounds firm-fleshed, lean
      white "soup" fish, such as
      whiting, cod, bass,
      flounder, or haddock,
      cleaned and cut into
      2-inch pieces
¼   cup olive oil
3   medium onions, chopped
2   medium leeks (white part
      only), thickly sliced
1   medium fennel bulb,
      coarsely chopped
6   medium tomatoes, peeled,
      seeded, and chopped
6   garlic cloves, crushed
6   sprigs of flat-leaf parsley
2   sprigs of fresh thyme or
      ½ teaspoon dried
1   bay leaf

1   teaspoon salt
½   teaspoon pepper
      Several drops of hot pepper
      sauce
1   teaspoon saffron threads
8   to 10 small red potatoes,
      peeled and cut into thick
      rounds
1½ pounds monkfish, cut into
      6 to 8 slices
¾   pound hake, halibut, or
      tilefish, cut into 1-inch
      pieces
2   pounds red snapper fillets,
      cut into 2-inch pieces
      Thin slices of toasted French
      bread
      Sauce Rouille (recipe
      follows)

1. Rinse soup fish in cold water and drain. Cut into large pieces. In a large stockpot or kettle, heat olive oil over medium heat. Stir in onions, leeks, and fennel. Cook until softened, about 5 minutes. Add tomatoes, garlic, parsley, thyme, and bay leaf. Simmer until blended and slightly thickened, about 10 minutes. Add soup fish and 10 cups water. Bring to a simmer, reduce heat to medium, and cook for 1 hour. Pass through a food mill or strain in several batches through a sieve, pressing down on solids. Discard solids and return strained soup to pot.

2. Season soup with salt, pepper, hot sauce, and saffron. Bring to a simmer over medium heat and add potatoes. Cook until potatoes are partially tender, about 10 minutes. Add monkfish, hake, and red snapper. Cover and cook until fish is firm and translucent, about 10 minutes.

3. To serve, use a slotted spoon to transfer fish to individual serving bowls, distributing fish evenly. Add several slices of potato to each bowl, then fill with soup. Serve with thin slices of toasted French bread spread with Sauce Rouille.

SAUCE ROUILLE
Makes about 1½ cups

1½ cups mayonnaise
¼ teaspoon salt
⅛ teaspoon freshly ground
black pepper
¼ teaspoon crushed hot red
pepper

5 garlic cloves, coarsely
chopped
1 teaspoon lemon juice

In a food processor, combine mayonnaise, salt, black pepper, hot pepper, garlic, and lemon juice. Puree until smooth. If not to be served at once, cover and refrigerate.

39 MOUCLADE
Prep: 8 minutes   Cook: 11 to 14 minutes   Serves: 6 to 8

This is an adapted recipe from a wonderful French food writer who makes complicated dishes easy. Mireille Johnston's flair for that elegant but simple touch is reflected below.

6 pounds mussels, scrubbed
clean and beards removed
4 cups dry white wine
1 large onion, finely chopped
2 bay leaves
4 tablespoons butter
6 tablespoons flour
3 garlic cloves, crushed
through a press

1 teaspoon curry powder
1 cup heavy cream
½ teaspoon salt
¼ teaspoon freshly ground
pepper
2 tablespoons lemon juice
1 tablespoon chopped parsley

1. In a large nonreactive stockpot, combine mussels, wine, onion, and bay leaves. Cover and cook over high heat, shaking pan and stirring once or twice, just until mussels open, 5 to 7 minutes. Remove to a bowl with a slotted spoon and separate mussels from the shells. Discard any mussels that have not opened. Set mussels aside; discard shells. Strain cooking broth through a sieve lined with a double thickness of dampened cheesecloth.

2. In a large saucepan, melt butter over medium heat. Add flour and cook, stirring, until lemon colored, 1 to 2 minutes. Whisk in strained mussel cooking liquid. Bring to a boil, whisking until thickened and smooth. Stir in garlic and curry powder. Boil over high heat until slightly reduced, about 5 minutes. Remove from heat and stir in cream.

3. Just before serving, add mussels to soup. Bring to a simmer over medium-low heat. Season with salt, pepper, and lemon juice. Ladle into large soup bowls and garnish with chopped parsley.

40   CIOPPINO
Prep: 15 minutes   Cook: 32 to 36 minutes   Serves: 6

This is San Francisco's answer to Marseille's bouillabaisse. If crab is available and affordable, by all means add some to the cioppino in place of or in addition to the scallops.

24 small hard-shell clams, such as littlenecks, scrubbed clean
½ cup dry white wine
2 pounds cod, rockfish, or bass fillets, cut into 2-inch pieces
1 pound medium shrimp, shelled and deveined
½ pound bay scallops or halved sea scallops
¼ cup olive oil
1 medium onion, finely chopped

1 garlic clove, minced
3 medium tomatoes, peeled, seeded, and chopped
3 tablespoons flour
3 cups Fish Stock (page 33) or bottled clam juice
3 cups dry red wine
1 tablespoon chopped fresh thyme leaves or 1 teaspoon dried
1 tablespoon chopped parsley
1 teaspoon salt
½ teaspoon freshly ground pepper

1. In a large kettle, combine clams with white wine. Cook, stirring, over medium-high heat until heated through, about 2 minutes. Cover, reduce heat to medium-low, and cook until clams have opened, 5 to 7 minutes. Remove clams in their shells to a bowl and set aside. Discard any that have not opened. Strain cooking liquid through a fine-mesh sieve lined with a double thickness of dampened cheesecloth. Rinse out kettle and pour in strained liquid.

2. Add cod and gently poach over low heat until firm, about 5 minutes. Add shrimp and scallops. Cover and cook until shrimp are bright pink and scallops are firm, about 5 minutes. Remove cover and set kettle with seafood aside.

3. In a large saucepan, heat olive oil over medium-high heat. Add onion and garlic. Cook, stirring, until softened, about 2 minutes. Add tomatoes, increase heat to high, and boil until thickened, 3 to 5 minutes. Sprinkle on flour and stir to blend. Pour in fish stock and red wine. Bring to a boil, stirring frequently. Add thyme, parsley, salt, and pepper. Cook until mixture is thickened, about 10 minutes.

4. Divide clams in shells, cod, shrimp, and scallops among 6 individual soup bowls. Ladle hot soup over shellfish and serve at once.

41   SEAFOOD GAZPACHO
Prep: 15 minutes   Cook: none   Chill: 2 hours   Serves: 6

4 large very ripe tomatoes, peeled, seeded, and diced
3 scallions (white part only), thinly sliced
½ medium green bell pepper, finely diced
1 medium cucumber, peeled, seeded, and finely diced
1 garlic clove, minced
3 tablespoons olive oil

3 tablespoons red wine vinegar
1 (8-ounce) bottle clam juice, chilled
½ teaspoon salt
¼ teaspoon freshly ground pepper
½ pound cooked shrimp, shelled, deveined, and finely diced

1. In a food processor, puree tomatoes until smooth. Transfer to a large mixing bowl. Stir in scallions, bell pepper, cucumber, and garlic. Drizzle olive oil and vinegar over vegetables. Stir just to blend. Cover and refrigerate for at least 2 hours or up to 24, until well chilled.

2. Just before serving, stir in cold clam juice, salt, and pepper. Ladle into serving bowls. Top each bowl with diced shrimp. Serve at once, very cold.

42   SEAFOOD GUMBO
Prep: 7 minutes   Cook: 1 hour 13 minutes   Serves: 4 to 6

3 tablespoons butter
1 medium onion, finely chopped
2 celery ribs, thinly sliced
1 garlic clove, minced
½ cup raw rice
1 (28-ounce) can Italian peeled tomatoes, drained and chopped
1½ pounds okra, sliced
2 cups Fish Stock (page 33) or bottled clam juice

2 teaspoons filé powder
1 bay leaf
Several sprigs of parsley
1 teaspoon salt
½ teaspoon freshly ground pepper
Pinch of cayenne
½ pound crabmeat, flaked and picked over
1 pint shucked oysters

1. In a large saucepan, melt butter over medium-high heat. Add onion, celery, and garlic. Cook until softened, about 2 minutes. Stir in rice and cook until glossy, about 1 minute. Add tomatoes, okra, fish stock, filé, bay leaf, parsley, salt, pepper, and cayenne. Increase heat to high and bring to a boil. Reduce heat to medium-low and cook, partially covered, until thickened, about 1 hour.

2. Add crab and oysters, reduce heat to medium, and simmer until heated through, about 10 minutes. Season to taste with additional salt and pepper if desired. Serve very hot.

43   EARLY FALL FISH SOUP

Prep: 15 minutes   Cook: 22 to 27 minutes   Serves: 6 to 8

2 medium carrots, finely chopped
1 medium celery rib, thinly sliced
1 medium onion, finely chopped
2 tablespoons olive oil
3 medium tomatoes, peeled, seeded, and diced
6 cups Fish Stock (page 33) or water
   Salt and pepper

2 pounds lean, firm-fleshed fish fillets or steaks (cod, halibut, haddock, grouper, bass, or tilefish)
2 small summer squash, halved lengthwise and sliced
1 cup cauliflower florets
1 cup broccoli florets
1 sweet potato, peeled and cut into ½-inch dice

1. In a large soup pot or kettle, combine carrots, celery, and onion. Add olive oil and cook over medium heat, stirring often, until softened, about 10 minutes. Add tomatoes and cook until they begin to give off their liquid, about 2 minutes. Add fish stock, increase heat to high, and bring to a boil. Season with salt and pepper to taste.

2. Reduce heat to medium-high. Trim fish of any skin and bones, cut into large chunks, and add to pot. Add squash, cauliflower, broccoli, and sweet potato. Simmer until vegetables are soft, 10 to 15 minutes. Season with salt and pepper to taste. Serve hot.

44   GINGERED CREAM OF SHRIMP SOUP

*Prep: 10 minutes   Stand: 15 minutes   Cook: 9 to 10 minutes
Serves: 4 to 6*

1 (1-inch) piece of fresh ginger, peeled and minced
2 cups heavy cream
2 cups Fish Stock (page 33) or bottled clam juice

½ pound medium shrimp, shelled and deveined
3 tablespoons butter
3 tablespoons flour
½ teaspoon salt
¼ teaspoon white pepper

1. In a small saucepan, combine ginger and cream. Bring to a simmer over medium-low heat, remove from heat, cover, and let stand for 15 minutes.

2. In a medium saucepan, bring fish stock to a boil. Add shrimp, reduce heat to medium, and cook until pink and curled, about 3 minutes. Remove and reserve 3 shrimp for garnish. Add ginger cream to remaining shrimp and stock.

3. In a blender or food processor, puree soup until shrimp are very finely ground, about 30 seconds. Strain through a fine-mesh sieve, pressing hard on solids to extract as much liquid as possible. Discard solids.

4. In a large saucepan, melt butter over medium heat. Add flour and cook, stirring, 1 to 2 minutes without allowing flour to color. Whisk in strained shrimp mixture. Bring to a boil, whisking until smooth and thickened. Reduce heat to low and simmer, stirring occasionally, 5 minutes. Season with salt and white pepper.

5. Cut reserved shrimp into tiny dice. Ladle soup into warmed bowls and garnish with a pinch of diced shrimp.

---

45   SHE CRAB SOUP
Prep: 7 minutes   Cook: 13 to 14 minutes   Serves: 4 to 6

She Crab Soup is a South Carolina specialty. There are probably as many variations as there are species of crabs in the world. The trick to the authentic version is the crab roe, often unobtainable outside of a limited locale. If it can be found in your market area, by all means substitute ½ cup of the delicacy for the egg yolk in the following recipe.

5 tablespoons butter	1 small onion, finely chopped
3 tablespoons flour	1 small celery rib, finely
1½ cups half-and-half	chopped
1½ cups milk	1 pound fresh or canned
½ teaspoon salt	crabmeat, picked over for
¼ teaspoon pepper	loose pieces of shell
2 tablespoons dry sherry	1 hard-boiled egg yolk
⅛ teaspoon cayenne	

1. In a large saucepan, melt 3 tablespoons butter over medium heat. Add flour and cook, stirring, until lemon colored, about 2 minutes. Whisk in half-and-half and milk. Raise heat to medium-high and bring to a boil, whisking constantly until smooth and thickened, 1 to 2 minutes. Stir in salt, pepper, sherry, and cayenne. Reduce heat to low and simmer 5 minutes.

2. Meanwhile, melt remaining 2 tablespoons butter in a medium skillet. Add onion and celery and cook over medium heat until softened, 2 to 3 minutes.

3. Add sautéed vegetables and crabmeat to thickened milk and half-and-half. Simmer over low heat for 5 minutes. Force egg yolk through a sieve into soup and serve hot.

46   SHRIMP AND ZUCCHINI SOUP
Prep: 7 minutes   Cook: 12 to 15 minutes   Serves: 4 to 6

2 tablespoons butter
1 small onion, finely chopped
1 medium carrot, halved
  lengthwise and thinly
  sliced
1 celery rib, thinly sliced
2 medium zucchini, quartered
  lengthwise and cut into
  ½-inch slices
½ pound medium shrimp,
  shelled, deveined, and
  cut into ½-inch pieces

2 tablespoons flour
4 cups Fish Stock (page 33) or
  2 (8-ounce) bottles clam
  juice mixed with 2 cups
  water
1 teaspoon salt
½ teaspoon freshly ground
  pepper

1. In a large saucepan, melt butter over medium-high heat. Add onion, carrot, and celery. Cook, stirring occasionally, until vegetables are softened, 2 to 3 minutes. Add zucchini and shrimp. Cook, stirring often, until shrimp turn light pink, about 2 minutes. Sprinkle on flour, reduce heat to low, and cook, stirring gently, 2 to 3 minutes.

2. Pour in fish stock. Increase heat to high and bring to a boil, stirring constantly, until soup is thickened, 1 to 2 minutes. Add salt and pepper, reduce heat to medium-low, and simmer 5 minutes. Serve at once in warmed bowls.

47   PORTUGUESE FISH SOUP
Prep: 5 to 7 minutes   Cook: 34 minutes   Serves: 4

4 slices bacon, finely chopped
1 tablespoon vegetable oil
1 small onion, chopped
1 medium carrot, cut into
  ½-inch dice
1 celery rib, thinly sliced
1 garlic clove, minced
3 medium tomatoes, peeled,
  seeded, and chopped

1 cup thinly shredded kale or
  spinach
4 cups Fish Stock (page 33),
  bottled clam juice, or
  water
2 pounds cod, cut into 1-inch
  pieces
½ teaspoon salt
¼ teaspoon pepper

1. In a large nonreactive saucepan, cook bacon with oil over medium heat until fat is rendered, about 1 minute. Add onion, carrot, celery, and garlic. Cook until vegetables are softened, about 2 minutes.

2. Add tomatoes and kale to the pan. Cook, stirring, until greens are wilted, about 1 minute. Pour in stock or water, reduce heat to medium, and simmer gently for 20 minutes. Add fish, salt, and pepper. Cook for an additional 10 minutes, or until fish is firm to the touch and opaque throughout.

48   MUSHROOM CLAM SOUP
Prep: 2 minutes   Cook: 5 minutes   Serves: 4

Add a half pound of thinly sliced fresh mushrooms if time permits.

2   (10¾-ounce) cans cream of
    mushroom soup
1   cup bottled clam juice
2   (6½-ounce) cans chopped
    clams
½   teaspoon imported sweet
    paprika

¼   teaspoon freshly ground
    pepper
2   tablespoons chopped
    pimiento

1. In a medium saucepan, combine soup and clam juice. Bring to a simmer over medium-high heat, about 2 minutes.

2. Stir in clams and their liquid. Reduce heat to low, stir in paprika and pepper, and simmer until warmed through, about 3 minutes. Serve in warmed bowls and garnish each with a sprinkling of chopped pimiento.

49   BILLI BI
Prep: 15 minutes   Cook: 8 to 10 minutes   Serves: 6

6   pounds small mussels
2   tablespoons butter
3   medium celery ribs, thinly
    sliced
1   small onion, finely chopped

1   cup dry white wine
    About 4 cups heavy cream
½   teaspoon salt
¼   teaspoon white pepper

1. Scrub mussels and remove hairy brown beards.

2. In a large stockpot or kettle, melt butter over medium-high heat. Add celery, reduce heat to medium, and cook, stirring, until softened, about 3 minutes. Remove celery with a slotted spoon and set aside.

3. In the same pot, combine mussels, onion, and wine. Cover and steam over medium heat until mussels have opened, 5 to 7 minutes. With a slotted spoon or skimmer, remove cooked mussels in shells to a large bowl to cool. Discard any that have not opened. Reserve mussel juices in pot. When cool enough to handle, remove mussels from their shells. Reserve about a third for garnish. Save remaining mussels for another use.

4. Strain mussel cooking liquid through a fine-mesh sieve lined with a double thickness of dampened cheesecloth. Measure liquid and add enough cream to measure 6 cups. Pour mixture into a large saucepan and add reserved cooked celery. Stir in salt and pepper. Warm through over low heat; do not boil.

5. Ladle into warmed individual serving bowls. Garnish each bowl with 2 or 3 mussels.

50   SHRIMP BISQUE
Prep: 15 minutes   Cook: 33 minutes   Serves: 6

½ pound medium shrimp	6 cups Fish Stock (page 33)
2 tablespoons butter	½ teaspoon salt
1 small onion, finely chopped	¼ teaspoon pepper
1 medium carrot, finely	Several sprigs of fresh
chopped	thyme or 1 teaspoon dried
1 celery rib, finely chopped	1 bay leaf
½ cup raw rice	½ cup heavy cream
¼ cup Cognac or brandy	Chopped fresh herbs or
½ cup dry white wine	croutons, for garnish

1. Shell and devein shrimp; reserve shells. Cut shrimp into ½-inch pieces. Refrigerate shrimp until just before serving.

2. In a large saucepan, melt butter over medium-high heat. Add onion, carrot, and celery. Cook, stirring often, until slightly softened, about 3 minutes. Add rice and cook, stirring, until translucent, about 2 minutes. Add shrimp shells and stir until they turn pink, about 1 minute. Pour in Cognac. Standing away from pan, carefully ignite with a match. When flames subside, add wine, bring to a boil, and boil over high heat until reduced by half, about 2 minutes.

3. Pour in fish stock; add salt, pepper, thyme, and bay leaf. Bring to a simmer, reduce heat to medium, and cook, uncovered, stirring often, until rice is tender, about 20 minutes. Remove bay leaf.

4. Transfer to a food processor and puree, in batches if necessary, until smooth. If desired for finer texture, work the soup through a fine-mesh sieve, pressing down on solids to extract as much liquid as possible. Discard solids.

5. Pour the bisque into a saucepan set over medium heat. Add pieces of shrimp and cook until done, about 5 minutes. Stir in cream, season to taste with additional salt and pepper, and serve in a warmed tureen or individual soup bowls. Garnish with chopped fresh herbs or croutons.

Five Quick Soups

The following quick recipes use canned and bottled convenience foods. Because they require little preparation, these soups can be put together at a moment's notice with ingredients that the average cook has on hand. Use your imagination to enhance the versatility of these quick and easy recipes:

   • Add thawed frozen fish fillets cut into chunks for an extra dimension.

   • Substitute canned crab, shrimp, or clams where desired or, conversely, use fresh seafood in place of called-for canned ingredients.

   • Substitute cream for clam broth or clam broth for cream where desired.

   • Whisk in a tablespoonful of tomato concentrate for color and enrichment of flavor.

   • A spoonful of sherry will add depth to almost any soup.

- Chopped fresh herbs are always welcome.
- Garnish quick soups with golden croutons, chopped fresh tomato, thin slices of hard-boiled eggs, rings of red, yellow, or green peppers, chopped cucumber, or thinly sliced scallion.

51 ITALIAN CLAM SOUP WITH MUSHROOMS
Prep: 15 minutes   Cook: 12 to 15 minutes   Serves: 4 to 6

¼ cup olive oil
½ pound fresh mushrooms, halved
1 teaspoon salt
½ teaspoon freshly ground pepper
1 small onion, thinly sliced
2 garlic cloves, minced
2 medium tomatoes, peeled, seeded, and chopped

1 tablespoon chopped fresh oregano or 1 teaspoon dried
3 dozen small clams, scrubbed clean
4 to 6 slices of Italian bread, lightly toasted
2 tablespoons freshly grated Parmesan cheese

1. In a medium skillet, heat 2 tablespoons olive oil over high heat. Add mushrooms and cook, tossing, until golden brown, about 3 minutes. Season with ½ teaspoon salt and ¼ teaspoon pepper. Set aside.

2. In a large saucepan or flameproof casserole, heat remaining 2 tablespoons olive oil over medium-high heat. Add onion and garlic and cook until softened, about 2 minutes. Add tomatoes, oregano, clams, and remaining ½ teaspoon salt and ¼ teaspoon pepper. Add 2 cups water, raise heat to high, and bring to a boil. Reduce heat to medium, cover, and simmer, stirring once or twice, until clams open, 7 to 10 minutes. Discard any clams that have not opened.

3. Place a slice of toasted bread in bottom of 4 or 6 large soup plates. Use a slotted spoon to arrange clams on top. Surround with reserved mushrooms. Ladle hot soup over all. Sprinkle with cheese and serve at once.

52 CREAM OF LOBSTER AND TOMATO SOUP
Prep: 2 minutes   Cook: 2 minutes   Serves: 4

2 (10¾-ounce) cans tomato soup
1 cup heavy cream
1 cup cooked lobster meat, chopped

⅓ cup chopped fresh basil or 2 teaspoons dried
¼ teaspoon freshly ground pepper

1. Combine soup and cream in a medium saucepan. Bring to a simmer over medium-high heat.

2. Stir in lobster and warm through, about 2 minutes. Remove from heat and stir in basil and pepper. Serve at once in warmed bowls.

53   OYSTER STEW
Prep: 5 minutes   Cook: 10 minutes   Serves: 4 to 6

2 tablespoons butter
2 pints shucked oysters, with
    liquor reserved
3 cups milk
1 cup half-and-half
½ teaspoon salt

¼ teaspoon ground white
    pepper
Oyster crackers or soda
    crackers, as
    accompaniment

In a large saucepan over medium heat, melt butter. Add oysters and reserved liquor. Pour in milk and half-and-half. Season with salt and white pepper. Reduce heat to low and simmer gently until oysters begin to curl slightly around the edges, about 10 minutes. Serve in warmed bowls with crackers.

54   ZESTY CRAB AND CELERY SOUP
Prep: 3 minutes   Cook: 2 minutes   Serves: 4

2 (10¾-ounce) cans cream of
    celery soup
⅔ cup dry white wine
2 (6-ounce) cans crabmeat,
    drained

1 cup heavy cream
1 teaspoon grated lemon zest
1 tablespoon chopped parsley
¼ teaspoon pepper
Lemon slices, for garnish

1. Heat soup gently over medium-low heat. Stir in wine. Pick over crab to remove any bits of shell and add crab to soup. Stir in cream, lemon zest, chopped parsley, and pepper.

2. Reduce heat to low and cook until warmed throughout, about 2 minutes. Serve in warmed bowls and garnish with thin slices of lemon.

55   SHRIMPY BLACK BEAN SOUP
Prep: 5 minutes   Cook: 2 minutes   Serves: 4 to 6

2 (15-ounce) cans black bean
    soup
2 tablespoons olive oil
½ teaspoon freshly ground
    pepper
2 (4¼-ounce) cans shrimp,
    drained

2 tablespoons dry sherry
2 tablespoons chopped
    cilantro
1 small onion, finely chopped
2 small jalapeño peppers,
    halved, seeded, and
    thinly sliced

1. In a large saucepan, combine black bean soup, olive oil, and pepper. Bring to a boil. Add shrimp and sherry, reduce heat to medium-low, and simmer until shrimp are heated through, about 2 minutes.

2. Serve in individual bowls and garnish each with a pinch of cilantro, a sprinkling of onion, and several thin slices of jalapeño.

Chapter 3

Fish in the Oven

Bake fish in a hot oven for best results. Times vary according to the species and thickness of fish. A guide to cooking fish to perfection has been devised by the Department of Fisheries of Canada. Called the Canadian Cooking Method, it has been proven to provide excellent results. The principle is that fish is measured at its thickest point and cooked for 8 to 10 minutes per inch or fraction thereof. Simply lay the fish fillet, steak, or whole fish on a flat work surface and measure with a ruler at its thickest point. A piece of fish that is 1½ inches thick will require a cooking time of 12 to 15 minutes, for example. If a fillet measures ½ inch, cook it for only 4 to 5 minutes. This rule applies to all methods of cooking, but is especially useful when baking. Increase cooking time to 18 to 20 minutes per measured inch of thickness for frozen fish.

Most fish are delicate enough to be baked quickly, but hearty varieties like tuna, monkfish, and swordfish can be braised slowly in a minimum amount of liquid. Oilier fish do well in the oven. Good choices are bluefish, mackerel, mullet, and salmon. Leaner fish, such as hake, halibut, perch, pike, snapper, sea bass, swordfish, and cod, need to be brushed with butter or oil or else cooked with wine or a sauce to prevent drying out in a hot dry oven.

Whole fish can be stuffed with a variety of ingredients and baked. This makes an elegant presentation when the fish is served on a large platter surrounded by colorful garnishes of greens, tomatoes, and halved hard-boiled eggs.

56 BAKED CATFISH WITH SWEET RED PEPPER SAUCE

Prep: 5 minutes   Cook: 13 minutes   Serves: 4

2 tablespoons butter
1 large red bell pepper, thinly
   sliced
1 garlic clove, minced
1 small onion, thinly sliced
½ cup dry white wine

4 catfish fillets, 4 to 6 ounces
   each
½ teaspoon salt
¼ teaspoon pepper
1 tablespoon chopped parsley

1. Preheat oven to 425°F. In a medium skillet, melt 2 tablespoons butter over medium-high heat. Add bell pepper, garlic, and onion. Reduce heat to medium-low, cover, and cook until softened, about 3 minutes. Remove from heat and pour in wine.

2. Place catfish fillets in a 9 x 13-inch baking dish. Season with salt and pepper. Pour bell pepper and wine mixture over fish. Cover dish with aluminum foil.

3. Bake 10 minutes, or until fish is firm and white throughout. Remove fish to a serving platter and cover to keep warm. Transfer contents of baking dish to a food processor. Puree until smooth. Pour over fish and sprinkle with parsley. Serve at once.

57 BREADED CATFISH

Prep: 5 minutes   Cook: 10 minutes   Serves: 4

1 egg
1 tablespoon milk
1 cup fresh bread crumbs
2 teaspoons chopped fresh
   thyme leaves or
   1 teaspoon dried
2 teaspoons chopped fresh
   rosemary or 1 teaspoon
   dried

4 catfish fillets, 4 to 6 ounces
   each
½ teaspoon salt
¼ teaspoon pepper
2 tablespoons melted butter

1. Preheat oven to 450°F. In a wide, shallow bowl, beat egg with milk until blended.

2. In a separate shallow bowl, combine bread crumbs with thyme and rosemary. Mix well. Dip fish in egg mixture, drain off excess, then immediately dredge in bread crumbs to coat both sides. Arrange on a buttered baking sheet and season with salt and pepper.

3. Drizzle melted butter over breaded fish. Bake 10 minutes, or until coating is lightly browned and fish fillets are opaque throughout. Serve hot.

58 FILLET OF FLOUNDER WITH CARROTS AND SNOW PEAS

Prep: 5 minutes   Cook: 14 to 16 minutes   Serves: 4

4 flounder fillets, about
    6 ounces each
½ teaspoon salt
¼ teaspoon pepper
2 tablespoons butter
2 medium carrots, cut into
    ¼-inch dice

2 ounces snow peas,
    stemmed, stringed, and
    cut into long thin strips
    (about 2 dozen)
¼ cup dry white wine or water

1. Preheat oven to 425°F. Arrange fish flat in a single layer in a 9 x 13-inch baking dish. Season with salt and pepper. Set aside.

2. In a small saucepan, melt butter over low heat. Add carrots, cover, and cook until slightly softened, 3 to 5 minutes. Stir in snow peas, cover, and cook 1 minute longer. Remove cover and pour in wine. Bring to a boil.

3. Pour vegetable mixture over fish and cover dish loosely with aluminum foil. Bake 10 minutes, or until fish is firm and opaque throughout.

59 CODFISH GRATIN

Prep: 5 minutes   Cook: 16 to 19 minutes   Serves: 4

This simple recipe can be dressed up with a variety of ingredients. Add ¼ pound sliced mushrooms to the sauce before baking. Or slice a ripe tomato, layer over fish, and then pour on the sauce. Add a tablespoon or so of fresh chopped herbs to the sauce. A half teaspoon of grated lemon rind can add an extra dimension. This dish can be a great way to use leftovers. Keep in mind that any addition should be of a subtle flavor, so that it does not overwhelm the delicate fish.

3 tablespoons butter
2 tablespoons flour
1 cup Fish Stock (page 33) or
    bottled clam juice
1 cup milk
½ teaspoon salt

¼ teaspoon pepper
1½ pounds cod fillets, cut into
    2-inch pieces
1 cup fresh bread crumbs
½ garlic clove, minced
1 tablespoon chopped parsley

1. In a small saucepan, melt 2 tablespoons butter over medium heat. Stir in flour and cook until lemon colored, about 2 minutes. Whisk in fish stock and milk, increase heat to high, and bring to a boil, whisking until smooth and thickened, 1 to 2 minutes. Reduce heat to low and simmer, stirring, 3 minutes. Season sauce with salt and pepper.

2. Preheat oven to 425°F. Place fish pieces in one layer in a lightly buttered baking dish. Pour sauce over fish. In a small mixing bowl, combine bread crumbs, garlic, and parsley. Sprinkle over top of sauce. Melt remaining 1 tablespoon butter and drizzle over crumbs. Bake 10 to 12 minutes, until bubbly and lightly browned.

60 CORN AND FLOUNDER MEDLEY
Prep: 5 minutes   Cook: 16 minutes   Serves: 4

This is a recipe that can be adapted to suit the culinary purist or the quick cooker. For the purist: Substitute 1 whole red pepper, roasted and peeled, for the bottled pimientos. Fresh corn in season is always better than canned or frozen (unless you're in a hurry!) . . . ditto with green beans. Fresh flounder fillets can be used in this recipe as well. Reduce the cooking time by about 5 minutes.

½ **pound fresh green beans (about 1 cup), or 1 (10-ounce) package frozen**
2 **cups corn kernels, fresh, canned, or thawed frozen**
1 **(4-ounce) jar pimientos, drained and cut into small dice**

2 **medium tomatoes, diced**
¾ **teaspoon salt**
¼ **teaspoon pepper**
2 **tablespoons butter**
2 **(8-ounce) packages frozen flounder fillets, thawed**

1. Preheat oven to 400°F. For fresh green beans, bring a large pot of salted water to a boil. Add beans and return to a boil. Boil rapidly for 1 minute. Drain and rinse under cold running water; drain again. If using frozen beans, thaw completely but do not cook.

2. In a medium bowl, combine green beans, corn, pimientos, and tomatoes. Season with ¼ teaspoon salt and ⅛ teaspoon pepper. Spoon into a buttered 9 x 13-inch baking dish and dot with 1 tablespoon butter.

3. Arrange fish on top, overlapping fillets if necessary. Dot with remaining butter and season with remaining salt and pepper. Cover with aluminum foil and place in oven. Bake 15 minutes, or until fish is tender and opaque throughout. Serve at once.

61 MUSTARDY BAKED BLUEFISH WITH CAPERS AND OLIVES
Prep: 3 minutes   Bake: 10 to 15 minutes   Serves: 4

2 **bluefish fillets, about ¾ pound each**
¼ **cup Dijon mustard**
2 **tablespoons chopped capers**

10 **oil-cured black olives, pitted and chopped**
½ **cup dry white wine**

1. Preheat oven to 425°F. Arrange fish skin side down without overlapping in a small baking dish. Spread mustard evenly over fish. Sprinkle with capers and olives. Add wine to pan.

2. Cover with aluminum foil and bake 10 to 15 minutes, or until fish is firm and flakes easily when tested with a fork. Cut each fillet in half and serve at once.

62   BAKED FLOUNDER WITH CUCUMBER AND MINT

Prep: 3 minutes   Cook: 13 to 15 minutes   Serves: 4

Mint loses its aromatic quality quickly, so for best flavor, chop the mint just before serving.

1 large cucumber, peeled,
   seeded, and very thinly
   sliced
1 tablespoon rice wine
   vinegar
4 flounder fillets, 6 to 8 ounces
   each, halved lengthwise

½ teaspoon salt
¼ teaspoon pepper
⅓ cup dry white wine or water
2 tablespoons chopped fresh
   mint leaves

1. Preheat oven to 425°F. In a large ovenproof skillet or oval flameproof gratin dish, combine cucumber, vinegar, and 2 tablespoons water. Cook over medium heat, stirring often, until cucumber is tender and most of liquid has evaporated, 3 to 5 minutes.

2. Arrange flounder fillets on top of cucumber slices. Season with salt and pepper. Pour on wine and cover tightly with aluminum foil.

3. Bake 10 minutes, or until fish is white, firm, and cooked through. Remove fish to individual serving plates and surround with cucumbers. Garnish with mint just before serving.

63   BAKED FISH WITH MUSHROOMS AND WHITE WINE

Prep: 5 minutes   Cook: 10 minutes   Serves: 4 to 6

2 tablespoons butter, softened
2 shallots, minced
4 medium mushrooms, thinly
   sliced
1 tablespoon lemon juice

2 pounds flounder or sole
   fillets
½ teaspoon salt
¼ teaspoon pepper
½ cup dry white wine

1. Preheat oven to 450°F. Spread softened butter over bottom of a 9 x 13-inch baking dish. Sprinkle shallots over bottom. In a small bowl, toss mushrooms with lemon juice. Set aside for 5 minutes, stirring gently once or twice.

2. Fold fish into small bundles by bringing tops and bottoms of fillets to meet in center, folding in thirds. Each bundle should be of uniform shape and size to ensure even cooking. Arrange in baking dish seam side down. Scatter mushrooms over fish and pour on wine. Loosely cover dish with aluminum foil.

3. Bake 10 minutes, or until fish is opaque throughout. Transfer fillets to a warm serving platter and spoon mushrooms and cooking juices over fish. Serve at once.

64 COD FILLETS WITH CREAMY LEEKS
Prep: 3 minutes   Cook: 24 to 30 minutes   Serves: 4

5 medium leeks, white and
    tender part of green
2 tablespoons butter
1 cup heavy cream

½ teaspoon salt
¼ teaspoon pepper
1½ pounds cod fillets, cut into
    4 equal pieces

1. Split leeks in half lengthwise and clean well under cold running water. Cut into ¼-inch slices. In a large saucepan, melt butter over medium-high heat. Add leeks and stir to coat. Reduce heat to low, cover, and cook, stirring often, until tender but not brown, 7 to 10 minutes.

2. Preheat oven to 450°F. Add cream to leeks. Raise heat to high and boil, stirring often, until thickened, about 5 minutes. Season with half of salt and pepper.

3. Scrape leeks into a 9 x 13-inch baking dish. Place fish on top, season with remaining salt and pepper, and cover dish with aluminum foil. Bake 12 to 15 minutes, or until cod is opaque throughout and firm to the touch.

65 SEAFOOD-STUFFED CABBAGE ROLLS WITH TOMATO SAUCE
Prep: 15 minutes   Cook: 28 to 33 minutes   Serves: 4

2 tablespoons olive oil
1 medium onion, finely
    chopped
1 medium celery rib, finely
    chopped
3 medium tomatoes, peeled,
    seeded, and coarsely
    chopped
¾ teaspoon salt
¼ teaspoon pepper

1 large head of cabbage
¾ pound firm-fleshed fish
    fillets (weakfish, scrod,
    flounder, or cod)
½ pound bay scallops or
    halved sea scallops
¼ cup chopped mixed fresh
    herbs (thyme, parsley,
    basil, and/or chives) or
    1 tablespoon dried

1. In a nonreactive medium saucepan, heat olive oil over medium heat. Add onion and celery and cook until softened, about 3 minutes. Add tomatoes, raise heat to medium-high, and cook, stirring often, until sauce is thickened, 7 to 10 minutes. Transfer to a food processor, add ½ teaspoon salt and ⅛ teaspoon pepper, and puree until smooth. Set tomato sauce aside.

2. Preheat oven to 375°F. Bring a large pot of water to a boil. Remove 12 of largest outer leaves from cabbage. Reserve remainder for another use. Plunge leaves into boiling water. Boil until limp, 3 to 5 minutes. Drain and rinse under cold running water. Lay out to drain on several layers of paper towels.

3. Cut fish into ½-inch cubes. In a mixing bowl, combine fish, scallops, herbs, and remaining salt and pepper. Toss to mix.

4. Lay cabbage leaves flat on a work surface. Cut out tough stem ribs. Place 2 to 3 tablespoons of fish mixture on one end of each leaf. Roll into a thick cylinder, holding in sides as you go. Place seam side down in an 8 x 11-inch baking dish. Pour tomato sauce over cabbage rolls. Bake 15 minutes, until sauce is bubbly and fish is cooked through.

66 BAKED CONFETTI FISH
Prep: 5 minutes   Cook: 15 to 17 minutes   Serves: 4

4 firm fish fillets, such as grouper, sea bass, haddock, or halibut, about 6 ounces each
2 tablespoons butter
½ medium red bell pepper, thinly sliced
½ medium yellow bell pepper, thinly sliced

½ medium green bell pepper, thinly sliced
1 medium onion, thinly sliced
1 garlic clove, minced
½ teaspoon salt
¼ teaspoon pepper
⅛ teaspoon ground cumin
½ cup dry white wine
1 tablespoon chopped parsley

1. Preheat oven to 425°F. Arrange fish flat on a 9 x 13-inch baking dish. In a large heavy skillet, melt butter over medium-high heat. Add bell peppers, onion, garlic, salt, pepper, and cumin. Reduce heat to medium and cook, stirring frequently, until softened, 5 to 7 minutes. Pour in wine, raise heat to high, and boil until liquid is reduced by half.

2. Spread pepper mixture over fish and cover loosely with foil. Bake 10 minutes, or until fish is firm to the touch and opaque throughout. Garnish with chopped parsley.

67 SESAME-SOY MAHI-MAHI WITH GINGER AND SCALLIONS
Prep: 2 minutes   Cook: 10 minutes   Serves: 4

4 mahi-mahi fillets, about 6 ounces each
½ cup soy sauce
2 teaspoons Asian sesame oil
1 (1-inch) piece of fresh ginger, peeled and grated

1 garlic clove, minced
½ teaspoon pepper
2 small scallions, thinly sliced

1. Preheat oven to 425°F. Arrange fish fillets flat in a baking dish. Sprinkle soy sauce, sesame oil, ginger, garlic, and pepper over fish. Cover dish loosely with aluminum foil.

2. Bake 10 minutes, or until fish is firm and opaque throughout. Garnish with thinly sliced scallions and serve at once.

68   FLOUNDER WITH SHIITAKE MUSHROOMS IN FRESH TOMATO SAUCE

Prep: 5 minutes   Cook: 16 minutes   Serves: 4

2   tablespoons olive oil
½   pound shiitake mushrooms, stemmed and thinly sliced
1   garlic clove, minced
½   cup dry white wine

2   medium tomatoes, peeled, seeded, and chopped
½   teaspoon salt
¼   teaspoon pepper
4   flounder fillets, about 6 ounces each

1. Preheat oven to 425°F. In a large skillet, heat olive oil over medium-high heat. Add mushrooms and garlic. Cook, tossing occasionally, until mushrooms are slightly wilted and lightly browned, about 3 minutes. Pour in wine, increase heat to high, and boil until reduced by half. Add tomatoes, salt, and pepper. Bring to a boil and cook, stirring occasionally, until slightly thickened, about 3 minutes.

2. Arrange flounder fillets in a baking dish large enough to hold them flat. Pour mushrooms and sauce over fish. Cover dish tightly with aluminum foil. Bake 10 minutes, or until fish is firm and opaque throughout.

69   MONKFISH BRAISED WITH FENNEL

Prep: 5 minutes   Cook: 38 to 40 minutes   Serves: 4

2   tablespoons olive oil
2   fennel bulbs, halved lengthwise and thinly sliced
1   medium onion, thinly sliced
1   (28-ounce) can Italian peeled tomatoes, drained and chopped
1   tablespoon minced fresh rosemary or ½ teaspoon dried

½   teaspoon salt
¼   teaspoon pepper
1   cup Fish Stock (page 33), bottled clam juice, or water
1½   pounds monkfish, cut into 2-inch pieces

1. Preheat oven to 375°F. In a large nonreactive skillet or flameproof casserole, heat olive oil over medium heat. Add fennel and onion and cook, stirring occasionally, until softened, about 5 minutes. Add tomatoes, rosemary, salt, and pepper. Cook over medium-high heat, stirring frequently, until tomatoes have thickened and vegetables are very soft, about 10 minutes. Pour in fish stock, raise heat to high, and boil until reduced by half, 3 to 5 minutes.

2. Place fish in a 9 x 13-inch baking pan and pour over fennel-tomato sauce. Cover dish loosely with aluminum foil. Bake 20 minutes, or until fish is firm and opaque throughout.

70   HALIBUT PARMESAN
Prep: 15 minutes   Cook: 28 to 30 minutes   Serves: 4

3 tablespoons olive oil
1 medium onion, finely
   chopped
1½ pounds fresh plum
   tomatoes, seeded and
   coarsely chopped, or
   1 (14-ounce) can Italian
   peeled tomatoes, drained
   and chopped
2 teaspoons chopped fresh
   oregano or 1 teaspoon
   dried

¼ teaspoon salt
⅛ teaspoon pepper
1 tablespoon tomato paste
   (optional)
2 pounds fresh halibut steaks,
   cut 1 inch thick
1 cup fresh bread crumbs
½ cup grated Parmesan cheese

1. Heat 2 tablespoons olive oil in a medium nonreactive saucepan. Add onion and cook until softened but not browned, 3 to 5 minutes. Stir in tomatoes and season with oregano, salt, and pepper. Stir in tomato paste for a deeper flavor, if desired. Reduce heat to medium-low and simmer, stirring frequently, until sauce is slightly thickened, about 10 minutes. Let cool slightly, then transfer to a food processor. Puree until smooth.

2. Preheat oven to 450°F. Pour tomato sauce into bottom of a 9 x 13-inch baking dish. Arrange fish on top. In a small bowl, combine bread crumbs and Parmesan cheese; toss to mix. Sprinkle evenly over fish. Drizzle remaining 1 tablespoon olive oil over crumbs.

3. Bake 15 minutes, or until Parmesan crumbs are lightly browned on top and fish is opaque throughout. Serve at once, spooning sauce around fish.

71   HONEY PECAN SALMON
Prep: 2 minutes   Cook: 17 to 20 minutes   Serves: 4

½ cup pecans, coarsely
   chopped
½ cup honey
2 tablespoons butter

1½ pounds salmon fillets, cut
   into 4 equal pieces
½ teaspoon salt
¼ teaspoon pepper

1. Preheat oven to 350°F. Spread pecans over bottom of a small baking sheet and bake about 5 minutes, or until lightly browned and toasted. Remove and let cool completely.

2. In a small saucepan, combine honey, butter, and toasted pecans. Cook over moderately high heat, stirring, until pecans are coated in a glossy glaze, about 5 minutes. Remove from heat and cover to keep warm.

3. Preheat oven to 425°F. Arrange salmon in a lightly buttered 9 x 13-inch baking dish. Pour warm pecans and glaze over fish and cover dish loosely with aluminum foil. Bake 7 to 10 minutes, or until fish is opaque in center.

72   MONKFISH CASSOULET

Prep: 5 minutes   Soak: 1 hour
Cook: 2 hours 9 minutes   Serves: 4 to 6

Once upon a time, monkfish was so plentiful and so undesirable that it was thrown back or sold for very little money by commercial fishermen. Not so today. It has become popular enough to fetch prices akin to those of nobler species. The mild taste is enhanced by pungent Mediterranean flavors in this recipe, and the beans make it a complete meal, though I like to serve this dish with plain white rice and a tossed salad.

½ pound dried Great Northern
   or navy beans, rinsed and
   picked over
2 whole cloves
1 medium onion, peeled
1 teaspoon salt
½ teaspoon pepper
1½ pounds monkfish
¼ cup olive oil
1 (28-ounce) can Italian peeled
   tomatoes, drained and
   chopped

1 garlic clove, minced
1 tablespoon fresh thyme
   leaves or 1 teaspoon dried
½ cup pitted oil-cured black
   olives
2 tablespoons chopped
   parsley
1 cup dry bread crumbs

1. Soak beans overnight in cold water to cover by 2 inches. Or place beans in a large saucepan and add water to cover by at least 2 inches. Bring to a boil, cover, and remove from heat. Let stand, covered, 1 hour. Drain beans. Place soaked beans in a large saucepan or flameproof casserole. Stick cloves in whole onion and bury onion in beans. Pour in 4 cups cold water. Bring to a boil over medium-high heat. Reduce heat to medium and simmer, partially covered, 1½ hours. Add ½ teaspoon salt and ¼ teaspoon pepper and continue to simmer until beans are tender, about 30 minutes longer. Remove and discard onion. Drain beans and spread in bottom of a 9 x 13-inch baking dish. Set aside, covered to keep warm.

2. Cut monkfish into 1-inch pieces. Heat 2 tablespoons olive oil in a large skillet, preferably nonstick. Add fish and cook over medium heat, stirring often, until fish is opaque and starts to give off moisture, about 3 minutes. Add tomatoes, garlic, thyme, olives, and parsley. Increase heat to medium-high. Cook, stirring and shaking pan, until juices thicken slightly, about 3 minutes. Season with remaining ½ teaspoon salt and ¼ teaspoon pepper. Pour fish and sauce over beans.

3. Preheat broiler and set broiling pan 4 to 6 inches from heat. Sprinkle bread crumbs over fish and beans. Drizzle remaining 2 tablespoons olive oil over bread crumbs. Broil about 3 minutes, or until bread crumbs are golden brown.

73 BAKED RED SNAPPER OLÉ

Prep: 10 minutes   Cook: 25 to 30 minutes   Serves: 4

1 red snapper, 4 to 5 pounds,
    cleaned and scaled, head
    and tail intact
½ teaspoon salt
¼ teaspoon pepper
1 small onion, thinly sliced
2 tablespoons olive oil
1 garlic clove, minced

4 fresh plum tomatoes,
    peeled, seeded, and diced
½ teaspoon grated lime zest
¼ teaspoon chili powder
1 tablespoon lime juice
½ cup loosely packed cilantro,
    chopped

1. Preheat oven to 425°F. Place fish in a 9 x 13-inch baking dish. Season with salt and pepper.

2. In a medium skillet, cook onion in olive oil over medium-high heat until softened, about 2 minutes. Add garlic and cook 1 minute longer. Stir in tomatoes, lime zest, and chili powder. Increase heat to high and cook until sauce is thickened and pulpy, about 2 minutes.

3. Pour tomato mixture over and around fish and cover dish loosely with aluminum foil. Bake 20 to 25 minutes, or until fish is opaque next to bone. Transfer fish to a large serving platter. Sprinkle with lime juice and cilantro and serve at once.

74 CITRUS BAKED SOLE WITH ORANGE

*Prep: 5 minutes   Marinate: 1 hour   Cook: 9 to 11 minutes
Serves: 4*

1½ pounds sole fillets
½ teaspoon salt
¼ teaspoon pepper
¼ cup fresh orange juice

¼ cup fresh lemon juice
1 whole orange
1 teaspoon cornstarch

1. Arrange fish in a baking dish large enough to hold fillets flat in a single layer. Season with salt and pepper. Add orange juice and lemon juice. Cover and refrigerate 1 hour.

2. Use a serrated knife to cut away peel from orange. Cut between membranes to remove whole sections. Place in a small bowl and set aside.

3. Preheat oven to 425°F. Remove fish from refrigerator and cover dish tightly with aluminum foil. Bake 8 to 10 minutes, until firm and opaque throughout.

4. With a wide spatula, carefully transfer fillets to individual serving plates. Pour cooking liquid into a small saucepan. Dissolve cornstarch in 2 tablespoons cold water. Stir into liquid in saucepan and bring to a boil over medium-high heat, stirring until thickened, about 1 minute. Spoon sauce over fillets. Garnish with orange sections.

75   EASY SNAPPER PARMESAN
Prep: 5 minutes   Cook: 10 minutes   Serves: 4

4 red snapper fillets, 4 to
   6 ounces each
⅓ cup mayonnaise
¼ cup plus 2 tablespoons
   grated Parmesan cheese
1 small onion, finely chopped

1 garlic clove, minced
2 tablespoons chopped
   parsley
½ teaspoon salt
¼ teaspoon pepper
   Lemon wedges

1. Preheat oven to 425°F. Arrange snapper fillets in a single layer on a lightly oiled baking sheet. In a small bowl, combine mayonnaise, ¼ cup Parmesan cheese, onion, garlic, parsley, salt, and pepper. Spread mixture evenly over snapper. Sprinkle remaining 2 tablespoons cheese on top.

2. Bake 10 minutes, or until fish begins to flake and Parmesan cheese is slightly browned. Serve with lemon wedges.

76   BRAISED PORGY WITH VEGETABLES
Prep: 10 minutes   Cook: 69 to 81 minutes   Serves: 4

4 whole porgies (about
   1 pound each), filleted,
   heads and bones reserved
2 tablespoons olive oil
1 small onion, chopped
1 cup dry white wine
½ teaspoon salt
2 medium tomatoes, peeled,
   seeded, and chopped
16 to 20 small red potatoes,
   scrubbed and cut in half

⅛ teaspoon pepper
1 medium yellow squash,
   halved lengthwise and
   sliced
1 medium zucchini, halved
   lengthwise and sliced
½ pound green beans, cut into
   ½-inch pieces

1. Cover fish fillets with plastic wrap and refrigerate until ready to cook. Rinse heads and bones under cold running water. Separate heads and cut bones into 2-inch segments.

2. In a large saucepan, heat olive oil over medium heat. Add onion and cook until softened, about 3 minutes. Add fish heads and bones and cook, stirring, 3 minutes. Pour in wine and 1 cup cold water. Add ¼ teaspoon salt, raise heat to high, and bring to a boil. Reduce heat to medium-low and simmer stock 20 minutes. Strain, discarding solids and reserving fish stock.

3. Preheat oven to 425°F. In a large oval gratin dish or rectangular glass baking dish, combine tomatoes, potatoes, ½ cup of fish stock, remaining salt, and pepper. (Reserve the remaining stock for another use. It freezes very well.) Place, uncovered, in preheated oven and bake, stirring occasionally, until potatoes are tender and liquid has slightly thickened, 30 to 40 minutes.

4. Place fish fillets on top of vegetables. Season with additional salt and pepper. Cover with foil and bake 10 minutes, or until fish is firm and opaque throughout.

5. Meanwhile, bring a large saucepan of salted water to a boil. Add yellow squash and zucchini, return to a boil, and drain immediately. Rinse under cold running water and drain on paper towels. Repeat this process with beans, cooking 1 to 2 minutes after water has returned to a boil. Spoon blanched squash, zucchini, and beans around fish. Cover again and bake until vegetables are warmed through, 2 to 3 minutes. Serve at once directly from dish.

77   FISH-STUFFED CABBAGE WITH MUSHROOMS

Prep: 15 minutes   Cook: 17 to 21 minutes   Serves: 4

Wolffish, or *loup de mer*, is one of those species that we used to look down on. Not any more! It is becoming a delicacy because of its increasing availability and tender, succulent flesh. Wolffish feeds on clams, oysters, and crabs in relatively deep waters. This results in a subtle yet complex flavor. Monkfish or bass makes an excellent substitution for the wolffish called for in the following recipe.

12 large cabbage leaves
2 tablespoons butter
6 scallions (white part only), finely chopped
1 garlic clove, minced
¼ pound mushrooms, thinly sliced

1 (28-ounce) can Italian peeled tomatoes, drained, seeded, and chopped
½ teaspoon salt
¼ teaspoon pepper
1½ pounds wolffish fillets, cut into 4 equal pieces

1. Cut tough rib ends from cabbage leaves. Bring a large pot of salted water to boil over high heat. Add cabbage leaves and boil until limp, 3 to 5 minutes. Drain and rinse under cold running water; drain again. Lay flat on paper towels and pat dry.

2. In a large nonreactive skillet, melt butter over medium-high heat. Add scallions and garlic. Cook, stirring, until slightly softened, about 1 minute. Add mushrooms and tomatoes. Increase heat to high and boil, stirring often, until sauce is slightly thickened, about 3 minutes. Season with salt and pepper and set aside.

3. Preheat oven to 425°F. Place 3 cabbage leaves together on a work surface, stem ends overlapping in center. Place a piece of fish in center. Season lightly with additional salt and pepper. Bring up ends and sides envelope fashion to completely cover the fish. Continue with remaining leaves and fish. Carefully transfer each to a buttered 9 x 13-inch baking dish, placing each bundle snugly next to the other, seam side down.

4. Spread tomato-mushroom mixture over bundles of fish. Cover dish loosely with aluminum foil. Bake 10 to 12 minutes, or until fish is firm and sauce is bubbly.

78   BAKED STUFFED FISH
Prep: 10 minutes   Cook: 20 minutes   Serves: 4

Whole fish are sometimes an excellent buy. They are often fresher than fillets as well. Count on a fish that weighs about 3 pounds to serve 4 people.

1 whole sea bass, snapper, or bluefish, about 3 pounds, cleaned and scaled, head and tail intact
1½ cups fresh bread crumbs
½ teaspoon salt
¼ teaspoon pepper

¼ pound mushrooms, finely chopped
2 scallions (white part only), thinly sliced
1 tablespoon chopped parsley
1 egg, lightly beaten

1. Preheat oven to 450°F. Rinse fish and pat dry. In a small bowl, combine bread crumbs, salt, pepper, mushrooms, scallions, and parsley. Add egg and stir to form a stiff stuffing. Fill cavity of fish with stuffing, packing in tightly. Secure opening with toothpicks. Place on a greased baking pan large enough to hold fish flat.

2. Bake until fish is firm and separates easily from bone, about 20 minutes. To serve, spoon out cooked stuffing and keep warm. Carefully cut fillets from either side of the backbone on both sides and lift to individual plates. Serve with a small amount of stuffing on the side.

79   CATALAN BAKED FISH WITH POTATOES AND OLIVES
Prep: 5 minutes   Cook: 1 hour 14 minutes   Serves: 4

Any olives will do for this recipe. My favorites are small green picholine imported olives. The ones with pits in them seem to have more flavor, but if you use them be sure to warn your guests first. Pitted green or black olives from a can or bottle will do just fine.

1 pound fresh plum tomatoes, peeled, seeded, and chopped, or 1 (28-ounce) can Italian peeled tomatoes, drained and chopped
10 small red potatoes, peeled and halved

2½ tablespoons olive oil
¾ teaspoon salt
½ teaspoon pepper
¼ pound (about 1 cup) olives
1½ pounds sea bass or cod fillets, about 1 inch thick, skin attached

1. Preheat oven to 375°F. In a large oval gratin or flameproof rectangular baking dish, combine tomatoes, potatoes, and 2 tablespoons olive oil. Season with ½ teaspoon salt and ¼ teaspoon pepper. Toss gently to mix. Bake, uncovered, stirring every 10 to 15 minutes, until tomatoes have given off liquid and potatoes are tender, about 1 hour.

2. Remove dish from oven and raise oven temperature to 425°F. Cut fish into 2-inch-wide strips. Lay fish skin side up over tomatoes and potatoes. Season with remaining ¼ teaspoon each salt and pepper. Sprinkle olives over top and return to oven. Bake, uncovered, 10 minutes, or until fish is firm and white throughout.

3. Remove from oven and turn oven setting to full broil. Brush skin of fish with remaining ½ tablespoon olive oil. Broil about 4 inches from heat about 4 minutes, or until fish and potatoes are lightly browned. Serve at once.

80   SEAFOOD PAELLA
Prep: 10 minutes   Cook: 32 minutes   Serves: 4

This classic seafood dish works best when done in a paella pan that measures 15 inches in diameter. These pans have convenient handles that facilitate oven cooking and are attractive enough to serve from directly. If a skillet or a wok is used, be sure that it is of sufficient size to hold the varied ingredients called for below. If fish stock is not available, use 2 bottles of clam juice mixed with 2 cups water.

¼ cup olive oil
½ pound medium shrimp, shelled and deveined
2 medium squid, cut into rings, tentacles discarded
1 pound skinless halibut, cut into 1½-inch pieces
1½ teaspoons salt
¼ teaspoon pepper
1 garlic clove, minced
1 medium red bell pepper, finely diced

2 to 3 medium tomatoes, peeled, seeded, and chopped
4 cups Fish Stock (page 33)
2 cups raw long-grain white rice
½ teaspoon saffron threads
12 mussels, scrubbed and debearded

1. In a paella pan, wok, or large skillet, heat olive oil over medium-high heat. Add shrimp, squid, and halibut and cook, turning often, until lightly browned, about 5 minutes. Season with ½ teaspoon salt and pepper. Remove seafood with a slotted spoon and set aside.

2. Add garlic and bell pepper to pan and cook 2 minutes. Add tomatoes and cook, stirring often, until softened, about 2 minutes longer. Pour in fish stock, increase heat to high, and bring to a boil. Stir in rice and remaining 1 teaspoon salt. Return to a boil and cook, stirring often, until liquid is slightly reduced, about 5 minutes. Add saffron, reduce heat to medium-low, and simmer undisturbed until tender, about 10 minutes. Meanwhile, preheat oven to 350°F.

3. Add reserved shrimp, squid, and halibut to rice. Bury mussels in rice, wrap pan or skillet loosely with aluminum foil, and transfer to oven. Bake until rice is very tender and ingredients are heated through, about 8 minutes. Remove from oven and serve directly from pan.

81   SWORDFISH STEAKS AL PESTO

Prep: 5 minutes   Cook: 10 to 12 minutes   Serves: 4

4 swordfish steaks, 4 to
   6 ounces each
1 cup loosely packed fresh
   basil leaves
1 garlic clove, peeled
¼ cup pine nuts

2 tablespoons grated
   Parmesan cheese
¼ teaspoon salt
⅛ teaspoon pepper
⅓ cup olive oil
   Lemon slices

1. Preheat oven to 425°F. Arrange fish steaks in a large lightly oiled baking dish. In a food processor, combine basil, garlic, pine nuts, Parmesan cheese, salt, and pepper. Puree until smooth. With machine on, slowly pour in olive oil. Process until pesto is well blended.

2. Spread pesto evenly over swordfish steaks. Cover dish loosely with aluminum foil. Bake until steaks are white throughout but still moist, 10 to 12 minutes. Garnish with thin slices of lemon.

82   BAKED WHITEFISH WITH SPINACH AND TOMATOES

Prep: 10 minutes   Cook: 25 to 27 minutes   Serves: 4

2 small carrots, chopped
1 celery rib, chopped
1 medium onion, chopped
2 tablespoons olive oil
1 (28-ounce) can Italian peeled
   tomatoes, drained and
   coarsely chopped

½ plus ⅛ teaspoon salt
¼ teaspoon pepper
2 pounds fresh spinach, stems
   removed and leaves well
   rinsed, or 2 (10-ounce)
   packages frozen
1 pound whitefish fillets

1. In a large nonreactive saucepan, combine carrots, celery, and onion. Stir in olive oil and cook over medium heat until vegetables are softened, 5 to 7 minutes. Add tomatoes, ½ teaspoon salt, and pepper. Cook over medium-low heat, stirring occasionally, until thick and pulpy, about 10 minutes. Transfer to a food processor and puree tomato sauce until smooth.

2. If using fresh spinach, plunge leaves in a large pot of rapidly boiling salted water. Return to a boil and immediately drain. Rinse under cold running water. If using frozen spinach, cook according to package directions. Use your hands to squeeze out excess moisture from spinach; coarsely chop.

3. Preheat oven to 425°F. Spread chopped spinach over bottom of a buttered 9 x 13-inch baking dish. Cut whitefish crosswise on the diagonal into ½-inch-thick slices. Layer over spinach and season with remaining ⅛ teaspoon salt. Spread tomato sauce over fish. Cover dish loosely with aluminum foil. Bake 10 minutes, or until sauce is bubbly and fish is firm and white. Serve at once.

Chapter 4

Fish in the Pan

Fish in the pan includes stir-frying, pan-frying, sautéing, and deep-frying. When done correctly, a crisp outside should encase a tender inside, protecting and sealing in flavor and moisture. There are some generalities that apply to all of these methods and a few more that are specific to deep-frying. Stir-frying is quick and self-explanatory, as is the popular method called blackening. Pan-frying requires a skillet just large enough to snugly hold the fish or shellfish being cooked without overcrowding. A mixture of butter and oil is called for in many of the pan-fried recipes in this book. The oil helps prevent the butter from burning, and we get to use flavorful butter at a higher temperature, which is important. If the fat is not hot enough, the crust won't form properly and the fish or shellfish will become soggy.

Frying has gotten a bum rap. There is nothing wrong with an occasional tasting of fried fish as long as it is just that: occasional fare, not everyday eating. An old-fashioned fish-fry with hushpuppies and cole slaw is as American as apple pie in many parts of the U.S. The important reminders for successful deep-frying are really very few. First of all, a deep-fat fryer with a preset level for measuring fat and a thermometer is a must for the true enthusiast. However, the same results can be had using a large, straight-sided saucepan and a trained eye for testing temperature with a piece of bread. Two to three inches of oil is necessary for successful frying. Tear off a small piece of bread and use it to test the temperature: Throw the bread into hot fat, allow it to come up to the surface, and time how long it takes to brown. If the piece of bread is done in 2 to 3 minutes, it means you're set to go. If not, continue heating until the test is correctly done. Never overcrowd the pan. Fry fish in one, two, or even three batches if necessary to prevent violating this cardinal rule of deep-fat frying. The temperature is lowered each time an ingredient is added. If too many items crowd the pan, the lower amount of heat will cause the fish to simmer, rather than fry, in the fat.

Most delicate fish fillets as well as croquettes and fish cakes need to be coated with flour, cornmeal, bread crumbs, cracker crumbs, or crushed cereal. Sometimes the ingredient to be fried is dipped in beaten egg before coating. Many times a quick dusting will be sufficient. Adding herbs and spices to coatings is a way to enhance flavor and make an interesting variation. Detailed instructions are given where appropriate in the following recipes.

83   FRIED CATFISH WITH SPICY RED PEPPER SAUCE

Prep: 5 minutes   Cook: 15 minutes   Serves: 4

Sally Belk, a friend, food writer, and editor, devised this recipe for her book *Around the Southern Table*. Substitute ocean perch or grouper for catfish if you prefer.

1   (7-ounce) jar pimientos, drained
2   teaspoons sugar
1   tablespoon red wine vinegar
2   tablespoons tomato paste
    Several drops of hot pepper sauce
    Pinch of cayenne

¾   teaspoon salt
1   cup vegetable oil
4   to 6 catfish fillets, about 6 ounces each
¼   teaspoon pepper
2   eggs, well beaten
1   cup cornmeal

1. In a food processor, puree pimientos with sugar and vinegar. Transfer to a small nonreactive saucepan and stir in tomato paste, hot sauce, cayenne, and ¼ teaspoon salt. Cook over low heat, stirring frequently, until warmed through and blended, about 5 minutes. Set red pepper sauce aside.

2. In a large skillet, heat oil over medium-high heat. Season fish fillets with pepper and remaining ½ teaspoon salt. Dip in eggs and then in cornmeal to coat both sides. Add to hot oil and fry, turning once, until golden brown, about 10 minutes. Drain on paper towels. Serve hot with sauce on the side.

84   77TH STREET STIR-FRY

*Prep: 5 minutes   Marinate: 20 minutes   Cook: 5 to 6 minutes
Serves: 4*

Serve this light, colorful dish over steamed white rice.

1½ pounds firm-fleshed fish fillets, about ½ inch thick, such as bass, cod, monkfish, mahi-mahi, grouper, or snapper
3   tablespoons rice wine vinegar
3   tablespoons soy sauce
3   tablespoons peanut oil
1   medium red bell pepper, thinly sliced
1   celery rib, thinly sliced

¼   pound snow peas, stemmed and stringed
1   (8-ounce) can sliced water chestnuts, drained
2   scallions (white and 1 inch of green), thinly sliced
2   teaspoons cornstarch
¾   cup Fish Stock (page 33), chicken broth, or water
½   teaspoon salt
¼   teaspoon pepper

1. Cut the fish crosswise on a slight diagonal into strips about ½ inch wide. In a large bowl, combine vinegar and soy sauce. Add fish and stir to coat. Cover and marinate at room temperature for 20 minutes.

2. In a wok or large skillet, heat 2 tablespoons peanut oil over high heat until hot but not smoking. Add bell pepper, celery, snow peas, water chestnuts, and scallions. Stir-fry over high heat until vegetables are slightly softened, about 2 minutes. Remove to a bowl and set aside.

3. Remove fish from marinade and reserve liquid. Add remaining 1 tablespoon peanut oil to wok. Add fish and stir-fry over high heat until opaque throughout, about 2 minutes. Return vegetables to wok.

4. In a small bowl, dissolve cornstarch in stock or water and pour over fish and vegetables in wok. Cook over medium-high heat, stirring, until slightly thickened, 1 to 2 minutes. Season with salt and pepper.

85 MUSHROOM-STUFFED FLOUNDER ROLLS WITH TOMATO-WINE SAUCE
Prep: 10 minutes   Cook: 18 to 20 minutes   Serves: 4

1 pound mushrooms,
   quartered
1 teaspoon lemon juice
1 small onion, coarsely
   chopped
¼ cup olive oil
¼ cup fresh bread crumbs
½ teaspoon salt
¼ teaspoon pepper
1 to 1½ pounds flounder
   fillets, halved lengthwise

1 cup flour
2 medium tomatoes, peeled,
   seeded, and chopped
¼ cup dry white wine
1 garlic clove, crushed
   through a press
1½ teaspoons fresh thyme
   leaves or ½ teaspoon
   dried

1. In a food processor, combine mushrooms, lemon juice, and onion. Process in several quick pulses until finely chopped, about 15 seconds. In a large skillet, heat 2 tablespoons olive oil over medium-high heat until hot but not smoking. Add mushroom mixture and cook, stirring, until liquid evaporates, about 5 minutes. Stir in bread crumbs, salt, and pepper. Set aside to cool.

2. Lay fish flat on a work surface and spread a small amount of mushroom stuffing evenly over each fillet. Starting at small end, roll up into a loose cylinder and secure with toothpicks.

3. Place flour in a shallow bowl or on a large plate. Coat each roll in flour to cover completely.

4. In a large skillet, heat remaining olive oil over medium-high heat. Add stuffed flounder rolls and reduce heat to medium. Cook until browned and crisp on one side, about 5 minutes. Carefully turn with a spatula and cook 5 minutes longer. Transfer to individual serving plates or a large platter and cover with foil to keep warm.

5. Add tomatoes to pan. Stir in wine, garlic, and thyme. Increase heat to high. Boil, stirring, until thickened and pulpy, 3 to 5 minutes. Season with additional salt and pepper to taste. Spoon sauce over rolls and serve at once.

86 FISH AND CHIPS

Prep: 15 minutes   Stand: 30 minutes
Cook: 10 to 14 minutes per batch   Serves: 4

Season fish and potatoes with additional salt and pepper while still hot for best results. For an authentic touch, sprinkle with vinegar, too. The English traditionally serve fish and chips with malt vinegar, but it is something of an acquired taste.

2 **pounds firm-fleshed white**
  fish fillets, such as shark,
  whiting, cod, haddock, or
  halibut
1¼ **cups flour**
2 **eggs, separated**
2 **tablespoons cold beer or**
  water

½ **teaspoon salt**
½ **cup milk**
2 **pounds all-purpose potatoes**
¼ **teaspoon pepper**
  Vegetable oil, for deep-
  frying

1. Rinse fish in cold water, pat dry, and set aside. In a food processor, combine flour, egg yolks, beer, ¼ teaspoon salt, milk, and ¼ cup cold water. Pulse several times to mix into a thin batter. Pour into a bowl, cover with plastic wrap, and let stand at room temperature for 30 minutes.

2. Peel potatoes and cut into ½-inch-thick sticks (French fries). Pat dry and season with pepper and remaining salt. Pour enough oil into a deep-fat fryer to measure 2 inches deep. Heat to 375°F. Add potatoes a handful at a time and fry until golden brown, 5 to 7 minutes. Drain on paper towels.

3. Dip fish into batter and fry, in batches without crowding, in same fat, turning frequently, until browned and crisp, 5 to 7 minutes. Drain on paper towels. Serve on a large platter, surrounded by French-fried potatoes.

87 BLACKENED CATFISH FILLETS

Prep: 3 minutes   Cook: 4 to 6 minutes   Serves: 4

This dish is adapted from a compilation of recipes put out by The Catfish Institute in Belzoni, Mississippi.

1 **tablespoon paprika**
1 **teaspoon onion powder**
1 **teaspoon garlic powder**
½ **teaspoon salt**
½ **teaspoon black pepper**
½ **teaspoon white pepper**

½ **teaspoon dried thyme leaves**
½ **teaspoon dried oregano**
4 **catfish fillets, about 6 ounces**
  each
4 **tablespoons butter, melted**

1. In a shallow bowl, combine paprika, onion powder, garlic powder, salt, black pepper, white pepper, thyme, and oregano. Mix well.

2. Dip fish fillets in melted butter, then in seasoning mixture. Heat a large heavy skillet, preferably cast iron, over high heat, until very hot. Add fish and cook, turning once, until blackened on both sides, 4 to 6 minutes.

88 FRIED CLAMS
Prep: 5 minutes   Cook: 6 to 8 minutes   Serves: 4

Season clams with lots of salt and pepper while they are still piping hot. Sprinkle with lemon juice for extra flavor.

24 littleneck or cherrystone clams, scrubbed clean and opened, or 3 (8-ounce) cans	**½ teaspoon salt**
½ cup flour	**¼ teaspoon pepper**
	2 eggs, beaten
	1 cup dried bread crumbs
	Vegetable oil

1. Dry clams between paper towels. If using canned clams, drain well and dry on paper towels.

2. In a shallow bowl, combine flour, salt, and pepper. In a separate bowl, beat eggs well with 1 tablespoon water. Spread out bread crumbs on a large plate or in a shallow bowl.

3. Roll clams in seasoned flour to coat. Shake off excess and transfer to beaten egg, turning to coat. Use a slotted spoon to transfer clams from eggs to bread crumbs. Toss and roll in crumbs until well coated.

4. Heat 2 inches of oil to 350°F in a deep-fat fryer. Fry clams, turning occasionally, until golden brown, 6 to 8 minutes. Drain on paper towels.

89 SOUTHERN FRIED CATFISH
Prep: 5 minutes   Cook: 10 minutes   Serves: 4

To make cracker crumbs, use your favorite store-bought crackers and grind them in a food processor. Alternatively, put the crackers in a plastic bag and pound with a rolling pin or flat of a large knife to pulverize.

For a memorable Southern breakfast—and I'm from Georgia—try serving catfish with grits and biscuits.

1 cup fresh cracker crumbs	**4 to 6 catfish fillets, about 6 ounces each**
½ teaspoon salt	**Vegetable oil**
¼ teaspoon pepper	
2 eggs	

1. In a shallow dish, combine cracker crumbs, salt, and pepper. In a medium bowl, beat eggs with 2 tablespoons water. Dip fillets in egg, then dredge in cracker crumbs to coat. Shake off excess crumbs.

2. Pour enough oil into a large nonstick skillet to measure 1 inch in depth. Heat oil to 365°F on a deep-frying thermometer. Fry fillets over medium-high heat, turning frequently, until golden brown, about 10 minutes. Drain on paper towels.

90   FLOUNDER PICCATA
Prep: 5 minutes   Cook: 6 to 8 minutes   Serves: 4

Serve with thin slices of lemon and sprigs of parsley for garnish. I like to accompany this tasty fish with linguine tossed with butter or with olive oil and garlic.

1 cup flour	2 tablespoons fresh lemon
½ teaspoon salt	juice
¼ teaspoon pepper	¼ teaspoon grated lemon zest
2 pounds flounder fillets	2 tablespoons chopped
4 tablespoons butter	parsley
2 tablespoons vegetable oil	1 tablespoon chopped capers

1. Combine flour, salt, and pepper in a shallow bowl or baking dish. Dredge fish in seasoned flour to coat both sides; shake off excess.

2. In a large skillet, melt 2 tablespoons butter in oil over medium-high heat. Add fish and cook, turning once, until browned outside and cooked through, 5 to 7 minutes. Remove to a platter and keep warm. Pour off all but 1 tablespoon of fat from skillet. Add remaining butter and cook over medium-high heat until browned, about 1 minute. Stir in lemon juice, lemon zest, parsley, and capers and pour over fish.

91   SESAME-COATED GROUPER
Prep: 3 minutes   Cook: 7 to 10 minutes   Serves: 4

Blanched snow peas are a visual and flavorful accompaniment to this dish. Shake a splash of soy sauce over fish for added zip.

4 boneless grouper steaks about 6 ounces each, or use swordfish, tuna, halibut, or cod	1½ cups unhulled sesame seeds
	½ teaspoon salt
	¼ teaspoon pepper
	2 tablespoons butter
1 cup flour	2 tablespoons vegetable oil
2 eggs, beaten	

1. Pat fish dry with paper towels. Have flour, eggs, and sesame seeds arranged for dipping in separate shallow bowls or on plates. Season fish with salt and pepper.

2. Coat each fish steak with flour and shake off excess. Dip into egg, then dredge in sesame seeds, turning to coat completely.

3. In a large skillet, melt butter in oil over medium-high heat. When bubbling subsides, add fish and cook, turning once, until brown and crispy outside and just opaque in center, 7 to 10 minutes. Drain on paper towels and serve at once.

92   FRIED OYSTERS
Prep: 3 minutes   Cook: 2 minutes per batch   Serves: 4

This recipe serves 4 as a main course or 6 as an appetizer. Serve oysters with your favorite bottled or homemade salsa.

Vegetable or olive oil
1 pint shucked oysters
1 cup cornmeal
½ teaspoon salt

¼ teaspoon pepper
Lemon or lime wedges, for
    garnish

1. Pour enough oil to measure 1 inch deep into an electric frying pan or deep-fat fryer. Heat to 365°F.

2. Meanwhile, drain oysters and discard liquid.

3. In a medium bowl, combine cornmeal, salt, and pepper. Dip oysters in cornmeal to coat all over; shake off excess. Add to hot oil in batches without crowding and fry until lightly browned, about 1 minute per side. Serve at once with lemon or lime wedges.

93   FRESH CODFISH CAKES
Prep: 8 minutes   Cook: 13 to 15 minutes   Serves: 4

Serve a spicy salsa or tartar sauce with these crispy cakes.

2 pounds cod fillets, cut into
    2-inch pieces
2 small onions, finely
    chopped
2 celery ribs, finely chopped
1 stick (4 ounces) butter
2 tablespoons chopped
    parsley

2 teaspoons grated lemon zest
1 cup fresh bread crumbs
2 teaspoons salt
½ teaspoon pepper
1 cup yellow cornmeal
¼ cup vegetable oil

1. In a food processor, puree fish until very smooth and light. Scrape into a bowl, cover, and refrigerate.

2. In a large skillet, cook onions and celery in 4 tablespoons butter over medium-high heat until softened, 3 to 5 minutes. Scrape into a large bowl and let cool slightly.

3. Add pureed fish, parsley, lemon zest, bread crumbs, salt, and pepper to onions and celery in bowl. Fold ingredients together until well blended.

4. Divide mixture into 8 equal portions. Use dampened hands to form round patties, each ¾ inch thick and about 3 inches in diameter. Dust lightly in cornmeal; shake off excess.

5. In a large skillet, melt remaining 4 tablespoons butter in vegetable oil over medium-high heat. Add patties and cook, turning once, until browned and crisp outside and cooked through in center, about 5 minutes per side. Drain briefly on paper towels and serve.

94   SHRIMP TEMPURA
Prep: 15 minutes   Chill: 4 hours   Cook: 4 to 6½ minutes   Serves: 4

1½ pounds extra-large shrimp
1½ cups flour
 1 teaspoon salt
 ¼ teaspoon pepper
 2 tablespoons butter, melted
    and cooled to tepid
 2 eggs, separated
 1 cup beer
    Vegetable oil

4 slices of sweet potato
4 slices of sweet onion
8 broccoli florets, about 1½
   inches in diameter
   Ginger-Sesame Dipping
   Sauce (recipe follows)

1. Slit shrimp down back and remove intestinal vein and shell; leave tails intact. Spread shrimp open to butterfly. Keep refrigerated until ready to cook.

2. In a large mixing bowl, combine flour, salt, pepper, butter, and egg yolks. Stir to blend, slowly pour in beer, and mix to form a thin batter. Cover and refrigerate for 4 to 6 hours.

3. When ready to cook, preheat oven to 200°F. Pour enough vegetable oil into a deep-fat fryer or large saucepan to measure about 2 inches deep. Heat to 375°F. Beat egg whites until stiff and fold into batter. In batches without crowding, dip shrimp into batter, one at a time, and drop into hot fat. Fry until lightly browned, 3 to 5 minutes. Drain on paper towels and keep warm in oven while frying vegetables.

4. Dip sweet potato slices into batter, one at a time, and fry for 1 to 1½ minutes, or until coating is crisp and light beige in color. Drain on paper towels, transfer to oven, and repeat with onion slices and broccoli florets. Serve at once, with individual bowls of Ginger-Sesame Sauce for dipping.

GINGER-SESAME DIPPING SAUCE
Makes about ⅔ cup

½ cup soy sauce
2 teaspoons Asian sesame oil
1½ teaspoons rice wine or other
    vinegar
 1 teaspoon sugar

2 scallions (white part only),
   minced
1½ teaspoons grated fresh
    ginger
 1 garlic clove, minced

In a small bowl, combine soy sauce, sesame oil, vinegar, and sugar. Stir to dissolve sugar. Mix in scallions, ginger, and garlic. Serve immediately or let stand at room temperature for up to 3 hours.

95   HALIBUT ORIENTAL
Prep: 5 minutes   Cook: 8 minutes   Serves: 4

Garnish halibut with several slices of pickled ginger or finely chopped scallions. Serve with plain white rice.

½ cup cornstarch
4 halibut steaks cut 1 inch
    thick, about 6 ounces each
½ cup soy sauce
¼ cup dry sherry
2 teaspoons rice wine vinegar

1 teaspoon minced fresh
    ginger
1 garlic clove, minced
1 tablespoon sugar
½ teaspoon pepper

1. Place cornstarch in a shallow bowl or plate. Add fish and turn to coat well.

2. In a small bowl, combine soy sauce, sherry, vinegar, ginger, garlic, sugar, and pepper. Stir to blend.

3. In a large, lightly oiled nonstick skillet, sauté halibut over medium-high heat, turning once, until lightly browned and crisp, about 1½ minutes per side. Pour soy mixture over fish and cook, uncovered, until fish is opaque throughout and sauce is thickened, about 5 minutes. Transfer halibut to individual serving plates and spoon sauce over.

96   SPICY FRIED SCALLOPS
Prep: 5 minutes   Cook: 3 to 4 minutes per batch   Serves: 4

For a less spicy touch, simply reduce the amount of cayenne. Spear these tasty morsels with toothpicks and serve with cocktails or plate them as a first course.

1½ pounds bay scallops or
    halved sea scallops
¼ cup flour
2 eggs
2 tablespoons milk

½ teaspoon pepper
½ teaspoon salt
1 cup cornmeal
1 teaspoon cayenne
Lemon or lime wedges

1. Rinse scallops under cold water and pat dry on paper towels. Place flour in a shallow bowl or plate, add scallops, and toss to coat lightly. Shake off excess.

2. In a shallow bowl, beat eggs, milk, pepper, and salt with a fork until blended. Combine cornmeal and cayenne in another shallow bowl or on a plate. Dip scallops in egg mixture, then in seasoned cornmeal. Toss and stir to coat completely. Shake off excess.

3. In an electric frying pan or deep-fat fryer, pour enough oil to measure 3 inches deep. Heat to 365°F. In batches without crowding, fry scallops until golden brown, 3 to 4 minutes. Drain on paper towels and serve hot with lemon or lime wedges.

97   HERB-CRUSTED FISH
Prep: 5 minutes   Cook: 7 to 8 minutes   Serves: 4

This recipe is for cuts from firm-fleshed fish that can be breaded and pan-fried in just a little oil, like a chicken or veal cutlet. Either steaks or fillets work well here. Garnish with lemon wedges and fresh parsley. Serve with boiled potatoes.

4 fish steaks or fillets, such as
   tuna, swordfish, catfish,
   grouper, or tilapia, about
   6 ounces each
2 cups fresh bread crumbs
1 tablespoon chopped fresh
   thyme leaves or
   1 teaspoon dried
1 tablespoon chopped fresh
   rosemary or 1 teaspoon
   dried

1 tablespoon chopped parsley
½ teaspoon salt
¼ teaspoon pepper
2 eggs, well beaten
2 tablespoons butter
2 tablespoons oil

1. Pat fish dry and set aside. In a large shallow bowl, combine bread crumbs, thyme, rosemary, parsley, salt, and pepper. Mix well.

2. Dip fish in eggs, then dredge in seasoned bread crumbs, turning and tossing to coat completely.

3. In a large skillet, melt butter in oil over medium-high heat. When bubbling subsides, add fish and cook, turning once, until browned and crisp outside and just opaque in center, 7 to 8 minutes. Drain on paper towels.

98   DEEP-FRIED SHRIMP
*Prep: 5 minutes   Soak: 15 minutes   Cook: 3 to 5 minutes per batch
Serves: 4*

Serve these crispy shrimp with lemon wedges or seafood cocktail sauce or tartar sauce for dipping.

1½ pounds large shrimp
1   cup milk
½   cup flour
½   cup cornmeal

½ teaspoon salt
¼ teaspoon pepper
   Vegetable oil

1. Slit shrimp down back and remove black vein and shell; leave tails intact. Spread shrimp open to butterfly. In a medium bowl, soak in milk for about 15 minutes.

2. In a shallow dish, combine flour, cornmeal, salt, and pepper. Pour enough oil to measure 2 inches deep into a deep-fat fryer. Preheat to 375°F. Drain shrimp and roll in flour/cornmeal mixture to coat. Fry in batches until golden brown, 3 to 5 minutes. Drain on paper towels.

99 DEEP-FRIED SMELTS

Prep: 17 minutes   Stand: 15 minutes
Cook: 4 to 5 minutes per batch   Serves: 4

16 to 20 medium smelts (about
   2 pounds), cleaned
1 cup flour
1 cup cornmeal
½ teaspoon salt

¼ teaspoon pepper
Vegetable oil, for deep-
   frying
Lemon wedges

1. Pat smelts dry and arrange on a large plate or platter. In a small bowl, combine flour, cornmeal, salt, and pepper. Sprinkle half this mixture over smelts and toss to coat. Let stand for 15 minutes.

2. In an electric frying pan or deep-fat fryer, pour in enough oil to measure about 3 inches deep. Heat to 375°F. Just before frying, sprinkle remaining half of flour/cornmeal mixture over smelts. Toss to coat again and shake off excess. Immediately plunge fish into hot oil. Fry in batches without crowding, turning once, until golden brown and crisp, about 4 to 5 minutes. Drain on paper towels and serve hot with lemon wedges.

100 SHADY VERANDA SHAD ROE

Prep: 4 minutes   Cook: 16 minutes   Serves: 4

Shad roe comes but once a year, sometime between April and June, depending on where you live, when the shad swim upriver to spawn.

½ pound sliced bacon
1 cup flour
½ teaspoon salt
¼ teaspoon pepper

4 small pair or 2 large pair
   shad roe, separated
½ cup red wine vinegar
2 tablespoons chopped capers

1. In a large nonreactive skillet, fry bacon over medium heat until crisp, about 3 minutes. Remove bacon strips and drain on paper towels. Reserve fat in skillet.

2. In a shallow bowl, combine flour, salt, and pepper. Dip shad roe in seasoned flour and shake off excess. Add roe to bacon fat in skillet and cook over medium heat, turning once, until firm and lightly browned, about 10 minutes. Remove to drain on paper towels.

3. Drain fat from skillet. Pour in vinegar and boil over medium-high heat, stirring often, until reduced by half, about 3 minutes. Add capers and stir until warmed through. Serve each roe with a small spoonful of sauce. Serve bacon strips as a garnish on the side.

101   SAUTÉED SOFT-SHELL CRABS

Prep: 1 minute   Cook: 6 minutes per batch   Serves: 4

Soft-shell crabs are such a treat that I like them cooked as simply as possible.

4 tablespoons butter	¼ teaspoon pepper
¼ cup vegetable oil	1 tablespoon chopped parsley
12 soft-shell crabs, cleaned	Lemon wedges
½ teaspoon salt	

1. In a large skillet, melt 2 tablespoons butter in 2 tablespoons oil over medium heat. Add half the crabs and raise heat to high. Cook, turning once, until lightly browned, about 3 minutes per side. Remove to a large platter; cover with foil to keep warm.

2. Repeat with remaining butter, oil, and crabs. Season with salt, pepper, and parsley. Serve at once, with lemon wedges on the side.

102   SOFT-SHELL CRABS SAG HARBOR

Prep: 5 minutes   Cook: 3 to 5 minutes per batch   Serves: 4

3 egg whites	Vegetable oil
1½ cups flour	12 soft-shell crabs, cleaned
1 teaspoon salt	Lemon or lime wedges
1 teaspoon pepper	

1. In a medium bowl, beat egg whites and ¼ cup water with a fork until frothy. In a large shallow bowl, combine flour, salt, and pepper.

2. In an electric frying pan or large skillet, heat 3 inches oil to 375°F. Dip crabs in egg whites and drain off excess. Transfer to flour and toss and turn to coat. Working in batches, fry crabs, turning occasionally, until golden brown and crispy, 3 to 5 minutes. Drain on paper towels and serve hot with lemon or lime wedges.

103   SOLE MEUNIÈRE

Prep: 5 minutes   Cook: 4 minutes   Serves: 4

For a special garnish, remove the peel and white pith from 2 lemons or limes. Cut the fruit into thin slices and use to top finished dish. Serve with steamed potatoes and buttered green beans.

½ cup flour
½ cup cornmeal
½ teaspoon salt
¼ teaspoon pepper
4 sole fillets, 4 to 6 ounces each
½ cup milk

4 tablespoons butter
2 tablespoons vegetable oil
2 tablespoons chopped parsley
1 tablespoon fresh lemon or lime juice

1. In a shallow bowl, combine flour, cornmeal, salt, and pepper. Dip sole in milk, then dredge in flour and cornmeal mixture to coat.

2. In a large skillet, melt 2 tablespoons of butter in oil over medium-high heat. Shake excess flour off dredged fish and arrange fish in pan. Cook, turning once, until browned and crisp, about 2 minutes on each side. Remove to serving plates. Drain off fat from pan.

3. Return skillet to heat and add remaining 2 tablespoons of butter, parsley, and lemon juice. Stir until butter is melted and well blended. Spoon a small amount of sauce over each fillet and serve.

104   CRISPY FRIED SQUID

Prep: 5 minutes   Cook: 2 minutes per batch   Serves: 4

This recipe serves 4 as a main course or 6 to 8 as an appetizer. Be sure to include a bowl of mayonnaise mixed with lemon juice or seafood cocktail sauce on the side for dipping

1 cup vegetable oil
2 pounds small squid, cleaned and cut into ½-inch rings, tentacles left whole
1 cup flour
2 egg whites

1 cup cornmeal
2 tablespoons chopped fresh oregano, or 1 teaspoon dried
1 teaspoon salt
½ teaspoon pepper
Lemon wedges

1. In an electric frying pan or deep-fat fryer, heat oil to 365°F. Pat squid dry with paper towels. Place flour in a shallow bowl or on a plate. Add squid and toss to coat; shake off excess.

2. In a small bowl, beat egg whites with a fork until frothy. In a separate bowl, combine cornmeal, oregano, salt, and pepper. Dip squid in egg whites, then in cornmeal, stirring or tossing to coat; shake off excess.

3. Working in batches if necessary, fry squid in hot oil, turning once, until lightly browned, about 2 minutes. Drain on paper towels and serve at once with lemon wedges.

105 TROUT ALMONDINE

Prep: 3 minutes   Cook: 10 to 12 minutes   Serves: 4

½ cup slivered almonds
2 tablespoons butter
2 tablespoons vegetable oil
1 cup flour
½ teaspoon salt

¼ teaspoon pepper
4 small whole trout, cleaned and scaled, heads and tails intact
½ cup dry white wine

1. In a large skillet, cook almonds in butter and oil over medium heat, stirring often, until lightly browned, 3 to 5 minutes. Remove skillet from heat. Remove almonds with a slotted spoon and set aside. Reserve remaining butter and oil.

2. In a shallow dish, combine flour, salt, and pepper. Dredge trout in seasoned flour to coat; shake off excess.

3. Cook trout in butter and oil in skillet over medium-high heat, turning once, until browned on both sides and opaque near bone, about 7 minutes. Remove to a platter and cover to keep warm. Return almonds to skillet, add wine, and raise heat to high. Bring to a boil, pour over fish, and serve at once.

106 SWORDFISH WITH SAUTÉED APPLES

Prep: 8 minutes   Cook: 12 to 15 minutes   Serves: 4

2 tablespoons butter
2 tablespoons vegetable oil
4 Golden Delicious apples, peeled, cored, and quartered

1½ pounds swordfish steaks, cut into 1½-inch pieces, or use tuna or shark
1 cup apple cider
¼ teaspoon salt
¼ teaspoon pepper

1. In a large nonstick skillet, melt butter in oil over medium-high heat. Add apples and cook, turning once, until lightly browned, 2 to 3 minutes. Transfer to a plate and set aside.

2. Add fish to skillet and cook over medium-high heat, turning once until lightly browned, about 3 minutes. Remove to a platter and cover with aluminum foil to keep warm.

3. Add cider to skillet and raise heat to high. Boil, stirring to scrape up bits left on bottom, until reduced by half, about 4 minutes. Return apples and fish to pan and cook, stirring gently, until fish is cooked through and liquid turns thick and syrupy, 3 to 5 minutes. Remove apples to a serving platter. Season fish with salt and pepper. Place in center of platter and surround with apples.

107 TUNA PROVENÇAL
Prep: 5 minutes   Cook: 11 to 15 minutes   Serves: 4

For a real Mediterranean treat, add chopped black olives to the tomatoes and serve with chick-peas. Swordfish can be used in place of tuna if desired.

4 (1-inch-thick) tuna steaks, about 6 ounces each
2 tablespoons olive oil
¼ cup dry white wine
2 medium ripe tomatoes, peeled, seeded, and chopped

1 tablespoon chopped fresh thyme leaves or 1 teaspoon dried
1 small garlic clove, crushed through a press
½ teaspoon salt
¼ teaspoon pepper

1. In a large nonreactive skillet, cook tuna in olive oil over medium-high heat, turning once, until browned and firm to touch, 7 to 9 minutes. Remove to a serving platter and cover with aluminum foil to keep warm.

2. Pour off fat in pan. Add white wine, increase heat to high, and boil, stirring constantly, until reduced by half, about 1 minute. Stir in tomatoes, thyme, and garlic. Reduce heat to medium and cook, stirring often, until thick and pulpy, 3 to 5 minutes. Season with salt and pepper. Spoon tomato sauce over tuna and serve.

108 TUNA HAWAIIAN
Prep: 1 minute   Cook: 10 to 13 minutes   Serves: 4

2 tablespoons olive oil
4 (1-inch-thick) tuna steaks, about 6 ounces each
½ cup fish stock, chicken broth, or dry white wine
1 (8-ounce) can unsweetened crushed pineapple, drained

2 teaspoons fresh lemon juice
½ teaspoon salt
¼ teaspoon pepper

1. In a large skillet, heat olive oil over medium-high heat until hot but not smoking. Add tuna and cook, turning once, until browned outside and firm to the touch, 7 to 9 minutes. Remove to a platter and cover with aluminum foil to keep warm.

2. Return skillet to heat. Pour in stock and increase heat to high. Boil, stirring frequently, until liquid is reduced by half, about 2 minutes. Stir in pineapple, lemon juice, salt, and pepper. Cook, stirring, until hot, 1 to 2 minutes. Spoon over tuna and serve at once.

109 FRITTO MISTO

Prep: 5 minutes   Cook: 2 to 5 minutes per batch   Serves: 4

Literally "mixed fry" in Italian, this is one of those regional dishes with hundreds of variations, depending upon what seafood is available. Substitute oysters or scallops for the shrimp. Use cleaned smelts or small fresh sardines in place of whitebait. (Whatever fish you use should be lean and firm.) Squash is perfect, as it cooks quickly and browns nicely, but halved mushrooms and blanched broccoli or cauliflower are good, too. Let your imagination and market availability be your guide. For a special garnish, fry several sprigs of fresh parsley until crisp just before serving. And be sure to taste it; its flavor is entrancing.

1   cup flour
½   teaspoon salt
1   tablespoon olive oil
2   egg whites
      Vegetable oil for deep-
        frying
¼   pound medium shrimp,
        shelled and deveined
½   pound small whitebait, left
        whole

½   pound assorted firm-fleshed
        fish fillets for frying, such
        as cod, perch, catfish,
        bass, or whiting, cut
        crosswise into ½-inch-
        wide strips
1   small zucchini, cut into
        1½-inch pieces
1   yellow squash, cut into
        1½-inch pieces
      Lemon wedges

1. Combine flour and salt in a medium bowl. Mix 2 cups cold water with olive oil and slowly pour into flour mixture, stirring constantly until smooth. Just before frying, beat egg whites until stiff and fold into batter.

2. Pour enough oil into a deep-fat fryer to measure 3 inches deep. Heat to 365°F. Dip shrimp into batter; then fry, stirring or turning occasionally, until golden brown and cooked through, about 3 minutes. Remove with a slotted spoon and drain on paper towels; cover to keep warm. Repeat with whitebait, reducing frying time to about 2 minutes. Dip fish strips in batter and fry until golden brown and crisp, about 5 minutes. Drain on paper towels. Finally, dip zucchini and yellow squash in batter and fry until crisp and golden brown, 2 to 3 minutes. Drain thoroughly on paper towels.

3. Arrange shrimp, whitebait, fish, and vegetables on a large serving platter. Garnish with lemon wedges.

110   SWORDFISH IN CURRIED CREAM SAUCE

Prep: 1 minute   Cook: 13 minutes   Serves: 4

Mixed steamed rice with currants or raisins and toasted pine nuts. Serve with this fish curry for a tempting Asian delight.

4 swordfish fillets, about 6 ounces each, or use cod, tuna, catfish, halibut, or tilefish	1 teaspoon curry powder, or to taste
2 tablespoons butter	1 cup heavy cream
2 tablespoons oil	½ teaspoon salt
	¼ teaspoon pepper

1. In a large skillet, cook fish in butter and oil over medium-high heat, turning once, until lightly browned and firm, about 7 minutes, depending on thickness. Remove fish to a platter and cover with aluminum foil to keep warm.

2. Discard all but about 2 teaspoons fat. Add curry powder and cook over medium-low heat, stirring, until light colored, about 1 minute. Pour in cream, increase heat to high, and bring to a boil. Boil, stirring often, until reduced by half, about 5 minutes. Season with salt and pepper.

3. Arrange fish on individual serving plates. Spoon some sauce over each fillet and serve at once.

Chapter 5

Flaming Fish

I was lucky enough to live in London for a few months during my youth. I had a small flat in the northern part of the city, and it just happened to be within walking distance of an incredible fish store. The owner, Steve, a crusty old sort if there ever was one, lived for fish. He sold it, he bought it, he ate it, and he spent his vacations going fishing in far parts of the world. He took over the business from his father, who shared his passion.

My stove was equipped with a real salamander, one of those British niceties akin to the electric teapot or the heated towel rack in the bathroom. A salamander is a broiler, usually located on top of the stove, with heat directed from above. It comes with an adjustable rack that can be moved up and down with ease: you never have to pull it out and fit it back into the slots as you do with a traditional gas broiler.

This is where I learned the real virtues of broiled fish. Glistening fillets of fresh fish from the North Sea, genuine sole from Dover, odd species this young American had never heard of (recommended so enthusiastically by Steve) were a few triumphs I'll never forget. Brown and crisp on the outside, tender and sweet on the inside, well seasoned, firm and hot . . . there really is nothing quite like broiled fish.

Broiling is one of the easiest ways to cook fish. Whole fish, fillets, and large chunks can all be prepared using this method. There are a few general rules to remember.

Thin fillets of lean fish like sole, flounder, whiting, or snapper dry out quickly and need to be basted frequently with butter or oil. Fattier fish like salmon, mackerel, bluefish, and tuna don't dry out as quickly and are good choices for broiling or grilling.

Preheat the broiler (after removing the broiling pan) for 10 to 15 minutes before starting. Oil the broiling pan before arranging food on it and place it 4 to 6 inches from source of heat. Be careful not to overcook. The Canadian Cooking Method described on page 45 is helpful. Tuck ends under thin fillets, measure at the thickest point, and cook for 8 to 10 minutes per inch or fraction thereof. There is no need to turn thin fillets when broiling. Thicker cuts should be turned once, carefully. Broil whole fish with heads and tails intact to prevent their drying out. Steaks and whole fish can be dusted lightly before broiling with cornmeal or flour for a crispy crust.

The same rules apply to grilling fish. Cooking times are the same as for baking and broiling. Start a charcoal fire 30 to 45 minutes in advance so that the coals have time to burn down to a gray ash. If the fire is too hot, the fish will char and not cook evenly. Be sure to baste frequently. Direct dry heat means that careful attention must be paid to prevent dried-out results.

A hinged grill is a good investment for the enthusiast. Fish is easier to turn over without breaking up flesh with the use of one of these contraptions. Be sure to oil the preheated grill before beginning and, as with broiling, cook 4 to 6 inches from the source of heat.

111   BROILED CATFISH WITH EGG RELISH
Prep: 5 minutes   Cook: 7 to 10 minutes   Serves: 4

2 hard-boiled eggs, finely
   chopped
2 tablespoons minced fresh
   herbs (parsley, rosemary,
   thyme, tarragon, or
   cilantro)

2 tablespoons mayonnaise
½ teaspoon salt
¼ teaspoon pepper
4 catfish fillets, 4 to 6 ounces
   each
2 tablespoons butter, melted

1. In a medium bowl, combine eggs, herbs, mayonnaise, ¼ teaspoon salt, and ⅛ teaspoon pepper. Cover with plastic wrap and refrigerate until ready to use.

2. Preheat broiler. Arrange fillets on a lightly buttered broiling pan. Brush with butter and season with remaining salt and pepper. Set about 4 inches from source of heat and broil 7 to 10 minutes, until opaque and slightly firm to the touch. Transfer fillets to individual serving plates. Top each with equal amounts of the egg mixture.

112   CLAM DIGGER'S DELIGHT
Prep: 3 minutes   Cook: 5 to 10 minutes   Serves: 4

This recipe serves four as an appetizer. Accompanied by a salad and a loaf of good bread, it would make a fine main course for two.

½ cup olive oil
3 tablespoons lemon juice
1 garlic clove, minced
1 tablespoon fresh oregano or
   1 teaspoon dried

½ teaspoon salt
¼ teaspoon pepper
2 dozen hard-shell clams,
   such as littleneck or
   cherrystone, scrubbed

1. Prepare a charcoal grill. In a medium bowl, combine olive oil, lemon juice, garlic, oregano, salt, and pepper.

2. Place clams on grill and cook until they pop wide open, 5 to 10 minutes. Discard any that do not open. Transfer to a serving dish, break off top shells, and drizzle olive oil mixture over clams. Serve at once.

113 BROILED BLUEFISH WITH QUICK SALSA
Prep: 4 minutes   Cook: 8 to 10 minutes   Serves: 4

Bluefish is a meaty fish with lots of flavor. This recipe takes minutes and is packed with taste sensations. Don't be afraid to improvise: Use lemon juice or vinegar if limes are not on hand. A tablespoon of dried herbs can be used in place of the cilantro, although crisp, clean flavor won't be quite the same. Instant couscous makes a perfect accompaniment for a quick meal.

2 medium tomatoes, chopped
2 tablespoons fresh lime juice
2 tablespoons chopped
    cilantro
¾ teaspoon salt

½ teaspoon pepper
2 pounds bluefish fillets, skin
    removed
2 tablespoons olive oil

1. Preheat broiler. In a medium bowl, combine tomatoes, lime juice, and cilantro. Season with ¼ teaspoon salt and ¼ teaspoon pepper and set salsa aside.

2. Cut fish into 4 equal pieces. Arrange on an oiled broiling pan in a single layer. Brush with olive oil and season with remaining ½ teaspoon salt and ¼ teaspoon pepper. Broil 8 to 10 minutes, until lightly browned outside and opaque in center. Serve hot with salsa.

114 BROILED BLUEFISH WITH CHEESY BREAD-CRUMB TOPPING
Prep: 3 minutes   Cook: 7 minutes   Serves: 4

2 tablespoons red wine
    vinegar
1 teaspoon Dijon mustard
½ teaspoon salt
½ teaspoon pepper
¼ cup olive oil

4 bluefish fillets, about
    6 ounces each
1 cup fresh bread crumbs
¼ cup grated Romano cheese
1 tablespoon chopped parsley
4 tablespoons butter, melted

1. In a medium bowl, combine vinegar, mustard, ¼ teaspoon salt, and ¼ teaspoon pepper. Stir to dissolve mustard. Slowly whisk in olive oil until smooth and emulsified. Set aside.

2. Preheat broiler. Place fish skin side down on an oiled broiling pan. In a small bowl, combine bread crumbs, cheese, parsley, and remaining ¼ teaspoon each salt and pepper. Mix well and sprinkle evenly over fish. Drizzle melted butter over crumbs. Broil about 4 inches from heat about 7 minutes, until browned outside and cooked through.

3. Remove cooked fish to serving plates and spoon about 1 tablespoonful of oil and vinegar mixture over each piece. Serve at once.

115 BROILED CATFISH WITH PINEAPPLE SALSA

Prep: 10 minutes   Stand: 30 minutes   Cook: 7 to 10 minutes
Serves: 4

1 cup fresh or canned
   unsweetened chopped
   pineapple
½ red bell pepper, finely diced
½ red onion, finely chopped
1 small garlic clove, minced
½ cup orange juice
2 tablespoons lemon or lime
   juice

1 tablespoon chopped parsley
½ teaspoon salt
½ teaspoon pepper
4 catfish fillets, 4 to 6 ounces
   each
2 tablespoons olive oil

1. In a medium bowl, combine pineapple, bell pepper, onion, garlic, orange juice, lemon juice, parsley and ¼ teaspoon each salt and pepper. Mix well, cover, and let salsa stand at room temperature for 30 minutes.

2. Preheat broiler. Brush fish with oil and arrange on an oiled broiling pan set about 4 inches from source of heat. Season with remaining ¼ teaspoon each salt and pepper. Broil 7 to 10 minutes, until opaque and slightly firm to the touch.

3. Spoon equal amounts of salsa in center of 4 individual serving plates. Top each with a catfish fillet and serve at once.

116 GRILLED COD WITH ORANGE BUTTER

Prep: 5 minutes   Freeze: 30 minutes   Cook: 10 minutes   Serves: 4

Substitute catfish for cod if desired. Sections of fresh orange make a nice garnish.

4 tablespoons butter, softened
1 teaspoon grated orange zest
2 teaspoons orange juice
2 teaspoons lemon juice
½ teaspoon salt

½ teaspoon pepper
4 pieces of cod fillet, 4 to
   6 ounces each
2 tablespoons olive oil

1. In a medium bowl, blend together butter, orange zest, orange juice, lemon juice, and ¼ teaspoon each salt and pepper. Place flavored butter on a small piece of plastic wrap, form into a 2-inch cylinder, and tightly twist ends closed. Freeze orange butter until firm, about 30 minutes.

2. Light a medium-hot fire in a grill or preheat broiler. Brush fish on both sides with olive oil and season with remaining ¼ teaspoon each salt and pepper. Place on a well-oiled grill or on a lightly oiled broiling pan about 4 inches from heat. Grill about 5 minutes per side, until firm to the touch. Remove to individual serving plates, top immediately with a thick slice of orange butter, and serve at once.

117 BROILED FLOUNDER WITH WINE AND THYME

Prep: 3 minutes   Cook: 6 minutes   Serves: 4

4 flounder fillets, about
  6 ounces each
¼ cup dry white wine
2 tablespoons butter, melted

2 teaspoons fresh chopped
  thyme or ½ teaspoon
  dried
½ teaspoon salt
½ teaspoon pepper

1. Preheat broiler. Arrange flounder on a lightly oiled broiling pan. Pour over wine, drizzle with butter, and season with thyme, salt, and pepper.

2. Broil 4 to 6 inches away from heat, without turning, about 6 minutes, until opaque throughout. Serve immediately.

118 GRILLED HALIBUT WITH PESTO

Prep: 7 minutes   Cook: 8 to 10 minutes   Serves: 4

1 cup loosely packed basil
  leaves
1 garlic clove, peeled
¼ cup pine nuts
2 tablespoons grated
  Parmesan cheese

½ teaspoon salt
½ teaspoon pepper
⅓ cup plus 2 tablespoons olive
  oil
4 small halibut steaks, about
  6 ounces each

1. In a food processor, combine basil, garlic, pine nuts, Parmesan cheese, ¼ teaspoon salt, and ¼ teaspoon pepper. Process until smooth. With machine on, slowly pour in ⅓ cup olive oil. Transfer pesto to a small bowl, cover, and set aside at room temperature.

2. Prepare charcoal grill or preheat broiler. Brush steaks on both sides with remaining 2 tablespoons oil. On a well-oiled grill over a medium-hot fire or on a lightly oiled broiling pan set about 4 inches from source of heat, grill halibut 4 to 5 minutes per side, until opaque and slightly firm to the touch.

3. Transfer to individual serving plates. Top each steak with a spoonful of pesto while hot and serve at once.

119   GRILLED LOBSTER WITH SAGE BUTTER

Prep: 4 minutes   Cook: 8 minutes   Serves: 4

1½ sticks (6 ounces) butter,
    melted
2 tablespoons chopped fresh
    sage or 1 teaspoon dried
1 teaspoon salt

½ teaspoon pepper
4 live lobsters, 1¼ to
    1½ pounds each
    Lemon wedges

1. Prepare a medium-hot fire in a charcoal grill equipped with a cover. In a medium bowl, combine butter, sage, salt, and pepper.

2. Kill the lobsters just before grilling by cutting through the heads and continuing to cut along the length of the bodies. Bend tail shells back to expose tail meat; with a nutcracker, gently crack claws.

3. Brush lobsters with sage butter. Place shell side down on a well-oiled grill. Cook, covered, about 3 minutes. Turn lobsters over and grill, covered, until meat is opaque but still moist, about 5 more minutes.

4. Just before serving, gently reheat remaining sage butter. Serve lobster with warmed butter and lemon wedges.

120   GRILLED MAKO SHARK WITH BLACK BEAN SALSA

Prep: 5 minutes   Cook: 8 to 10 minutes   Serves: 4

¾ cup cooked black beans
1 medium tomato, seeded and
    chopped
¼ cup grated red onion
¼ cup plus 2 tablespoons olive
    oil
2 tablespoons red wine
    vinegar

1 teaspoon salt
⅛ teaspoon cayenne
1½ pounds mako shark, about
    1 inch thick, cut into
    4 pieces
¼ teaspoon pepper

1. Prepare charcoal grill or preheat broiler. In a medium bowl, combine beans, tomato, onion, ¼ cup olive oil, vinegar, ½ teaspoon salt, and cayenne. Mix well, cover, and set salsa aside at room temperature.

2. Brush shark on both sides with remaining 2 tablespoons olive oil. Season with remaining ½ teaspoon salt and the pepper. Arrange on a well-oiled grill over a medium-hot fire or on a lightly oiled broiling pan under the broiler, about 4 inches from source of heat. Broil 4 to 5 minutes per side, until fish lightly springs back when gently pressed in center.

3. Transfer to individual serving plates and top with equal amounts of the black bean salsa.

121 BROILED MULLET

Prep: 2 minutes   Cook: 8 minutes   Serves: 4

Common from the Carolinas southward and especially popular along the gulf coast of Florida, Alabama, and Louisiana, this often overlooked species is delicious broiled.

4 mullet fillets, about 6 ounces
    each
¼ cup red wine vinegar
4 teaspoons olive oil

½ teaspoon salt
¼ teaspoon pepper
¼ teaspoon paprika

1. Preheat broiler. Place fish on a lightly oiled broiling pan and spoon about 1 tablespoon vinegar over each fillet. Drizzle each with 1 teaspoon olive oil and season with salt and pepper.

2. Broil 4 to 6 inches from heat about 8 minutes, until lightly browned. Remove from oven, dust with paprika, and serve at once.

122 GRILLED SQUID

Prep: 5 minutes   Marinate: 30 minutes
Cook: 4 to 5 minutes per batch   Serves: 4

Quick, high-temperature cooking ensures tender, tasty squid. To help accomplish this, Chris Schlesinger and John Willoughby in *The Thrill of the Grill* suggest using a clean brick covered with foil to weight down squid and intensify heat while grilling. Serve this dish with a mixed green salad and oven-roasted potatoes.

½ cup olive oil
3 tablespoons lemon juice
2 garlic cloves, minced
1 teaspoon salt

½ teaspoon pepper
2 pounds small squid,
    cleaned, bodies and
    tentacles separated

1. In a 9 x 13-inch nonreactive baking dish, combine olive oil, lemon juice, garlic, salt, and pepper. Add squid and turn to coat. Cover with plastic wrap and marinate at room temperature for 30 minutes, turning once or twice.

2. Light a hot fire in a grill. Drain squid and reserve marinade. Place 3 to 4 squid bodies close to each other on a well-oiled grill and weight down with a clean brick covered in foil. Cook, turning once, 1½ to 2 minutes per side. Remove brick, baste once on each side with reserved marinade, and cook, uncovered, an additional 30 seconds on each side. Repeat until all squid are cooked. Brick is not necessary to grill tentacles. Cook tentacles until crisp, about 2 minutes. Slice bodies into ¼-inch rings and serve immediately.

123 GRILLED SALMON WITH LIME MINT BUTTER

Prep: 5 minutes   Freeze: 30 minutes   Cook: 6 to 10 minutes
Serves: 4

4 tablespoons butter, softened
2 teaspoons lime juice
1 tablespoon chopped fresh
    mint
1 teaspoon salt

½ teaspoon pepper
4 salmon steaks, 1 inch thick
    (4 to 6 ounces each)
2 tablespoons olive oil

1. Prepare charcoal grill or preheat broiler. Combine butter, lime juice, mint, ½ teaspoon salt, and ¼ teaspoon pepper in a medium bowl and use a fork to mix thoroughly. Place on a small piece of plastic wrap, form into a 2-inch-long cylinder, and twist ends tightly closed. Freeze until firm, about 30 minutes.

2. Brush salmon steaks on both sides with oil and season with remaining salt and pepper. On a well-oiled grill over a medium-hot fire or on a lightly oiled broiling pan under the broiler, cook salmon 3 to 5 minutes per side, until slightly firm and opaque in center. Transfer steaks to individual serving plates and top each with a thick slice of the flavored butter.

124 GRILLED SALMON STEAKS TERIYAKI

Prep: 3 minutes   Marinate: 30 minutes   Cook: 8 to 10 minutes
Serves: 4

⅓ cup soy sauce
2 tablespoons dry sherry
1 tablespoon Asian sesame oil
1 tablespoon grated fresh
    ginger or 1 teaspoon
    ground

1 garlic clove, minced
½ teaspoon pepper
4 salmon steaks, 1 inch thick
    (4 to 6 ounces each)

1. Prepare charcoal grill or preheat broiler. In a 9 x 13-inch nonreactive baking dish, combine soy sauce, sherry, sesame oil, ginger, garlic, and pepper. Marinate salmon in mixture for 30 minutes at room temperature or 2 hours in the refrigerator, turning frequently.

2. On a well-oiled grill over a medium hot fire or on a lightly oiled broiling pan under the broiler, cook the salmon 4 to 5 minutes per side, until slightly firm and opaque. Serve immediately.

125   BROILED MACKEREL
Prep: 2 minutes   Cook: 6 to 8 minutes   Serves: 4

¼ cup mayonnaise
2 teaspoons Dijon mustard
½ teaspoon salt

½ teaspoon pepper
4 mackerel fillets, 6 to
   8 ounces each

1. Preheat broiler. In a small bowl, combine mayonnaise, mustard, salt, and pepper. Stir to blend well. Arrange mackerel fillets on a lightly oiled broiling pan and spread equal amounts of mayonnaise-mustard mixture evenly over each.

2. Broil 4 to 6 inches away from heat, without turning, 6 to 8 minutes, until golden brown on top and opaque throughout. Serve hot.

126   BROILED FLOUNDER
Prep: 2 minutes   Cook: 6 minutes   Serves: 4

4 flounder fillets, about
   6 ounces each
2 tablespoons lemon juice

3 tablespoons butter, melted
½ teaspoon salt
¼ teaspoon pepper

1. Preheat broiler. Arrange fillets on a lightly oiled broiling pan and drizzle with lemon juice and butter. Season with salt and pepper.

2. Broil 4 to 6 inches from heat, without turning, about 6 minutes, until opaque throughout and lightly browned.

127   GRILLED OYSTERS
Prep: 5 minutes   Cook: 5 to 10 minutes   Serves: 4

If shallots are not available, substitute a finely chopped small onion.

½ cup red wine vinegar
2 medium shallots, finely
   chopped
½ teaspoon salt

¼ teaspoon pepper
2 dozen oysters in the shell,
   well scrubbed

1. Prepare charcoal grill. In a medium bowl, combine vinegar, shallots, salt, and pepper.

2. Place oysters on grill flat side up and cook 4 inches from coals until they pop open, 5 to 10 minutes. Transfer to a serving dish, discarding any that do not open. Break off top shells and discard. Loosen flesh of oysters in shells and drizzle with vinegar and shallot mixture.

128 BROILED SWORDFISH WITH ANCHOVY BUTTER

Prep: 5 minutes   Soak: 10 minutes   Freeze: 30 minutes
Cook: 10 minutes   Serves: 4

1 (2-ounce) can anchovies, drained
½ cup milk
4 tablespoons butter, softened
2 teaspoons lemon juice
½ teaspoon salt

½ teaspoon pepper
4 swordfish steaks, 1 inch thick (about 6 ounces each)
2 tablespoons olive oil

1. In a medium bowl, soak anchovies in milk for 10 minutes to remove excess saltiness. Drain, discard milk, and pat anchovies dry with paper towels. Chop fine.

2. In a small bowl, combine anchovies with butter, lemon juice, ¼ teaspoon salt, and ¼ teaspoon pepper. Mix with a fork until well blended. Place on a small piece of plastic wrap, form into a 2-inch-thick cylinder, and twist ends tightly closed. Freeze until firm, about 30 minutes.

3. Prepare charcoal grill or preheat broiler. Brush swordfish with oil and season with remaining salt and pepper. Place on a well-oiled grill or broiling pan. Cook about 4 inches from source of heat, about 5 minutes per side, until lightly browned and slightly firm to the touch. Top each with a thick slice of the flavored butter and serve at once.

129 SHRIMP TERIYAKI

Prep: 5 minutes   Marinate: 30 minutes   Cook: 4 minutes   Serves: 4

1½ pounds large shrimp, shelled and deveined, tails left on
¼ cup soy sauce
2 tablespoons vegetable oil

1 tablespoon grated fresh ginger
2 tablespoons lemon juice
½ teaspoon salt
¼ teaspoon pepper

1. Cut shrimp down the back, almost in half but leaving them whole. Open to butterfly.

2. In a medium bowl, combine soy sauce, oil, ginger, and lemon juice. Add shrimp, turning to coat, season with salt and pepper, cover, and marinate in refrigerator for 30 minutes.

3. Prepare charcoal grill or preheat broiler. Remove shrimp from marinade and arrange on oiled grill or broiling pan. Broil about 4 inches from heat about 2 minutes on each side, brushing frequently with marinade, until pink and curled.

130 SWORDFISH KEBABS WITH FRESH TOMATO SALSA

Prep: 5 minutes   Marinate: 30 minutes   Cook: 10 minutes
Serves: 4 to 6

3 medium tomatoes, quartered	2 swordfish steaks, cut 1 inch thick (about 1 pound each)
1 garlic clove, minced	
1 small onion, chopped	2 tablespoons olive oil
1 teaspoon salt	12 medium mushrooms, wiped clean and halved
1 cup cilantro, loosely packed	
¼ cup lime juice	¼ teaspoon pepper

1. In the bowl of a food processor, combine tomatoes, garlic, onion, ½ teaspoon salt, cilantro, and 1 tablespoon lime juice. In several quick pulses, process until thick and pulpy. Leave at room temperature if salsa is to be used right away. If made in advance, cover and refrigerate until ready to serve.

2. Cut swordfish into 1½-inch chunks and place in a medium bowl. Add remaining 3 tablespoons lime juice and oil. Cover with plastic wrap and marinate 30 minutes at room temperature or 2 hours in the refrigerator. Turn and toss frequently.

3. Preheat broiler. Using four 12-inch skewers, prepare kebabs by alternating swordfish and mushrooms. Season with remaining salt and pepper. Arrange on an oiled broiling pan and broil about 4 inches from source of heat about 10 minutes, turning frequently, until fish is opaque and mushrooms are lightly colored. Serve at once with salsa on the side.

131 BROILED SHAD ROE

Prep: 2 minutes   Cook: 10 minutes   Serves: 4

From January to March, shad run along the East Coast, providing devotees with plenty of sumptuous roe. One of the best ways to prepare this seasonal specialty is simply to broil it. Serve with crisp bacon and scrambled eggs for a sensational breakfast dish. A single lobe may not be enough for hearty appetites. A double lobe per person is a gracious plenty.

4 shad roe, single or double lobe	½ teaspoon salt
4 tablespoons butter, melted	¼ teaspoon pepper

1. Preheat broiler. Lightly oil a broiling pan and arrange roe on top. Brush liberally with butter, season with salt and pepper, and set pan about 5 inches from source of heat.

2. Broil about 5 minutes per side, brushing frequently with butter, until dark brown and sizzling.

132 SUMPTUOUS SUMMER KEBABS

Prep: 7 minutes Marinate: 30 minutes Cook: 10 minutes
Serves: 4

2 tuna steaks, 1 inch thick, cut into 1½-inch cubes
2 swordfish steaks, 1 inch thick, cut into 1½-inch cubes
1 cup dry white wine
¼ cup plus 2 tablespoons olive oil
1 tablespoon chopped fresh thyme leaves or 1 teaspoon dried
1 medium onion, very thinly sliced
1 teaspoon salt
½ teaspoon pepper
1 large red or green bell pepper, cored, seeded, and cut into 1-inch squares
12 cherry tomatoes
6 large mushrooms, wiped clean and halved

1. In a large bowl, combine tuna, swordfish, wine, olive oil, thyme, onion, ½ teaspoon salt, and ¼ teaspoon pepper. Toss to mix, cover with plastic wrap, and marinate for 30 minutes at room temperature or 2 hours refrigerated. Toss or stir frequently.

2. Prepare charcoal grill or preheat broiler. Remove fish from marinade and drain on paper towels. Reserve marinade. On four 12-inch skewers, alternate fish, bell pepper squares, tomatoes, and mushrooms, dividing equally. Season kebabs with remaining salt and pepper. Place on a well-oiled grill or broiling pan. Cook 4 to 6 inches from heat about 10 minutes, turning often and basting from time to time with reserved marinade, until fish is lightly browned and firm.

133 WHITING BROILED WITH SOY SAUCE AND SESAME

Prep: 2 minutes Cook: 4 minutes Serves: 4

Have the fishmonger clean, dress, butterfly, and remove the bone from the whiting.

4 small whiting, boned
2 tablespoons soy sauce
2 teaspoons sesame seeds
¼ teaspoon crushed hot red pepper

1. Preheat broiler. Place fish skin side down without touching each other on a lightly oiled broiling pan and sprinkle with soy sauce, sesame seeds, and hot pepper.

2. Broil 4 inches from heat about 4 minutes without turning, until sesame seeds are lightly toasted and fish is opaque throughout.

134   SKIPPER'S BROILED SOFT-SHELL CRABS

Prep: 5 minutes   Marinate: 1 hour   Cook: 6 to 8 minutes   Serves: 4

½ cup olive oil
1 stick (8 ounces) butter,
   melted
3 tablespoons lemon juice
2 shallots, finely chopped

2 cloves garlic, minced
1 teaspoon salt
½ teaspoon pepper
8 large or 12 medium soft-
   shell crabs, cleaned

1. In a large nonreactive baking dish, combine olive oil, butter, lemon juice, shallots, garlic, salt, and pepper. Add crabs and turn to coat. Cover with plastic wrap and marinate for 1 hour, refrigerated.

2. Prepare charcoal grill or preheat broiler. Drain crabs and reserve marinade. Arrange crabs on their backs on a well-oiled grill or on a lightly oiled broiling pan. Broil 4 to 5 inches from heat 3 to 4 minutes per side, basting frequently with reserved marinade, until lightly browned. Serve immediately.

135   BROILED SNAPPER WITH CILANTRO-LIME BUTTER

*Prep: 3 minutes   Freeze: 30 minutes   Cook: 7 to 10 minutes
Serves: 4*

4 tablespoons butter, softened
2 teaspoons lime juice
1 tablespoon chopped cilantro
1 teaspoon salt

½ teaspoon pepper
4 snapper fillets, 4 to 6 ounces
   each
2 tablespoons vegetable oil

1. In a medium bowl, use a fork to combine butter, lime juice, cilantro, ½ teaspoon salt, and ¼ teaspoon pepper. Place on a small piece of plastic wrap, form into a 2-inch-long cylinder, and twist ends tightly closed. Freeze until firm, about 30 minutes.

2. Preheat broiler. Brush fillets on both sides with oil and season with remaining salt and pepper. Arrange on a lightly oiled broiling pan. Broil 4 inches from the heat 7 to 10 minutes without turning, until completely white. Serve on individual serving plates and top each with a thick slice of the flavored butter.

136   BROILED TILEFISH WITH LEMON HERB BUTTER

Prep: 2 minutes   Freeze: 30 minutes   Cook: 6 to 10 minutes
Serves: 4

4 tablespoons butter, softened
1 teaspoon grated lemon zest
1½ tablespoons chopped fresh
    herbs (parsley, thyme,
    rosemary, basil, tarragon,
    or chives) or 1½ teaspoons
    dried

1 teaspoon salt
½ teaspoon pepper
4 tilefish steaks, cut ½ inch
    thick, 4 to 6 ounces each

1. In a medium bowl, blend butter, lemon zest, herbs, ½ teaspoon salt, and ¼ teaspoon pepper. Place on a small piece of plastic wrap, form into a 2-inch-thick cylinder, and twist ends tightly closed. Freeze lemon herb butter until firm, about 30 minutes.

2. Preheat broiler. Season fish with remaining ½ teaspoon salt and ¼ teaspoon pepper. On a lightly oiled broiling pan, broil the fish 4 inches from heat, 3 to 5 minutes per side, turning once, until firm and opaque throughout. Remove to serving plates and immediately top with a thick slice of lemon herb butter. Serve at once.

137   SIZZLING SKEWERED SHRIMP

Prep: 5 minutes   Marinate: 30 minutes   Cook: 4 minutes   Serves: 4

Serve shrimp on skewers hot off the grill or right from the broiler on a bed of hot rice. Each guest can slide the shrimp off and put the skewer aside.

20 large shrimp, shelled and
    deveined
½ cup vegetable oil
3 tablespoons lime juice

½ to 1 teaspoon crushed hot
    red pepper, to taste
1 teaspoon salt

1. In a medium bowl, combine shrimp, oil, lime juice, hot pepper, and salt. Toss to mix, cover with plastic wrap, and marinate 30 minutes at room temperature or 1 hour refrigerated. Toss or stir frequently.

2. Prepare charcoal grill or preheat broiler. Remove shrimp from marinade and thread securely on four 12-inch-long skewers. Brush lightly with marinade. On a well-oiled grill over a medium-hot fire or on a lightly oiled broiling pan under the broiler, cook shrimp about 2 minutes per side, until lightly browned and curled. Serve immediately.

138 CHILIED TROUT

Prep: 3 minutes   Cook: 10 minutes   Serves: 6

1 tablespoon tomato paste	½ teaspoon salt
2 teaspoons chili powder	6 whole trout, about 8 ounces
1 tablespoon olive oil	each, cleaned and scaled
1 teaspoon fresh lemon juice	

1. Preheat broiler. In a small bowl, combine tomato paste, chili powder, olive oil, lemon juice, and salt. Stir to blend well.

2. Lay fish out on a work surface. Use fingers to rub each side with about 1 teaspoonful of chili paste, or to taste.

3. Place fish on a well-oiled broiling pan. Broil about 4 inches from heat about 5 minutes per side, until skin is dark amber and flesh springs back slightly when pressed at its thickest part.

139 SASSY TUNA

Prep: 3 minutes   Cook: 8 to 10 minutes   Serves: 4

¾ cup cooked fresh, canned, or frozen corn	¼ cup plus 2 tablespoons olive oil
½ cup finely chopped red bell pepper	1 teaspoon salt
3 tablespoons balsamic vinegar	½ teaspoon pepper
	4 tuna steaks, 1 inch thick (about 6 ounces each)

1. Prepare charcoal grill or preheat broiler. In a medium bowl, combine corn, bell pepper, vinegar, ¼ cup olive oil, ½ teaspoon salt, and ¼ teaspoon pepper. Cover and set aside at room temperature.

2. Brush tuna steaks on both sides with remaining 2 tablespoons olive oil and season with remaining salt and pepper. On a well-oiled grill over a medium-hot fire or on a lightly oiled broiling pan under the broiler, cook tuna 4 to 5 minutes per side, until center is still barely translucent.

3. Transfer steaks to individual serving plates and top with equal amounts of corn-pepper mixture.

140 BROILED TROUT CALYPSO

Prep: 2 minutes   Cook: 6 to 8 minutes   Serves: 4

4 trout, 8 to 12 ounces each,
    boned and butterflied
¼ cup fresh lime juice
4 teaspoons butter, melted

½ teaspoon ground cumin
½ teaspoon salt
¼ teaspoon cayenne

1. Preheat broiler. Arrange trout skin side down without touching each other on a lightly oiled broiling pan. Spoon about 1 tablespoon of lime juice over each fish. Drizzle each with 1 teaspoon butter and season with cumin, salt, and cayenne.

2. Broil 4 to 6 inches from heat 6 to 8 minutes without turning, until lightly browned outside and opaque throughout.

Chapter 6

On the Light Side

Poaching and steaming are the purist ways of cooking fish. Natural juices are sealed in and not a bit of fat is needed to provide a healthful, flavorful end result. Leaner fish that benefit from moisture during cooking are cod, halibut, monkfish, snapper, flounder, sole, sea bass, and tilefish. Pink and moist poached salmon falls into its own special category. Shellfish can be poached or steamed, too.

The utensil used for poaching depends on the size and kind of fish. Fillets and steaks can be poached in a large skillet. Larger whole fish need to be cooked in a fish poacher to ensure satisfactory results. Rectangular poachers come in varying sizes with handles to facilitate transferring from stove-top to counter for cooling. Fish poachers have a perforated rack. The rack also helps to lower and raise the fish from the cooking liquid. These pans are expensive and not a part of many home kitchens. A roasting pan long enough to hold the fish flat and deep enough to contain enough liquid to completely cover the fish works well, too. You may wrap a large whole fish in cheesecloth, allowing for extra cloth to extend from either end for lifting in and out of the pan.

Poaching liquid can be as simple as salted water or it can be embellished with aromatic vegetables, wine, or even milk. Simmer poached fish gently; do not allow liquid to boil or it will cause the flesh to break. Cooking times vary according to size and species. The Canadian Cooking Method described on page 45, basically 10 minutes for every inch of fish at its thickest point, is helpful when determining doneness.

Steaming fish means cooking over, rather than immersing in, simmering water. The same fish mentioned above are good for steaming, as are most kinds of shellfish. Again, the utensil used is important. A Chinese bamboo steamer that can be set over simmering water and covered tightly is ideal. These come in stacks, which makes it possible to steam vegetables at the same time, as in the Steamed Scallops with Wilted Spinach recipe in this chapter. Metal steamers are available, too. Both are relatively inexpensive and can be used for cooking a variety of foods. Alternatively, a collapsible steaming basket can be set in a large saucepan with a tight-fitting lid for similar results. Whole fish need the space that a real steamer provides, while fillets and small steaks can be effectively cooked in the basket. Either way, an inch or two of water in the bottom of the pan is all that is needed for successful steaming. Watch the water level closely and add additional water as necessary to prevent scorching.

Poached or steamed fish lends itself to an array of sauces and condiments to bring out flavor and add pizzazz. Lightly steamed or sautéed vegetables make good side dishes. Try sprinkling rice or boiled potatoes with fresh herbs or mixing with chopped fresh tomato as accompaniments.

141   WHOLE POACHED SALMON
Prep: 10 minutes   Cook: 60 to 70 minutes   Chill: 3 hours   Serves: 4

A whole poached salmon makes an elegant centerpiece for a small cocktail party. The decoration can be as simple or as elaborate as desired. Surround with lettuce leaves, lemon or lime wedges, hard-boiled eggs, tomato wedges, olives, and sprigs of fresh parsley. For a special touch, cover with aspic and layer thin overlapping slices of cucumber to resemble scales.

To ensure accuracy of cooking time, lay salmon flat and measure at its thickest point. Cook 10 minutes per inch of thickness, after the liquid is simmering.

Sauce Gribiche is my favorite accompaniment to poached salmon. Mayonnaise blended with a handful of fresh herbs, grated lemon zest, and lots of salt and pepper makes a quick and easy sauce, too.

1 small onion, thickly sliced	1 whole salmon, 6 to
1 carrot, coarsely chopped	8 pounds, cleaned, with
1 celery rib, thickly sliced	head and tail intact
1 tablespoon salt	2 recipes Sauce Gribiche
2 cups dry white wine	(page 11)

1. In a large stockpot, combine 4 quarts water with onion, carrot, celery, and salt. Bring to a boil over high heat. Reduce heat to medium and simmer, uncovered, for 15 minutes. Add wine and simmer 10 minutes longer.

2. Strain mixture into a large fish poacher with a removable rack. (Alternatively, strain liquid into a roasting pan large enough to hold salmon flat and wrap fish in cheesecloth, leaving about 12 inches of cloth extending from both sides to facilitate handling.) Bring liquid to a simmer over medium-high heat, lower salmon into liquid, reduce heat to medium-low, and poach 45 minutes to 1 hour, until a thermometer inserted in thickest part registers 140°F. Remove from heat and let salmon cool in its cooking liquid.

3. Using 2 spatulas, carefully transfer poached salmon to a large serving platter. Remove skin, cover, and refrigerate until chilled, at least 3 hours or overnight. Pass Sauce Gribiche separately on the side.

142 STEAMED COD WITH GREEN TOMATO AND APPLE SALSA

Prep: 5 minutes   Stand: 1 hour   Cook: 7 to 10 minutes   Serves: 4

Early summer finds green tomatoes in abundance. Two or three tomatillos, a small variety found in Latin American markets, can be used as a substitute in this recipe.

1 small Granny Smith apple, cored and cut into ¼-inch dice
1 medium green tomato, cored and cut into ¼-inch dice
½ red onion, thinly sliced
1 tablespoon chopped fresh mint or 1 teaspoon dried
2 tablespoons olive oil
2 tablespoons fresh lime juice
1 teaspoon salt
½ teaspoon pepper
4 cod fillets, about 6 ounces each

1. In a medium bowl, combine apple, green tomato, red onion, mint, olive oil, lime juice, and half the salt and pepper. Stir to blend, cover, and let salsa stand at room temperature for 1 hour.

2. Season cod fillets with remaining ½ teaspoon salt and ¼ teaspoon pepper. In a large covered saucepan fitted with a steamer rack or in a Chinese bamboo steamer, steam fish over high heat until firm and opaque, 7 to 10 minutes. Transfer to individual serving plates and serve hot with salsa.

143 STEAMED FLOUNDER WITH RED TOMATO SALSA

Prep: 5 minutes   Stand: 1 hour   Cook: 7 to 10 minutes   Serves: 4

2 medium tomatoes, cored and cut into ¼-inch dice
1 small onion, finely diced
2 tablespoons olive oil
1 tablespoon white wine vinegar
2 tablespoons chopped fresh basil or parsley
1 teaspoon salt
½ teaspoon pepper
4 flounder fillets, about 6 ounces each

1. In a small bowl, combine tomatoes, onion, olive oil, vinegar, basil, ½ teaspoon salt, and ¼ teaspoon pepper. Stir to blend, cover, and let salsa stand at room temperature for 1 hour.

2. Season fillets with remaining ½ teaspoon salt and ¼ teaspoon pepper. In a large covered saucepan fitted with a steamer rack or in a Chinese bamboo steamer, steam fish over boiling water until firm and opaque, 7 to 10 minutes. Transfer to individual serving plates and serve with a spoonful of salsa.

144   SPICY STEAMED BLUE CRABS
Prep: 2 minutes   Cook: 12 to 15 minutes   Serves: 4

For best results, steam crabs in a large pot with a removable rack. Alternatively, fit a large saucepan with a steaming rack, cover, and cook in batches as described below. Provide guests with nutcrackers and metal picks to remove the succulent crabmeat. Warm melted butter seasoned with garlic and salt makes a flavorful dipping sauce.

1 cup beer	10 whole peppercorns
1 tablespoon fresh lemon	2 bay leaves
juice	16 live blue crabs
3 garlic cloves, peeled	¼ cup crab boil seasoning
1 teaspoon salt	

1. In a large saucepan fitted with a steaming rack or a Chinese bamboo steamer, combine beer, lemon juice, garlic, 1 teaspoon salt, peppercorns, bay leaves, and 1 cup water. Bring to a boil over high heat.

2. Meanwhile, toss or sprinkle crabs with crab boil. Pile into saucepan or steamer, cover tightly, and steam over high heat until bright red, 12 to 15 minutes. If using a bamboo steamer, cook in batches as necessary. Transfer to a large platter or bowl for serving.

145   STEAMED FLOUNDER WITH MUSHROOM STUFFING
Prep: 5 minutes   Cook: 10 to 13 minutes   Serves: 4

1 small onion, quartered	1 tablespoon minced chives or
6 medium mushrooms,	parsley
quartered	1 teaspoon salt
1 tablespoon fresh lemon	½ teaspoon pepper
juice	4 flounder fillets, about
2 tablespoons butter	6 ounces each, halved
¼ cup fresh bread crumbs	lengthwise
	½ teaspoon paprika

1. Finely chop onion and mushrooms with lemon juice in a food processor or by hand. In a large skillet, melt butter over medium-high heat. Add mushroom mixture and cook until smooth and pasty, about 3 minutes. Remove from heat. Stir in bread crumbs, herbs, ½ teaspoon salt, and ¼ teaspoon pepper.

2. Lay 4 flounder fillet halves flat on a work surface. Spread each with about 2 tablespoons of mushroom stuffing. Top with remaining halves. Transfer to a large steaming rack, sprinkle with paprika, cover, and steam over high heat until opaque throughout, 7 to 10 minutes. Serve at once.

146   MUSSELS, CLAMS, AND OYSTERS STEAMED IN WINE AND HERBS

Prep: 5 minutes   Cook: 5 to 7 minutes   Serves: 4

1 cup dry white wine	12 mussels, scrubbed and
4 sprigs of fresh thyme or	beards removed
1 teaspoon dried	12 littleneck clams, scrubbed
4 sprigs of fresh rosemary or	12 oysters, scrubbed
1 teaspoon dried	4 garlic cloves, minced
1 teaspoon salt	3 shallots, minced
½ teaspoon pepper	
¼ to ½ teaspoon cayenne, to taste	

1. In a large steamer or stockpot, combine wine, thyme, rosemary, salt, pepper, cayenne, and 1 cup water. Bring to a boil over high heat.

2. In a large bowl or pan, toss mussels, clams, and oysters with garlic and shallots. Add to steamer or stockpot, cover, and steam, stirring occasionally, until shells open, 5 to 7 minutes. Discard any shellfish that do not open. With a slotted spoon, transfer shellfish to 4 individual serving bowls.

3. Strain cooking liquid through a fine-mesh sieve lined with a double layer of cheesecloth. Pour equal amounts of strained liquid over each serving. Serve at once.

147   POACHED SNAPPER WITH ORANGE

Prep: 5 minutes   Cook: 8 to 11 minutes   Serves: 4

1 tablespoon olive oil	4 snapper fillets, about
1 garlic clove, minced	6 ounces each
¼ cup dry white wine	2 teaspoons grated orange zest
¼ cup fresh orange juice	1 tablespoon chopped parsley
½ teaspoon salt	1 large orange, peeled and cut
½ teaspoon pepper	into sections

1. In a large nonreactive skillet, heat olive oil over medium heat. Add garlic and cook, stirring constantly, until soft and fragrant, about 1 minute. Pour in wine, orange juice, ¼ teaspoon salt, and ¼ teaspoon pepper. Stir to combine. Gently place fish on top.

2. Sprinkle each snapper fillet with equal amounts of orange zest, parsley, and remaining ¼ teaspoon each salt and pepper. Cover skillet and poach until fish is opaque throughout, 6 to 8 minutes. With a slotted spatula, transfer fillets to a platter and cover with aluminum foil to keep warm.

3. Raise heat to high and boil remaining liquid, stirring occasionally, until reduced to about 3 tablespoons, 1 to 2 minutes. Spoon sauce over snapper and garnish with orange sections.

148 CHILLED POACHED SALMON STEAKS WITH DILLED YOGURT SAUCE

Prep: 3 minutes   Cook: 10 minutes   Chill: 2 hours   Serves: 4

1 cup dry white wine
1 small onion, coarsely
    chopped
1 celery rib, coarsely chopped
2 garlic cloves, peeled
1 bay leaf
¾ teaspoon salt
½ teaspoon pepper

4 salmon steaks, 1 inch thick
    (6 to 8 ounces each)
1 cup plain yogurt
2 teaspoons fresh lemon juice
1 tablespoon chopped fresh
    dill or 1 teaspoon dried
Sprigs of fresh dill

1. In a large nonreactive skillet or flameproof casserole, combine wine, onion, celery, garlic, bay leaf, ½ teaspoon salt, ¼ teaspoon pepper, and 1 cup water. Bring to a boil over high heat. Add salmon steaks, reduce heat to medium-low, cover, and poach until fish flakes, about 10 minutes. Remove to a platter with a slotted spatula and let cool to room temperature. Cover and refrigerate until thoroughly chilled, at least 2 hours.

2. Meanwhile, in a small bowl, combine yogurt, lemon juice, chopped dill, and remaining ¼ teaspoon each salt and pepper. Stir to blend well, cover, and refrigerate sauce until chilled, at least 2 hours.

3. Arrange salmon steaks on 4 individual serving plates. Top with a table-spoonful of dilled yogurt sauce and garnish with sprigs of fresh dill. Pass remaining sauce on the side.

149 FLOUNDER POACHED WITH TRICOLORED PEPPERS

Prep: 3 minutes   Cook: 5 to 7 minutes   Serves: 4

1 cup dry white wine
2 tablespoons olive oil
½ green bell pepper, thinly
    sliced
½ red bell pepper, thinly
    sliced

½ yellow bell pepper, thinly
    sliced
½ teaspoon salt
½ teaspoon pepper
4 flounder fillets, about
    6 ounces each

1. In a large nonreactive skillet or flameproof casserole, combine wine, olive oil, sliced bell peppers, salt, pepper, and ½ cup water. Bring to a boil over high heat.

2. Add flounder fillets, reduce heat to medium-low, cover, and simmer until flounder flakes and is opaque throughout, 5 to 7 minutes. With a slotted spatula, transfer fillets with peppers to individual serving plates and serve immediately.

150   STEAMED SEA BASS WITH BEET RELISH

Prep: 7 minutes   Stand: 1 hour   Cook: 7 to 10 minutes   Serves: 4

2 small canned or fully
   cooked beets, cut into
   tiny dice
1 (1-inch) piece of fresh
   ginger, peeled and
   minced, or ½ teaspoon
   ground ginger
2 teaspoons grated orange zest

1 scallion, thinly sliced
¼ cup fresh orange juice
2 tablespoons olive oil
1 teaspoon salt
½ teaspoon pepper
4 sea bass fillets, about 6
   ounces each

1. In a medium bowl, combine beets, ginger, orange zest, scallion, orange juice, olive oil, ½ teaspoon salt, and ¼ teaspoon pepper. Stir to blend. Cover and let stand at room temperature for 1 hour.

2. Season sea bass fillets with remaining ½ teaspoon salt and ¼ teaspoon pepper. In a large covered saucepan fitted with a steamer rack or in a Chinese bamboo steamer, steam fish over high heat until firm and opaque, 7 to 10 minutes. Transfer to individual serving plates and garnish with a spoonful of beet relish on the side.

151   STEAMED SCALLOPS WITH WILTED SPINACH AND LEMON CREAM SAUCE

Prep: 5 minutes   Cook: 10 to 12 minutes   Serves: 4

1 cup heavy cream
½ teaspoon grated lemon zest
1 tablespoon fresh lemon
   juice
¾ teaspoon salt
½ teaspoon pepper

1 pound fresh spinach (about
   4 cups loosely packed),
   tough stems removed
1 pound bay scallops or
   halved sea scallops

1. To prepare sauce, pour cream into a large nonreactive saucepan. Add lemon zest and bring to a boil over high heat. Boil until reduced by half, about 5 minutes. Remove from heat and stir in lemon juice, ¼ teaspoon salt, and ¼ teaspoon pepper. Set aside, covered to keep warm.

2. Spread spinach leaves evenly on a steaming rack and season with remaining ½ teaspoon salt and ¼ teaspoon pepper. Scatter scallops on top of spinach, cover pan, and steam over high heat until scallops are opaque throughout and spinach is warm and wilted, 5 to 7 minutes. Divide spinach and scallops evenly among 4 individual serving plates, spoon a small amount of lemon cream sauce on top, and serve at once.

152   STEAMED SEA BASS WITH HERB BUTTER

Prep: 6 minutes   Freeze: 30 minutes   Cook: 4 to 6 minutes   Serves: 4

4 tablespoons butter, softened
2 teaspoons fresh lemon juice
1 teaspoon fresh thyme leaves
  or ¼ teaspoon dried
¾ teaspoon salt
½ teaspoon pepper
1 cup dry white wine

1 small onion, coarsely
  chopped
1 celery rib, coarsely chopped
2 garlic cloves, peeled
3 sprigs of parsley
4 sea bass fillets, about
  6 ounces each

1. In a medium bowl, combine butter, lemon juice, thyme, ¼ teaspoon salt, and ¼ teaspoon pepper, stirring with a fork until blended. Place on a small piece of plastic wrap, form into a 2-inch-long cylinder, and twist ends tightly closed. Freeze until firm, about 30 minutes.

2. Preheat oven to 375°F. In a medium nonreactive saucepan, combine wine, onion, celery, garlic, parsley, remaining ½ teaspoon salt and ¼ teaspoon pepper, and 1 cup water. Bring to a boil over high heat. Pour liquid into a broiler pan fitted with a lightly oiled rack. Arrange fillets on rack, cover loosely with aluminum foil, and steam in oven until fish flakes and is opaque throughout, 4 to 6 minutes. Remove fillets with a spatula to 4 individual serving plates and top each with a thick slice of herb butter. Serve immediately.

153   STEAMED SHRIMP WITH SOY AND GINGER

Prep: 3 minutes   Cook: 3 to 4 minutes   Serves: 4

Line a large platter with lettuce leaves, pile shrimp in the center, and surround with lemon and lime wedges. Serve shrimp in shells and let guests peel their own.

3 tablespoons soy sauce
1 (1-inch) piece of fresh
  ginger, peeled and
  minced
2 scallions (white part only),
  thinly sliced

2 garlic cloves, minced
½ to 1 teaspoon crushed hot
  red pepper, to taste
1½ pounds medium shrimp
½ cup sake or dry white wine
¼ teaspoon salt

1. In a large bowl, combine soy sauce, ginger, scallions, garlic, and hot pepper. Add shrimp and toss to coat thoroughly.

2. Meanwhile, in a large covered saucepan fitted with a steaming rack or a Chinese bamboo steamer, combine sake, salt, and 1 cup water. Bring to a boil over high heat. Add shrimp, cover, and steam, stirring occasionally, until bright pink and curled, 3 to 4 minutes. Serve hot; or let cool to room temperature, cover, and refrigerate until thoroughly chilled.

154   WHOLE STEAMED TROUT STUFFED WITH CRAB

Prep: 3 minutes   Cook: 10 minutes   Serves: 4

Farm-raised trout are increasingly available as aquaculture becomes more and more important as an industry. Look for these easy-to-prepare fish in grocery stores and in regional farmers' markets.

¼ cup fresh bread crumbs
½ pound crabmeat
2 teaspoons chopped fresh marjoram or ½ teaspoon dried
1 teaspoon salt

½ teaspoon pepper
2 tablespoons butter, melted
4 whole trout, 6 to 8 ounces each, cleaned, head and tail intact

1. In a small bowl, combine bread crumbs, crab, marjoram, ½teaspoon salt, and ¼ teaspoon pepper. Add butter and toss lightly to mix.

2. Season inside cavity of trout with remaining salt and pepper. Loosely fill with crab stuffing and secure with toothpicks.

3. Place trout flat on a steaming rack set over simmering water. Steam, covered, until fish is firm when pressed in center, about 10 minutes. Remove toothpicks and serve at once.

Chapter 7

Fish in a Flash

Heat bothers me, and it seems as if in every place I've ever lived, I wind up having my everyday eating area in the kitchen. For this reason, I plan meals in the summer months that keep cooking to a minimum. During those dog days of July and August when the misery of it all comes to a head in the evening, just when I'm ready to have my dinner, I'll do anything to find relief. This is where I first learned the merits of having a microwave oven. After years of shunning this new-fangled device, I found that rather than heating a traditional oven to 400°F to bake my favorite summer food, fish, I could achieve the same results in less time without the discomfort of more hot air.

No matter what time of year, I found that fish works well in the microwave. A high water content makes it easy for penetrating waves of heat-producing vibrations to cook fish and shellfish evenly and efficiently. Fillets, steaks, and whole fish can be prepared with a minimum of fuss. Crab, shrimp, clams, and mussels are good candidates as well.

Power levels vary from machine to machine. All the recipes here call for fish to be cooked on High power and were developed using a 700-watt microwave. Check manufacturer's instructions for your particular machine. A few general guidelines are helpful when cooking fish in the microwave:

Place fish in a microwave-safe dish deep enough to allow an inch or so of space between it and the microwave-safe plastic wrap used for cover. Fold back one corner of the wrap to allow steam to escape during cooking. Tuck under ends of thin fillets for even cooking and arrange around outer edge of the dish. After cooking for times indicated in recipes, cover tightly and let fish stand for 2 to 3 minutes before serving to absorb flavor and moisture. Pour off accumulated juices and save for making a sauce, flavoring soups, or pouring over cooked fish.

Lemon juice, white wine, or bottled clam juice, used in small amounts, can be added to fish just before microwaving for added flavor. Fresh herbs, spices, and quick-cooking vegetables like thinly sliced peppers, finely chopped onions, cucumbers, spinach, and diced zucchini are good additions, too.

To use the microwave properly requires some reading and practicing. Here are a few fish recipes that are simple enough for the novice to execute but interesting enough for the enthusiast to enjoy.

155   BLUEFISH WITH LEMON-ROSEMARY MAYONNAISE

Prep: 3 minutes   Cook: 5 to 7 minutes   Serves: 4

¼ cup mayonnaise
2 tablespoons minced onion
1 tablespoon fresh lemon
   juice
½ teaspoon dried rosemary,
   crumbled

½ teaspoon salt
¼ teaspoon pepper
4 bluefish fillets, 6 to 8 ounces
   each

1. In a medium bowl, combine mayonnaise, onion, lemon juice, rosemary, salt, and pepper. Stir to blend well. Spread equal amounts evenly on each fillet.

2. Place fillets in a large microwave-safe dish and cover with microwave-safe plastic wrap, folding back one edge to allow steam to escape. Cook on High until opaque throughout, 5 to 7 minutes. Remove from microwave and let stand for 2 minutes, covered, before serving.

156   BLUEFISH WITH MUSTARD AND CAPERS

Prep: 4 minutes   Cook: 5 to 7 minutes   Serves: 4

4 tablespoons butter, softened
1 tablespoon Dijon mustard
1 tablespoon capers, chopped
½ teaspoon salt

¼ teaspoon pepper
4 bluefish fillets, 6 to 8 ounces
   each
¼ teaspoon paprika

1. In a small bowl, mix butter and mustard with a fork until smooth. Add capers, salt, and pepper and blend well. Spread equal amounts evenly over each fillet. Sprinkle paprika on top.

2. Place fillets in a large microwave-safe dish and cover with microwave-safe plastic wrap, folding back one edge to allow steam to escape. Cook on High until opaque throughout, 5 to 7 minutes. Let stand for 2 minutes, covered, before serving.

157   CATFISH MORNAY
Prep: 4 minutes   Cook: 8 to 9 minutes   Serves: 4

1 pound catfish fillets, cut into 1-inch pieces	1 tablespoon flour
¼ cup dry white wine	½ cup heavy cream
¾ teaspoon salt	1 cup shredded Swiss cheese (about 4 ounces)
½ teaspoon pepper	2 cups cooked white rice
1 tablespoon butter	¼ cup dry bread crumbs

1. In a large microwave-safe casserole, combine fish, wine, and ¼ teaspoon each salt and pepper. Cover with microwave-safe plastic wrap and turn back one corner to allow steam to escape. Cook on Medium until barely opaque, about 3 minutes. Drain off liquid and set aside, covered.

2. In a 2-cup glass measuring cup, heat butter on High power until melted, 35 to 45 seconds. Remove from microwave and blend in flour with a fork. Pour in cream and add remaining ½ teaspoon salt and ¼ teaspoon pepper. Cook on High for 1 minute. Remove from microwave, stir, and cook on High 30 to 60 seconds longer, until slightly thickened. Add ½ cup of cheese to sauce while hot and stir well to blend.

3. Spread rice evenly over bottom of a large microwave-safe casserole and arrange fish on top. Spoon sauce over fish and sprinkle remaining cheese and bread crumbs on top. Cook, uncovered, on High until bubbly and heated through, 3 to 4 minutes. Serve hot.

158   CATFISH WITH SPINACH AND PEPPERS
Prep: 5 minutes   Cook: 9 minutes   Serves: 4

1 red bell pepper, thinly sliced	¾ teaspoon salt
1 garlic clove, minced	½ teaspoon pepper
1 tablespoon olive oil	4 catfish fillets, about 6 ounces each
2 pounds fresh spinach, well rinsed, large stems removed (about 8 cups)	1 tablespoon fresh lemon juice

1. Combine bell pepper, garlic, and olive oil in a large microwave-safe casserole. Toss to coat with oil. Cover with microwave-safe plastic wrap. Cook on High power until tender, about 4 minutes, stirring once.

2. Remove casserole from oven and pile on spinach. Season with ¼ teaspoon each salt and pepper. Arrange fillets on top and season with remaining ½ teaspoon salt and ¼ teaspoon pepper. Cover with microwave-safe plastic wrap and turn back one corner to allow steam to escape.

3. Cook on High until fish is opaque throughout, about 5 minutes. Let stand, covered, for 3 minutes. Sprinkle with lemon juice just before serving.

159 CATFISH WITH TOMATOES AND MUSHROOMS

Prep: 6 minutes   Cook: 15 to 17 minutes   Serves: 4

1 tablespoon olive oil
1 small onion, finely chopped
1 garlic clove, minced
1 (14-ounce) can Italian peeled tomatoes, drained and chopped

¾ teaspoon salt
½ teaspoon pepper
4 catfish fillets, about 6 ounces each
¼ pound mushrooms, thinly sliced

1. In a large microwave-safe casserole, combine olive oil, onion, and garlic. Toss to mix. Cover with microwave-safe plastic wrap and cook on High power until tender, 3 to 4 minutes.

2. Stir in tomatoes and ¼ teaspoon each salt and pepper. Cover again with plastic wrap and turn back one corner to allow steam to escape. Cook on High power until thick and bubbly, stirring once, about 8 minutes.

3. Place fish on top of tomato mixture, add mushrooms, and season with remaining ½ teaspoon and ¼ teaspoon pepper. Cover and cook on High until fish is opaque throughout, 4 to 5 minutes. Remove from oven and let stand, covered, for 3 minutes before serving.

160 GARLICKY ZAPPED CLAMS

Prep: 5 minutes   Cook: 5 to 7 minutes   Serves: 4

Serve these easy, delicious clams as a first course with fresh bread for dipping in flavorful cooking liquid

20 littleneck clams, scrubbed clean
3 tablespoons olive oil
5 garlic cloves, minced
2 shallots, minced

1 tablespoon chopped parsley
½ teaspoon salt
½ teaspoon crushed hot red pepper
Lemon wedges

1. Place clams in a round, microwave-safe 3-quart casserole. In a small bowl, combine olive oil, garlic, shallots, parsley, salt, and hot pepper. Stir to blend well, then pour over clams.

2. Cover dish with microwave-safe plastic wrap and make several small slits with a knife to allow steam to escape. Microwave on High until clams open, 5 to 7 minutes. Discard any that do not open.

3. Divide clams equally among 4 individual serving bowls, drizzle on cooking liquid from casserole, garnish with lemon wedges, and serve immediately.

161   BREADED COD
Prep: 3 minutes   Cook: 8 minutes   Serves: 4

4 skinless cod fillets, about
  6 ounces each
¼ cup olive oil

½ teaspoon salt
½ teaspoon pepper
1 cup seasoned bread crumbs

1. Brush fillets liberally on both sides with olive oil and season with salt and pepper. Place bread crumbs in a shallow bowl, add fillets, and turn several times to coat well.

2. Arrange fish in a single layer on a large microwave-safe dish. Cover loosely with wax paper and cook on Medium until fish is opaque throughout and lightly browned on top, about 8 minutes. Remove from microwave and let stand, covered, for 2 minutes before serving.

162   MICROWAVE PROVENÇAL FISH FILLETS
Prep: 5 minutes   Cook: 8 minutes   Serves: 4

2 medium tomatoes, peeled,
  seeded, and chopped
1 tablespoon white wine
  vinegar
2 tablespoons olive oil
1 garlic clove, minced
1 tablespoon chopped fresh
  herbs (thyme, rosemary,
  tarragon, or basil) or
  ¾ teaspoon dried

½ teaspoon salt
¼ teaspoon pepper
4 skinless fresh fish fillets
  (cod, scrod, grouper, or
  whitefish), about
  6 ounces each

1. In a small bowl, combine tomatoes, vinegar, olive oil, garlic, herbs, salt, and pepper. Stir well to blend.

2. Arrange fish fillets in a microwave-safe dish large enough to hold them in a single layer. Pour tomato mixture over fish and cover with microwave-safe plastic wrap; fold over one edge to allow steam to escape. Cook on Medium until fillets are opaque throughout, about 8 minutes. Remove from microwave and let stand, covered, for 2 to 3 minutes before serving.

163 MICROWAVED SALMON STEAKS WITH CUCUMBER AND MINT

Prep: 4 minutes   Cook: 15 to 18 minutes   Serves: 4

1 medium cucumber, peeled,
  halved lengthwise,
  seeded, and thinly sliced
1 tablespoon butter
¾ teaspoon salt

½ teaspoon pepper
4 salmon steaks, 1 inch thick
  (6 to 8 ounces each)
1 tablespoon chopped fresh
  mint

1. In a large microwave-safe casserole, combine cucumber slices, butter, ¼ teaspoon salt, and ¼ teaspoon pepper. Cook on High, stirring once, until tender, about 3 minutes.

2. Remove from microwave, arrange fish on top, and season with remaining ½ teaspoon salt and ¼ teaspoon pepper. Cover dish with microwave-safe plastic wrap and fold back one corner to allow steam to escape. Cook on Medium 7 minutes. Turn steaks over and cook until fish is opaque in center, 5 to 8 minutes longer. Sprinkle mint over salmon just before serving.

164 SALMON WITH CREAMED LEEKS

Prep: 3 minutes   Cook: 12 minutes   Serves: 4

2 medium leeks (white and
  tender green), halved
  lengthwise and thinly
  sliced
1½ pounds salmon fillets, cut
  into 4 equal pieces

1 cup heavy cream
½ teaspoon salt
½ teaspoon pepper

1. Arrange leeks on bottom of a microwave-safe dish. Place fish skin side down on top. Pour cream around leeks and season all over with salt and pepper. Cover with microwave-safe plastic wrap and turn back one corner to allow steam to escape. Cook on High for 3 minutes. Turn fish over, cover again with plastic wrap, and cook until fish springs back when pressed with a finger, about 2 minutes longer. Remove fish to a serving platter, covered to keep warm, and set aside.

2. Cover leeks and cream and cook on High until leeks are tender and cream is thickened, stirring once, about 7 minutes. Spoon hot sauce and leeks over fish and serve at once.

165 MICROWAVE SCROD WITH SWEET AND SOUR CARROTS

Prep: 5 minutes   Cook: 13 minutes   Serves: 4

4 medium carrots, peeled and cut into ¼-inch slices (about 2 cups)	½ teaspoon pepper
1 tablespoon butter	4 scrod fillets, about 6 ounces each
2 tablespoons honey	1 tablespoon fresh lemon juice
1 teaspoon Dijon mustard	½ teaspoon grated lemon zest (optional)
¾ teaspoon salt	

1. In a large microwave-safe casserole, combine carrots, butter, honey, mustard, ¼ teaspoon salt, and ¼ teaspoon pepper. Cover with microwave-safe plastic wrap and turn back one corner to allow steam to escape. Cook on High until slightly tender, about 5 minutes, stirring after 2 minutes.

2. Arrange fish fillets over carrots and season with lemon juice, lemon zest, and remaining ½ teaspoon salt and ¼ teaspoon pepper. Cover with plastic wrap, turn back one corner to allow steam to escape, and cook on Medium until fish is opaque throughout, about 8 minutes, turning after 5 minutes. Remove from microwave and let stand for 2 minutes, covered, before serving.

166 SEA BASS WITH SOY SAUCE AND RICE WINE VINEGAR

Prep: 5 minutes   Cook: 20 minutes   Serves: 2

1 whole bass, 2 to 3 pounds, head and tail intact	1 tablespoon rice wine vinegar
2 tablespoons soy sauce	½ teaspoon pepper
2 scallions, thinly sliced	
1 (1-inch) piece of fresh ginger, peeled and grated	

1. Arrange fish flat on a large microwave-safe serving platter. In a small bowl, combine soy sauce, scallions, ginger, vinegar, and pepper. Stir well to blend and pour over fish.

2. Cover platter with microwave-safe plastic wrap and turn back one corner to allow steam to escape. Cook on Medium until fish is opaque throughout, about 20 minutes, turning once. Let rest for 2 minutes, covered, and serve at once.

167   CRUNCHY SHRIMP
Prep: 5 minutes   Cook: 2 minutes   Serves: 4

4 cups loosely packed flaked
   corn cereal
1 teaspoon salt
½ teaspoon pepper

½ teaspoon paprika
2 eggs
1½ pounds medium shrimp,
   shelled and deveined

1. In a food processor, combine corn cereal, salt, pepper, and paprika. Process until finely ground and pour crumbs into a shallow bowl.

2. In a medium bowl, beat eggs until frothy. Add shrimp to bowl and toss to coat with egg. One at a time, remove shrimp, letting excess egg drain back into bowl, and add to seasoned crumbs. Dredge until shrimp is covered in crumbs; remove shrimp to a sheet of wax paper. Repeat until all shrimp are coated.

3. Arrange shrimp on outer rim of a microwave-safe dish (do in two batches, if necessary). Cover with microwave-safe plastic wrap and fold back one edge to allow steam to escape. Cook on High for 2 minutes. Remove from microwave and let stand, covered, for 1 minute, before serving.

168   TROUT WITH WINE AND TARRAGON
Prep: 2 minutes   Cook: 12 to 15 minutes   Serves: 2

Try filling cavity with fresh herb sprigs, shallots, or garlic for added flavor, if desired. Serve with couscous mixed with halved raisins and toasted nuts.

2 whole trout, 6 to 8 ounces
   each, head and tail intact
¼ cup dry white wine
1 tablespoon minced fresh
   tarragon or 1 teaspoon
   dried

¾ teaspoon salt
½ teaspoon pepper

1. Place fish on a large microwave-safe platter, pour wine over fish, and sprinkle with tarragon. Season with salt and pepper. Cover with microwave-safe plastic wrap and turn one edge over to allow steam to escape.

2. Cook on Medium until fish springs back when pressed in center and is opaque near bone, 12 to 15 minutes. Let stand, covered, for 2 minutes before serving.

Chapter 8

Seafood Under Wraps

From the French term for paper package, *en papil-lote* is one of the best ways to seal in juices when cooking lean fish. Brushed lightly with oil or butter, fish is enveloped in paper or aluminum foil with seasonings, crimped around the edges to form a tight seal, and baked in a hot oven until puffed and golden. The fish is served right out of the oven, in its wrapping, to be opened by the diner at the table. Parchment paper is excellent for this technique, but foil is more readily available and works just as well. (Some acids, like wine or lemon juice, will slightly discolor foil, but don't be put off; it is completely harmless.)

Quick-cooking finely chopped onion, mush-rooms, tomatoes, or any aromatic vegetable can be added to the package for flavor. Fresh herbs, chopped and sprinkled over fish just before sealing and cooking, make a lovely addition. Soy sauce, ginger, garlic, and curry are some of the enhancements used in the following recipes. The imaginative cook will be able to mix and match similar ingredients to provide an interesting dish using this most simple cooking method.

Thin, delicate fillets of fresh fish like sole, flounder, pompano, or snapper do well *en papillote*. Catfish, orange roughy, tilefish, grouper, and salmon fillets are good candidates, too. The sealing in of juices prevents drying out, providing essential moisture to fish that are susceptible to the rigors of oven heat.

Cooked couscous, rice, or potatoes can be added to the package before sealing. The result is a surprisingly easy one-dish meal that needs only a garnish of green vegetables or a tossed salad to round out a quick lunch or dinner menu. Fish wrapped in parchment can be served right on the plate. Bring foil-wrapped packets to the table, so guests can enjoy the burst of aroma when they pierce the center of the papillote with their knives. Just warn everyone to be careful of the hot steam. Then transfer the fish and any other contents of the package to the plate and dispose of the foil before eating.

169   CHILI-LIME BLUEFISH
Prep: 2 minutes   Cook: 10 to 12 minutes   Serves: 4

4 bluefish fillets, about
    6 ounces each
¼ cup olive oil
¼ cup fresh lime juice

½ teaspoon chili powder
¼ teaspoon salt
1 tablespoon chopped cilantro
    or parsley

1. Preheat oven to 425°F. Arrange fish on 4 pieces of foil that measure 12 inches wide by 15 inches long. Spoon 1 tablespoon olive oil over each fillet. Sprinkle each with 1 tablespoon lime juice and dust with about ⅛ teaspoon chili powder. Season lightly with salt. Sprinkle cilantro over all.

2. Fold top of foil over bottom and crimp edges tightly to seal. Arrange packets on a baking sheet in a single layer. Bake 10 to 12 minutes, or until foil is puffed and fish is opaque throughout.

170   BLUEFISH EN PAPILLOTE
Prep: 3 minutes   Cook: 10 to 12 minutes   Serves: 4

4 bluefish fillets, 4 to 6 ounces
    each
¼ teaspoon salt
¼ teaspoon pepper

¼ cup olive oil
2 garlic cloves, minced
½ cup grated Parmesan cheese

1. Preheat oven to 425°F. Place fillets in the center of 4 pieces of foil that measure 12 inches wide by 15 inches long. Season with salt and pepper. Drizzle 1 tablespoon olive oil over each piece of fish and scatter garlic on top. Sprinkle 2 tablespoons grated cheese over each fillet.

2. Fold top of foil over bottom and crimp edges tightly to seal. Place packets in a large baking dish in a single layer. Bake 10 to 12 minutes, or until foil is puffed and fish is opaque throughout.

171   CATFISH CAPERS
Prep: 3 minutes   Cook: 10 to 12 minutes   Serves: 4

4 catfish fillets, 4 to 6 ounces
    each
½ teaspoon salt

¼ teaspoon pepper
4 teaspoons drained capers
¼ cup dry white wine

1. Preheat oven to 425°F. Place fish fillets in center of 4 pieces of well-buttered foil that measure 12 inches wide and 15 inches long. Season with salt and pepper.

2. Sprinkle 1 teaspoon capers and 1 tablespoon wine over each fillet. Fold top over bottom and crimp edges tightly to seal. Place on a baking sheet and bake 10 to 12 minutes, or until foil is puffed and fish is tender and opaque throughout.

172 CALICO CORN AND PEPPER FISH BOATS
Prep: 5 minutes   Cook: 10 to 12 minutes   Serves: 4

4 fish fillets (mackerel,
  bluefish, mahi-mahi, or
  salmon), 4 to 6 ounces
  each
½ teaspoon salt
¼ teaspoon pepper

2 cups cooked fresh, canned,
  or frozen corn
1 medium red bell pepper,
  finely diced
1 garlic clove, minced
4 tablespoons butter, melted

1. Preheat oven to 425°F. Lay fish flat on 4 pieces of foil that measure 12 inches wide and 15 inches long. Season with salt and pepper. Sprinkle equal amounts of corn, bell pepper, and garlic over each fish fillet and drizzle 1 tablespoon melted butter.

2. Fold top of foil over bottom and crimp edges tightly to seal. Arrange packets on a baking sheet in a single layer. Bake 10 to 12 minutes, or until foil is puffed and fish flakes easily.

173 DIJON DIVINE FISH FILLETS
Prep: 5 minutes   Cook: 10 to 12 minutes   Serves: 4

Black peppercorns blend well with the mustard in this recipe. Try using pink or green peppercorns for a colorful variation. To crush, seal peppercorns in a plastic bag. Use a mallet, a rolling pin, or the flat side of a large knife to crush.

1 cup fresh bread crumbs
2 tablespoons Dijon mustard
4 tablespoons butter, melted
½ teaspoon salt
4 dark fish fillets (mackerel,
  bluefish, tuna, or mullet),
  4 to 6 ounces each

2 teaspoons black
  peppercorns, finely
  crushed

1. Preheat oven to 425°F. In a medium mixing bowl, combine bread crumbs, mustard, butter, and salt.

2. Place fillets on 4 pieces of foil that measure 12 inches wide and 15 inches long. Spread about 3 tablespoons of mustard crumbs evenly over each fillet. Sprinkle about ½ teaspoon crushed pepper over each fillet.

3. Fold top of foil over bottom and crimp edges tightly to seal. Arrange packets on a baking sheet in a single layer. Bake 10 to 12 minutes, or until foil is puffed and fish is cooked through.

174   FISH PROVENÇAL EN PAPILLOTE
Prep: 3 minutes   Cook: 10 to 12 minutes   Serves: 4

4 ounces firm white fish fillets
    (flounder, snapper, bass,
    catfish, or orange
    roughy), about 6 ounces
    each
3 medium tomatoes, peeled,
    seeded, and chopped

2 garlic cloves, finely minced
1 tablespoon fresh thyme
    leaves or 2 teaspoons
    dried
¼ teaspoon salt
⅛ teaspoon pepper
¼ cup olive oil

1. Preheat oven to 425°F. Tear off 4 pieces of foil that measure about 12 inches wide and 15 inches long. Place 1 fillet on each piece of foil. Spoon equal amounts of tomato over each of the fillets. Sprinkle with garlic and thyme. Season with salt and pepper. Drizzle 1 tablespoon of oil over each fillet. Fold top of foil over bottom and crimp edges tightly to seal.

2. Arrange foil packages on a large baking sheet in a single layer. Bake 10 to 12 minutes, until foil is puffed and fish is cooked through.

175   FISH FILLETS WITH SNOW PEAS
Prep: 3 minutes   Cook: 10 to 12 minutes   Serves: 4

4 fish fillets (trout, flounder,
    sole, snapper, bass, or
    salmon), 4 to 6 ounces
    each
½ teaspoon pepper
20 snow pea pods, stemmed,
    stringed, and cut
    lengthwise into thin
    strips

¼ cup vegetable oil
¼ cup soy sauce
4 teaspoons toasted sesame
    seeds

1. Preheat oven to 425°F. Lay fish flat on 4 pieces of foil that measure 12 inches wide and 15 inches long. Season with pepper. Divide snow peas equally among the fillets and drizzle with 1 tablespoon each of oil and soy sauce. Sprinkle each fillet with 1 teaspoon sesame seeds.

2. Fold top of foil over bottom and crimp edges tightly to seal. Arrange on a baking sheet in a single layer. Bake 10 to 12 minutes, until foil is puffed and fish is cooked through.

176 SHERRIED FISH WITH ALMONDS EN PAPILLOTE

Prep: 2 minutes   Cook: 10 to 12 minutes   Serves: 4

½ cup toasted almonds
2 tablespoons butter
¼ cup dry Spanish sherry
4 firm-fleshed fish fillets
     (mackerel, bluefish,
     grouper, mahi-mahi, or
     catfish), about 6 ounces
     each

½ teaspoon salt
¼ teaspoon pepper

1. In the bowl of a food processor, combine almonds, butter, and sherry. Puree until smooth.

2. Preheat oven to 425°F. Arrange fillets in center of 4 pieces of foil that measure 12 inches wide and 15 inches long. Season with salt and pepper. Spread one-fourth of the almond mixture over each fillet. Fold top of foil over bottom and crimp edges tightly to seal.

3. Arrange packets on a baking sheet in a single layer. Bake 10 to 12 minutes, until foil is puffed and fish is cooked through.

177 GREEK-STYLE FISH IN FOIL WITH OLIVES AND FETA CHEESE

Prep: 5 minutes   Cook: 10 to 12 minutes   Serves: 4

4 firm-fleshed fish
     fillets(salmon, bass,
     perch, mahi-mahi,
     mullet, or bluefish), 4 to 6
     ounces each
¼ cup olive oil

4 ounces feta cheese
1 cup pitted black olives,
     preferably kalamata,
     coarsely chopped
2 teaspoons fresh lemon juice
½ teaspoon pepper

1. Preheat oven to 425°F. Place fish fillets in center of 4 pieces of foil that measure 12 inches wide and 15 inches long. Drizzle 1 tablespoon olive oil over each. Crumble equal amounts of cheese over each fillet and scatter olives on top. Sprinkle each fillet with a small amount of lemon juice and season with pepper.

2. Fold top of foil over bottom. Crimp edges tightly to seal. Arrange packets on a baking sheet in a single layer. Bake 10 to 12 minutes, until foil is puffed and fish is opaque throughout.

178   FISH STEAKS WITH ASPARAGUS AND WHITE WINE

Prep: 5 minutes   Cook: 10 to 12 minutes   Serves: 4

Many larger fish such as tilefish, code, tuna, swordfish, and grouper are cut into slices and sold as "steaks." These fish are perfect for cooking *en papillote*. For a special touch, substitute strips of homemade roasted red bell pepper for the pimientos.

4 **fish steaks, cut about 1 inch thick (4 to 6 ounces each)**
½ **teaspoon salt**
¼ **teaspoon pepper**
4 **tablespoons butter, melted**
20 **asparagus spears, trimmed of all but 1 inch of stem and peeled**

2 **whole pimientos, cut into long thin strips**
¼ **cup dry white wine**

1. Preheat oven to 425°F. Place fish steaks in center of 4 pieces of foil that measure 12 inches wide and 15 inches long. Season with salt and pepper. Pour 1 tablespoon butter over each steak. Top each with 5 asparagus spears and strew over equal amounts of pimiento strips. Sprinkle each with 1 tablespoon white wine.

2. Fold top of foil over to meet bottom. Crimp edges tightly to seal. Place on a baking sheet in a single layer. Bake 10 to 12 minutes, until foil is puffed and fish is cooked through.

179   BARBECUED KINGFISH

Prep: 1 minute   Cook: 10 to 12 minutes   Serves: 4

Kingfish, also known as king mackerel, is popular in the South, where it thrives in warm ocean waters. Use your favorite bottled or homemade barbecue sauce for this simple, down-home fish dish. For extra zip, sprinkle with several drops of hot pepper sauce before sealing in foil.

4 **pieces of kingfish fillet, about 6 ounces each**
½ **teaspoon salt**

¼ **teaspoon pepper**
½ **cup barbecue sauce**

1. Preheat oven to 425°F. Center fish on 4 pieces of foil that measure 12 inches wide and 15 inches long. Season with salt and pepper. Spoon 2 tablespoons of barbecue sauce over each fillet.

2. Fold top of foil over bottom. Crimp edges tightly to seal. Arrange packets on a baking sheet in a single layer. Bake 10 to 12 minutes, or until foil is puffed and fish is opaque throughout.

180   COOL AS A CUCUMBER SALMON
Prep: 3 minutes   Cook: 11 to 13 minutes   Serves: 4

4 pieces of salmon fillet, 4 to
   6 ounces each
1 medium cucumber, peeled,
   seeded, and thinly sliced
1 cup plain yogurt

½ teaspoon salt
¼ teaspoon pepper
2 tablespoons chopped fresh
   dill or 2 teaspoons dried

1. Preheat oven to 425°F. Arrange salmon on 4 pieces of foil that measure about 15 inches long and 12 inches wide.

2. Bring salted water to boil in a medium saucepan. Add cucumber slices and return to a boil over high heat. Cook for 30 seconds. Drain and rinse under cold running water; drain well. Pat dry on paper towels.

3. Spread ¼ cup yogurt over each piece of salmon. Top with cucumber slices. Season with salt and pepper and sprinkle with dill. Fold top of foil over bottom and crimp edges tightly to seal.

4. Arrange packets on a large baking sheet in a single layer. Bake 10 to 12 minutes, or until foil is puffed and fish is cooked through.

181   FLOUNDER AND FENNEL WITH FRESH TOMATOES
Prep: 5 minutes   Cook: 15 to 19 minutes   Serves: 4

2 fennel bulbs, trimmed of
   greens, about ¾ pound
   each
2 tablespoons unsalted butter
¼ teaspoon salt
⅛ teaspoon pepper

1 tablespoon fresh thyme
   leaves or 1 teaspoon dried
2 medium tomatoes, peeled,
   seeded, and chopped
4 flounder fillets, 4 to 5 ounces
   each

1. Cut fennel in half lengthwise and remove tough inner core. Cut into thin slices. In a large saucepan, melt butter over medium heat. Add fennel, salt, pepper, and thyme. Reduce heat to low, cover, and cook, stirring occasionally, until tender, 5 to 7 minutes.

2. Preheat oven to 425°F. Butter 4 pieces of foil that measure 12 inches wide and 15 inches long. On the bottom half of each piece, place one-fourth of cooked fennel. Lay fish over fennel and top with one-fourth of chopped tomatoes.

3. Fold over top part of foil and crimp edges together tightly to seal. Arrange packets in a single layer on a baking sheet. Bake 10 to 12 minutes, until foil is puffed and fish is cooked through.

182   FOILED FLUKE

Prep: 3 minutes   Cook: 10 to 12 minutes   Serves: 4

4 fluke fillets, 4 to 6 ounces
   each
½ cup sour cream
4 medium mushrooms, thinly
   sliced

1 small red bell pepper, thinly
   sliced
½ teaspoon salt
¼ teaspoon pepper

1. Preheat oven to 450°F. Place each fillet on bottom half of a piece of aluminum foil that measures 12 inches wide and 15 inches long. Spread 2 tablespoons of sour cream over each fillet. Divide mushrooms and pepper strips evenly among fillets. Season with salt and pepper.

2. Fold top of foil over bottom. Crimp edges tightly to seal. Arrange packets on a baking sheet in a single layer. Bake 10 to 12 minutes, until foil is puffed and fish flakes easily.

183   FLOUNDER FLORENTINE WITH MUSHROOMS EN PAPILLOTE

Prep: 7 minutes   Cook: 17 to 19 minutes   Serves: 4

5 medium mushrooms, thinly
   sliced
¼ cup olive oil
2 medium tomatoes, peeled,
   seeded, and chopped
1 pound fresh spinach,
   cleaned, large stems
   removed, or 1 (10-ounce)
   package frozen, thawed

½ teaspoon salt
¼ teaspoon pepper
4 flounder fillets (or use sea
   bass, sole, or orange
   roughy), 4 to 6 ounces
   each

1. In a medium skillet, cook mushrooms in olive oil over high heat, stirring often, until lightly browned, about 2 minutes. Add tomatoes and cook, stirring, until water has evaporated, about 3 minutes. Add spinach and cook, stirring often, until completely wilted, about 2 minutes. Remove from heat and season with salt and pepper.

2. Preheat oven to 425°F. Brush 4 pieces of aluminum foil that measure 12 inches wide and 15 inches long with olive oil. Divide mushroom and spinach mixture among pieces of foil, spreading on bottom half. Lay a fish fillet on top of each and season with salt and pepper.

3. Fold over top of foil to meet bottom. Crimp edges closed tightly to seal. Arrange packets on a baking sheet in a single layer. Bake 10 to 12 minutes, or until foil is puffed and fish flakes easily.

184   MAHI-MAHI WITH RED AND YELLOW PEPPERS

Prep: 3 minutes   Stand: 10 minutes   Marinate: 30 minutes
Cook: 17 to 22 minutes   Serves: 4

1 red bell pepper
1 yellow bell pepper
1 garlic clove, minced
¼ teaspoon ground cumin
1 tablespoon fresh lemon
    juice
    Olive oil for brushing

1 pound mahi-mahi, or
    other mild-flavored firm-
    fleshed fish fillets such as
    monkfish, grouper, tuna,
    or swordfish
½ teaspoon salt
¼ teaspoon pepper

1. Preheat broiler. Arrange whole peppers on a broiling pan. Broil peppers until charred on all sides, 7 to 10 minutes, turning frequently. Transfer to a paper bag and close tightly. Let stand for 10 to 15 minutes to soften skin. Remove from bag and rub off blackened skin. Remove cores and seeds and cut peppers into long thin strips.

2. In a small bowl, combine pepper strips, garlic, cumin, and lemon juice. Marinate at room temperature for about 30 minutes.

3. Preheat oven to 425°F. Tear off 4 strips of aluminum foil that measure about 12 inches wide and 15 inches long. Brush with olive oil. Divide the pepper mixture on the centers of the 4 pieces of foil. Cut fish into 2-inch pieces, divide into 4 equal parts, and place on the peppers. Season with salt and pepper. Fold over the top pieces of the foil and crimp the edges closed to form a tight seal. Place on a baking sheet in a single layer. Bake 10 to 12 minutes, until foil is puffed and fish flakes easily.

185   SEA BASS WITH SOY AND GINGER

Prep: 2 minutes   Cook: 10 to 12 minutes   Serves: 4

4 sea bass or orange roughy
    fillets, 4 to 6 ounces each
1 tablespoon minced fresh
    ginger

¼ cup soy sauce
2 teaspoons Asian sesame oil
¼ teaspoon pepper

1. Preheat oven to 425°F. Place fish fillets in center of 4 pieces of aluminum foil that measure about 12 inches wide and 15 inches long. Sprinkle ginger evenly over fish. Drizzle 1 tablespoon soy sauce and ½ teaspoon sesame oil over each. Season with pepper.

2. Fold over top of foil to meet bottom. Crimp edges closed tightly to seal. Arrange packets on a baking sheet in a single layer. Bake 10 to 12 minutes, until foil is puffed and fish is opaque throughout.

186   SEAFOOD MEDLEY
Prep: 3 minutes   Cook: 10 to 12 minutes   Serves: 4

2 cups cooked rice
½ pound bay scallops or
   halved sea scallops
½ pound medium shrimp,
   shelled and deveined
½ pound crabmeat

4 tablespoons butter, melted
¼ cup fresh lemon juice
¼ teaspoon salt
¼ teaspoon pepper
1 tablespoon chopped parsley

1. Preheat oven to 425°F. Place half cupfuls of rice in center of 4 pieces of foil that measure 12 inches wide and 15 inches long. Top mounds of rice with equal portions of scallops, shrimp, and crabmeat. Drizzle 1 tablespoon butter over each mound and sprinkle with equal amounts of lemon juice. Season with salt and pepper. Add a touch of parsley.

2. Fold top foil over bottom and crimp edges to seal tightly. Arrange packets in a single layer on a baking sheet. Bake 10 to 12 minutes, until foil is puffed and fish is opaque.

187   FOILED SOLE WITH BRUSSELS SPROUTS, CAULIFLOWER, AND TOMATO
Prep: 5 minutes   Cook: 15 to 17 minutes   Serves: 4

24 Brussels sprouts, halved
1 cup 1-inch cauliflower
   florets
1½ tablespoons butter, softened
2 medium tomatoes, peeled,
   seeded, and chopped

1 tablespoon fresh thyme
   leaves or 1 teaspoon dried
4 sole fillets, 4 to 6 ounces each
½ teaspoon salt
¼ teaspoon pepper

1. Bring 2 medium saucepans of salted water to a boil. Cook Brussels sprouts and cauliflower separately until soft, about 2 minutes for cauliflower and 5 minutes for Brussels sprouts. Drain and rinse under cold running water; drain well. Pat dry on paper towels.

2. Preheat oven to 425°F. Tear off 4 pieces of aluminum foil that measure about 12 inches wide and 15 inches long. Brush with butter. On bottom half of each piece, place equal amounts of Brussels sprouts, cauliflower, chopped tomatoes, and thyme. Cut fish into 2-inch pieces and place on and around the vegetables. Season with salt and pepper to taste.

3. Fold over top piece of foil and crimp edges closed to form a tight seal. Arrange packets on a baking sheet in a single layer. Bake 10 to 12 minutes, until foil is puffed and fish flakes easily.

188 SEAFOOD COUSCOUS
Prep: 3 minutes   Stand: 10 minutes   Cook: 10 to 12 minutes
Serves: 4

Instant couscous works perfectly for this dish. Simply follow package instructions for best results. Serve in foil and let guests open at table or remove fish with couscous to individual plates just before serving.

2 tablespoons butter	½ pound medium shrimp,
¾ teaspoon salt.	shelled and deveined
1 cup couscous	½ pound haddock, cut into
1 cup heavy cream	4 pieces
1 teaspoon saffron threads	¼ teaspoon pepper
½ pound bay scallops or	
halved sea scallops	

1. In a medium saucepan, combine butter, ½ teaspoon salt, and 1½ cups water. Bring to a boil and stir in couscous. Cover, remove from heat, and let stand 5 minutes.

2. Combine cream and saffron in a small saucepan. Bring just to a simmer over medium-low heat. Stir, cover, let stand for 5 minutes to soften saffron.

3. Meantime, preheat oven to 425°F. Lightly butter 4 pieces of foil that measure 12 inches wide and 15 inches long. Place about one-fourth of couscous in center of each piece of foil.

4. Top couscous with equal portions of scallops, shrimp, and haddock. Season with remaining ¼ teaspoon salt and the pepper. Pour about ¼ cup of the saffron cream over each mound of seafood.

5. Crimp edges tightly to seal. Arrange packets in a single layer on a baking sheet. Bake 10 to 12 minutes, until foil is puffed and fish is cooked through.

189 SNAPPER FILLETS WITH GARBANZO BEANS
Prep: 3 minutes   Cook: 10 to 12 minutes   Serves: 4

4 snapper fillets, 4 to	4 sun-dried tomatoes, cut into
6 ounces each	thin strips
½ teaspoon salt	2 cups cooked or canned
¼ teaspoon pepper	garbanzo beans
¼ cup olive oil	(chick-peas)

1. Preheat oven to 425°F. Lay fish fillets flat on 4 pieces of foil that measure 12 inches wide and 15 inches long. Season with salt and pepper. Drizzle 1 tablespoon oil over each fillet. Divide strips of sun-dried tomato over fillets and surround each with ½ cup beans.

2. Fold top of foil over bottom. Crimp edges tightly to seal. Arrange packets on a baking sheet in a single layer. Bake 10 to 12 minutes, until foil is puffed and fish flakes easily.

190   MONKFISH WITH CURRIED FRUIT

Prep: 3 minutes   Soak: 10 minutes   Cook: 14 to 16 minutes
Serves: 4

¾ pound assorted dried fruits:
   raisins, pitted prunes,
   dried apricots, or dried
   apple rings
6 tablespoons butter
¼ cup minced onion

2 teaspoons curry powder
1 to 1¼ pounds monkfish, cut
   into ½-inch-thick slices
¼ teaspoon salt
⅛ teaspoon pepper

1. Cut fruit into ¼-inch dice and place in a bowl. Pour in enough warm water to cover. Soak for 10 minutes. Drain and squeeze gently with your hands to remove excess moisture.

2. In a small saucepan, melt butter over medium heat. Add onion and cook until slightly softened, about 2 minutes. Add curry and cook, stirring, until onion is soft, about 2 minutes longer. Stir in fruit and remove from heat.

3. Preheat oven to 425°F. Divide monkfish slices among 4 pieces of foil that measure 12 inches wide by 15 inches long, arranging them in center. Season with salt and pepper. Spoon one-fourth of curried fruit mixture over each portion of fish. Fold over foil and crimp edges tightly to seal. Arrange packets on a baking sheet in a single layer. Bake 10 to 12 minutes, or until foil is puffed and fish is cooked through.

Chapter 9

Nautical Noodles

Pasta and seafood are a marriage made in heaven. Tender morsels of fish and shellfish complement the earthy flavor and texture of cooked noodles.

Dried pasta comes in many shapes and sizes. Since it has an indefinite shelf-life, several different varieties are always handy in an active kitchen. Imported and domestic brands are easily available—a change from the days when most stores carried only macaroni and spaghetti. The pasta craze hit us in the eighties and hasn't lost its momentum yet. Fresh pasta is a different animal. Although it's fun to make and increasingly available in local supermarkets, for this fish lover it doesn't have the meaty character needed for most of the recipes in this chapter.

Tuna, bluefish, mackerel, swordfish, and catfish are my favorite choices for Nautical Noodles. These fish hold up to the tossing, baking, or saucing that pasta requires—unlike delicate fillets, which tend to flake into nothing and get lost in the sauce. Shellfish and pasta are always a good combination—shrimp, crab, and lobster are hard to beat. Clams with linguine is not a pasta classic without a reason, for example. It is one of those age-old meldings of flavors that are simply meant to be.

While the ingredients in this chapter look expensive at first glance, remember that tuna, swordfish, lobster, crab, and scallops can be stretched to feed more people when mixed with pasta. Substitute surimi (see page 209), canned crab, or frozen shrimp for increased savings.

In general, cream-based sauces are good with flat or hollow-shaped pastas like fettuccine, spaghetti, macaroni, linguine, ziti, or penne. Their broad surfaces allow sauce to cling to and thoroughly coat them. Tomato-based sauces are best with shaped pastas like shells, spirals (fusille), or bow ties (farfalle). These will hold chunks of textured sauce rather than just a coating.

To cook pasta, add to a large pot of boiling salted water. Return to a boil and cook uncovered until tender but still firm and not mushy. Start timing for the recipes in this chapter after the water has come back to a boil. Remove a piece toward the end of the specified time, cool under cold running water, and taste to make sure it is properly done before draining. There should be a slight resistance to the bite (hence the term *al dente*). Drain at once and proceed according to recipe.

191 FETTUCCINE WITH CATFISH IN MUSTARD DILL SAUCE

Prep: 10 to 12 minutes   Cook: 8 to 10 minutes   Serves: 4

1 **pound dried fettuccine**	1 **tablespoon chopped parsley**
2 **tablespoons butter**	1 **tablespoon chopped fresh**
3 **tablespoons flour**	**dill**
2 **cups milk**	¼ **cup Dijon mustard**
1 **pound catfish fillets, cut into**	¼ **teaspoon salt**
1½-inch pieces	

1. In a large pot of boiling salted water, cook pasta until tender but still firm, 8 to 10 minutes. Drain well and keep warm.

2. Meanwhile, in a medium saucepan, melt butter over medium-high heat. Stir in flour and cook, stirring constantly, until bubbly and lemon colored, about 2 minutes. Gradually whisk in milk, raise heat to high, and cook, whisking frequently, until thickened and smooth, 2 to 3 minutes. Add catfish, parsley, and dill. Reduce heat to low and cook until fish is opaque throughout, 3 to 4 minutes. Remove from heat and stir in mustard and salt.

3. Place pasta in a large serving bowl. Pour catfish and sauce over pasta, toss well, and serve at once.

192 CATFISH PASTA PRIMAVERA

Prep: 5 to 7 minutes   Cook: 10 to 12 minutes   Serves: 4

This dish is pretty with three different colors of peppers, but if only red and/or green is available, do not hesitate to increase the amount of a single hue and make the pasta anyway.

1 **pound ziti or penne**	1 **cup dry white wine or**
2 **tablespoons butter**	**chicken stock**
½ **red bell pepper, cut into**	1 **pound catfish fillets, cut into**
long thin strips	**1-inch chunks**
½ **yellow bell pepper, cut into**	½ **teaspoon salt**
long thin strips	¼ **teaspoon pepper**
½ **green bell pepper, cut into**	½ **cup grated Parmesan cheese**
long thin strips	2 **tablespoons chopped**
1 **cup green peas, fresh or**	**parsley**
frozen	
3 **scallions (white part only),**	
thinly sliced	

1. In a large pot of boiling salted water, cook pasta until tender but still firm, 10 to 12 minutes. Drain well.

2. Meanwhile, in a large nonreactive skillet, melt butter over medium-high heat. Add bell peppers, peas, and scallions. Cook, stirring occasionally, until tender, 3 to 5 minutes. Remove vegetables with a slotted spoon and set aside.

3. Pour wine into skillet and bring to a boil over high heat. Add catfish, return to a boil, reduce heat to medium, and simmer until fish flakes easily, about 3 minutes. Return vegetables to skillet, season with salt and pepper, and toss gently to coat.

4. Toss pasta with vegetables and fish. Sprinkle with Parmesan cheese and parsley. Serve at once.

---

193 CRAB AND SPINACH MANICOTTI WITH MORNAY SAUCE

Prep: 20 minutes   Cook: 35 to 47 minutes   Serves: 4

With its lush filling and light cheese sauce, this dish is definitely company fare. It will serve four as a main course, but six to eight as a starter.

1 (10-ounce) package frozen chopped spinach
2 garlic cloves, minced
¼ cup plus 1 tablespoon minced onion
3 tablespoons butter
1 egg, lightly beaten
1 cup ricotta cheese
½ cup grated Parmesan cheese
½ pound fresh crabmeat

1 teaspoon salt
1 teaspoon pepper
⅛ teaspoon grated nutmeg
1 (12-ounce) package manicotti shells (about 16)
2 tablespoons flour
2 cups milk
½ cup dry white wine
1 cup grated Swiss cheese

1. Cook spinach in a medium saucepan of boiling salted water, covered, until spinach is thawed and bright green, 3 to 5 minutes. Drain well. Use hands to squeeze out excess water. In a skillet, cook garlic and 1 tablespoon onion in 1 tablespoon butter over medium heat until softened, 1 to 2 minutes. Add spinach, stir to blend, and cook until heated through, about 2 minutes. Remove from heat.

2. In a medium bowl, combine spinach mixture, egg, ricotta, Parmesan cheese, crabmeat, ½ teaspoon salt, ½ teaspoon pepper, and nutmeg. Cover and set aside.

3. In a large pot of boiling salted water, cook manicotti shells until tender but still firm, about 10 minutes. Drain and rinse under cold running water; drain well.

4. In a medium nonreactive saucepan, melt remaining 2 tablespoons butter over medium-high heat. Add remaining ¼ cup onion and cook, until soft, 2 to 3 minutes. Add flour and cook, stirring, 1 to 2 minutes. Whisk in milk, raise heat to medium, and cook, stirring frequently, until thickened and bubbly, 3 to 5 minutes. Stir in wine and cheese. Remove from heat and stir until cheese is melted.

5. Preheat oven to 350°F. Lightly oil a large lasagne pan. Stuff each shell with about 2 tablespoons of crab and spinach mixture and arrange in pan. Pour cheese sauce over pasta. Bake 15 to 20 minutes, until lightly browned on top.

194   PENNE WITH BROCCOLI, ANCHOVY, AND GARLIC

Prep: 2 minutes   Cook: 12 to 15 minutes   Serves: 4 to 6

1 pound penne	2 tablespoons anchovy paste
¼ cup olive oil	2 cups broccoli florets
4 garlic cloves, thinly sliced	¼ teaspoon pepper

1. Bring a large pot of salted water to a boil over high heat. Add penne, return to a boil, and cook until tender, 10 to 12 minutes. Measure out and reserve ½ cup pasta cooking water. Drain pasta.

2. Meanwhile, in a medium saucepan, heat olive oil over medium-low heat. Add garlic and cook, stirring often, until softened, 2 to 3 minutes. Add anchovy paste and stir to blend. Remove from heat and set aside.

3. In a large saucepan, bring a large amount of salted water to a boil over high heat. Add broccoli, return to a boil, and cook until tender, about 3 minutes. Drain well and add to skillet with garlic-anchovy mixture.

4. Add reserved ½ cup pasta cooking water to broccoli and anchovy mixture. Bring to a simmer over medium-high heat. Cook, stirring occasionally, until warmed through, 2 to 3 minutes.

5. Transfer pasta to a large bowl. Add broccoli and sauce, season with pepper, and toss well. Serve at once.

195   SWORDFISH, MUSHROOMS, AND PENNE IN BRANDY CREAM SAUCE

Prep: 4 minutes   Cook: 10 to 12 minutes   Serves: 4 to 6

1 pound penne or ziti	½ teaspoon pepper
2 tablespoons butter	1 pound swordfish, cut into
2 tablespoons vegetable oil	1-inch pieces
½ pound medium	¼ cup Cognac or brandy
mushrooms, halved	1 cup heavy cream
½ teaspoon salt	1 tablespoon chopped parsley

1. In a large pot of boiling salted water, cook penne until tender but still firm, 10 to 12 minutes. Drain well.

2. Meanwhile, in a large skillet, melt 1 tablespoon butter in 1 tablespoon oil over medium-high heat. Add mushrooms, season with ¼ teaspoon salt and ⅛ teaspoon pepper, and cook, stirring and tossing frequently, until well browned, 3 to 4 minutes. Transfer to a plate and set aside.

3. Add remaining 1 tablespoon each butter and oil to skillet and melt over medium-high heat. Add swordfish, season with remaining salt and pepper, and cook, turning, until lightly browned on all sides, 2 to 3 minutes. Remove tuna to a plate. Pour off any fat from pan.

4. Pour Cognac into skillet, raise heat to high, and boil, scraping up browned bits from bottom of pan, until reduced by half, about 1 minute. Pour in cream and cook, whisking often, until reduced by one-third, 2 to 3 minutes. Return mushrooms and tuna to skillet, stir in parsley, and cook until warmed through, about 1 minute longer. Toss pasta with swordfish, mushrooms, and sauce.

196   SQUID IN RED PEPPER SAUCE OVER PASTA

Prep: 10 minutes   Stand: 10 minutes   Cook: 20 to 26 minutes
Serves: 4

1 large red bell pepper	½ teaspoon salt
2 tablespoons butter	¼ teaspoon pepper
1 tablespoon olive oil	1 pound linguine
1 small onion, chopped	½ cup heavy cream
2 garlic cloves, minced	¼ cup dry white wine
1½ pounds squid, cleaned, cut	⅛ teaspoon cayenne
into ½-inch rings, and	¼ cup chopped cilantro or
tentacles cut in half	parsley

1. Roast pepper directly over a gas flame or under broiler as close to heat as possible, turning, until blackened all over, 7 to 10 minutes. Place in a bag and let stand for 10 to 15 minutes to soften skin. Rub off blackened skin and remove stem, ribs, and seeds.

2. In a large skillet, melt butter with olive oil over medium-high heat. Add onion and garlic and cook, stirring often, until softened, 2 to 3 minutes. Add squid and season with ¼ teaspoon each salt and pepper. Cook, stirring constantly, until lightly browned, about 3 minutes. Transfer to a medium bowl and set aside.

3. In a large pot of boiling salted water, cook linguine until tender but still firm, 8 to 10 minutes. Drain well.

4. Meanwhile, in a food processor, puree roasted red pepper with 2 tablespoons water until smooth. Transfer to a medium nonreactive saucepan. Add cream, wine, cayenne, and remaining ¼ teaspoon salt. Cook over medium-high heat, stirring frequently, until thickened, 2 to 3 minutes. Add squid and cook, stirring, until just warmed through, 1 to 2 minutes. Remove from heat and stir in cilantro. In a large serving bowl, toss pasta with squid and sauce.

197 PENNE WITH BLUEFISH AND MUSTARD SAUCE

Prep: 3 minutes   Cook: 16 to 20 minutes   Serves: 4

2 tablespoons olive oil
2 bluefish fillets, 6 to
    8 ounces each
1 pound penne
½ cup dry white wine

½ cup heavy cream
¼ cup Dijon mustard
½ teaspoon salt
¼ teaspoon pepper
1 tablespoon chopped parsley

1. In a large skillet, heat olive oil over medium-high heat. Add bluefish and cook, turning once, until fish flakes easily with a fork, 6 to 8 minutes. Transfer to a plate and set aside.

2. Bring a large pot of salted water to a boil over high heat. Add pasta, return to a boil, and cook, stirring occasionally, until tender, 10 to 12 minutes.

3. Meanwhile, add wine to fish skillet. Bring to a boil over high heat and cook, stirring, until reduced by half, 2 to 3 minutes. Pour in cream and continue boiling until thickened, 3 to 5 minutes longer. Remove sauce from heat and whisk in mustard, salt, and pepper until well blended. Cut bluefish into ½-inch pieces, add to sauce, and stir gently to coat.

4. Drain pasta well and transfer to a large bowl. Pour sauce with bluefish over pasta, sprinkle on parsley, and toss to blend. Serve at once.

198 MUSSELS MARINARA OVER SPAGHETTI

Prep: 10 minutes   Cook: 31 to 35 minutes   Serves: 4 to 6

3 dozen mussels
2 tablespoons olive oil
1 green bell pepper, chopped
1 medium onion, chopped
3 garlic cloves, minced
1 (16-ounce) can stewed
    tomatoes, drained and
    chopped

¼ cup chopped fresh basil or
    1 teaspoon dried
2 bay leaves
1 cup dry white wine
¼ teaspoon salt
¼ teaspoon pepper
1 pound spaghetti
½ cup grated Parmesan cheese

1. Scrub mussels well under cold running water. Pull out or cut off brown hairy beards with a small sharp knife.

2. In a large nonreactive saucepan, heat olive oil over medium heat. Add bell pepper, onion, and garlic. Cook, stirring occasionally, until softened, 3 to 5 minutes. Add tomatoes, basil, and bay leaves. Cover and cook until slightly thickened, about 10 minutes. Reduce heat to low. Stir in wine, salt, and pepper. Continue to cook, uncovered, stirring occasionally, until sauce is reduced and concentrated in flavor, about 10 minutes longer.

3. In a large pot of boiling salted water, cook spaghetti until tender but still firm, 8 to 10 minutes. Drain well. Transfer to a large serving bowl.

4. Meanwhile, add mussels to tomato sauce. Raise heat to medium-high, cover, and cook, stirring occasionally, until mussels open, 5 to 7 minutes. Discard any mussels that do not open.

5. Pour mussels and sauce over spaghetti. Toss to mix. Sprinkle with Parmesan cheese and serve at once.

199   LINGUINE WITH RED CLAM SAUCE
Prep: 8 minutes   Cook: 19 to 21 minutes   Serves: 4

24 littleneck or cherrystone
       clams, shucked, liquid
       reserved, or 3 (6½-ounce)
       cans chopped clams with
       their liquid
 2 tablespoons butter
 3 tablespoons olive oil
 3 garlic cloves, minced
 1 medium onion, chopped
 1 (28-ounce) can Italian peeled
       tomatoes, drained and
       chopped
 1 cup bottled clam juice or
       chicken stock

 2 tablespoons chopped fresh
       basil or 1 teaspoon dried
 1 teaspoon dried oregano
 1 bay leaf
 1 pound linguine
 ½ cup dry white wine
 ½ teaspoon salt
 ¼ teaspoon black pepper
 ¼ teaspoon crushed hot red
       pepper
 ¼ cup grated Parmesan cheese
       (optional)

1. Coarsely chop clams; refrigerate until used. In a medium saucepan, heat butter and oil over medium heat. Add garlic and onion and cook, stirring frequently, until soft, about 3 minutes. Add tomatoes, reserved clam liquid, bottled clam juice, basil, oregano, and bay leaf. Raise heat to medium-high and cook, stirring often, until sauce is slightly thickened, about 5 minutes. Remove from heat and cover to keep warm.

2. In a large pot of boiling salted water, cook linguine until tender but still firm, 8 to 10 minutes. Drain well.

3. Add chopped clams, wine, salt, black pepper, and hot pepper to sauce. Cook over medium heat, stirring occasionally, 3 minutes.

4. Divide pasta among 4 large soup plates. Ladle clam sauce over pasta and sprinkle 1 tablespoon Parmesan cheese on top of each serving, if you like.

200   SPAGHETTI ALLA PUTTANESCA

Prep: 5 to 7 minutes   Cook: 17 minutes   Serves: 4 to 6

The following classic recipe is adapted from Giuliano Bugialli's book *Bugialli on Pasta.*

¼ cup olive oil
2 garlic cloves, minced
1 (28-ounce) can Italian peeled tomatoes, drained and chopped
½ cup pitted oil-cured black olives, chopped
1 (2-ounce) can flat anchovy fillets, drained and coarsely chopped

2 tablespoons capers, coarsely chopped
2 tablespoons tomato paste
¼ teaspoon salt
¼ teaspoon black pepper
¼ teaspoon crushed hot red pepper
1 pound spaghetti

1. In a large nonreactive saucepan or flameproof casserole, heat olive oil over medium-high heat. Add garlic and cook, stirring frequently, until lightly browned, about 2 minutes. Stir in tomatoes, olives, anchovies, capers, and tomato paste. Season with salt, black pepper, and hot pepper. Cook, stirring occasionally, until slightly thickened and well blended, about 15 minutes.

2. Meanwhile, bring a large pot of salted water to a boil over high heat. Add pasta, return to a boil, and cook, stirring occasionally, until tender, 8 to 10 minutes. Drain well and transfer to a large bowl. Add sauce and toss well to blend. Serve at once.

201   SHRIMP AND BROCCOLI OVER PASTA

Prep: 3 minutes   Cook: 14 to 18 minutes   Serves: 4 to 6

1 pound linguine
1 pound broccoli, cut into 1-inch florets
3 tablespoons butter
1 pound shrimp, shelled and deveined
3 tablespoons olive oil

½ medium red bell pepper, finely diced
2 garlic cloves, minced
½ cup dry white wine
½ teaspoon salt
¼ teaspoon pepper
¼ cup grated Romano cheese

1. In a large pot of boiling salted water, cook linguine until tender but still firm, 8 to 10 minutes. Drain well.

2. Meanwhile, in a large saucepan of boiling salted water, cook broccoli until just tender, about 2 minutes. Drain into a colander, rinse under cold running water, and drain well.

3. In a large nonreactive skillet, melt butter over medium heat. Add shrimp and cook, turning once, until pink and curled, 2 to 3 minutes. Remove shrimp to a plate and set aside. (Do not overcrowd pan. Cook in two batches if necessary, using additional butter if needed.)

4. In same skillet, heat olive oil over medium-high heat. Add red bell pepper and garlic and cook, stirring occasionally, until tender, 2 to 3 minutes. Pour in wine, raise heat to high, and boil until reduced by half, about 2 minutes. Return broccoli and shrimp to pan, lower heat to medium, and season with salt and pepper. Cook, stirring frequently, until heated through, 2 to 3 minutes.

5. In a large serving bowl, toss linguine with broccoli and shrimp. Sprinkle with Romano cheese and serve at once.

202 CORKSCREWS WITH CRAB AND SPINACH

Prep: 2 minutes   Cook: 10 to 12 minutes   Serves: 4

Use a mixture of halved yellow cherry tomatoes and halved red ones for a colorful variation.

1 **pound fusille (corkscrew pasta) or penne**	½ **pound crabmeat**
2 **tablespoons olive oil**	½ **teaspoon salt**
2 **garlic cloves, coarsely chopped**	¼ **teaspoon pepper**
12 **cherry tomatoes, halved**	¼ **cup grated Parmesan cheese**
1 **pound fresh spinach, chopped, or 1 (10-ounce) package frozen chopped, thawed**	

1. In a large pot of boiling salted water, cook pasta until tender but still firm, 10 to 12 minutes. Drain and transfer to a large bowl.

2. Meanwhile, in a large skillet, heat oil over medium-high heat. Add garlic and cook, stirring often, until lightly browned, about 2 minutes. Add tomatoes and cook, stirring occasionally, until slightly softened, about 2 minutes. Add spinach and cook, stirring, until slightly wilted, about 2 minutes. Stir in crab, season with salt and pepper, and cook until warmed through, 1 to 2 minutes.

3. Toss pasta with crab and vegetables. Sprinkle Parmesan cheese on top and serve at once.

203 SALMON, SNOW PEAS, AND PASTA IN DILL CREAM SAUCE

Prep: 3 minutes   Cook: 11½ to 15 minutes   Serves: 4

¼ pound snow peas, stemmed
   and stringed
1 pound dried fettuccine
2 fresh salmon fillets, about
   1 pound total
¾ teaspoon salt

½ teaspoon pepper
2 tablespoons butter
1 cup heavy cream
1 tablespoon fresh lime juice
1 tablespoon chopped fresh
   dill or 1 teaspoon dried

1. In a large saucepan of boiling salted water, cook snow peas over high heat until bright green and crisp-tender, 30 to 60 seconds. Drain, rinse under cold running water, and drain well.

2. In a large pot of boiling salted water, cook fettuccine until tender but still firm, 8 to 10 minutes. Drain well.

3. Meanwhile, season salmon with ½ teaspoon salt and ¼ teaspoon pepper. Meanwhile, melt butter in a large skillet over medium-high heat. Cook salmon, turning once, until lightly browned and firm, 6 to 8 minutes. Transfer salmon to a plate and set aside.

4. Add cream to skillet and stir in lime juice. Boil over high heat until reduced by half, 3 to 4 minutes. Add snow peas to reheat and remove from heat. Stir in dill and remaining salt and pepper.

5. Place pasta in a large serving bowl. Use fingers to shred salmon into large pieces. Add to bowl and toss with cream and snow peas.

204 PASTA WITH SHRIMP AND GARLIC-MUSTARD SAUCE

Prep: 3 minutes   Cook: 10 to 12 minutes   Serves: 4

1 pound bow tie (farfalle) or
   rotelle pasta
2 tablespoons olive oil
2 tablespoons butter
4 garlic cloves, minced
1 pound shrimp, shelled and
   deveined
½ cup dry white wine

2 tablespoons fresh lemon
   juice
1 tablespoon Dijon mustard
¼ teaspoon dried thyme leaves
½ teaspoon salt
¼ teaspoon pepper
¼ cup grated Parmesan cheese

1. In a large pot of boiling salted water, cook pasta until tender but still firm, 10 to 12 minutes. Drain well.

2. Meanwhile, heat olive oil and butter over medium-high heat in a large skillet. Add garlic and cook, stirring, until softened and fragrant, about 1 minute. Add shrimp and cook, turning once, until pink and curled, 2 to 3 minutes. With a slotted spoon, remove shrimp to a plate and set aside.

3. Add wine and lemon juice to skillet, raise heat to high, and boil until reduced by half, 2 to 3 minutes. Reduce heat to medium. Whisk in mustard and thyme. Return shrimp to skillet, season with salt and pepper, and cook until heated through, 1 to 2 minutes.

4. Divide pasta among 4 individual serving plates. Top with equal amounts of shrimp mixture and sprinkle Parmesan cheese on top.

---

205   SHRIMP, SCALLOPS, AND SAFFRON ORZO
Prep: 3 minutes   Cook: 10 to 11 minutes   Serves: 4

1½ cups chicken stock, canned broth, or water
1 cup orzo (rice-shaped pasta)
½ teaspoon saffron threads
3 tablespoons butter
¼ pound shrimp, shelled and deveined
¼ pound bay scallops or halved sea scallops

1 small onion, finely, chopped
¼ pound mushrooms, quartered
¼ teaspoon salt
¼ teaspoon pepper

1. In a medium saucepan, bring chicken stock and 1½ cups water to a boil over high heat. Add orzo, return to a boil, reduce heat to medium-high, and cook until almost tender, about 7 minutes. Measure out ¼ cup pasta cooking liquid into a small bowl. Add saffron and set aside. Drain orzo into a sieve.

2. Meanwhile, in a large skillet, melt 1 tablespoon butter over medium-high heat. Add shrimp and cook, turning, until curled and pink, 2 to 3 minutes. Remove to a plate and cover to keep warm.

3. Melt another 1 tablespoon butter in skillet over medium-high heat. Add scallops and cook, stirring and tossing, until firm and lightly browned, 2 to 3 minutes. Add to plate with shrimp and cover to keep warm.

4. Melt remaining 1 tablespoon butter in skillet. Add onion, mushrooms, and ⅛ teaspoon each salt and pepper. Cook over medium-high heat, stirring often, until lightly browned, 2 to 3 minutes.

5. Return shrimp and scallops to skillet. Add orzo and saffron mixture. Season with remaining ⅛ teaspoon each salt and pepper. Cook, stirring, 1 minute to heat through and serve immediately.

206 ANGEL HAIR PASTA WITH CRAB AND VEGETABLES

Prep: 10 minutes   Cook: 10 to 16 minutes   Serves: 4

2 tablespoons butter
1 cup thinly sliced cooked or canned artichoke hearts
1 medium red bell pepper, cut into long thin strips
1 carrot, cut into long thin strips
1 zucchini, cut into long thin strips

1 cup heavy cream
½ pound lump crabmeat
¼ teaspoon salt
⅛ teaspoon pepper
1 pound angel hair or vermicelli pasta
¼ cup grated Parmesan cheese

1. In a large skillet, melt butter over medium-high heat. Add artichoke hearts, bell pepper, carrot, and zucchini. Cook, stirring, until softened, 3 to 5 minutes. Pour in cream, raise heat to high, and boil until reduced by half, 3 to 5 minutes. Add crab and season with salt and pepper. Simmer 1 minute. Remove from heat and cover to keep warm.

2. In a large pot of boiling salted water, cook pasta until tender but still firm, 3 to 5 minutes. Drain and transfer to a large serving bowl.

3. Pour crab and vegetables with sauce over pasta. Toss and serve at once, sprinkled with Parmesan cheese.

207 SCALLOPS WITH LEMON CAPER SAUCE OVER PASTA

Prep: 2 minutes   Cook: 10 to 12 minutes   Serves: 4

3 tablespoons olive oil
1 tablespoon fresh lemon juice
Grated zest of 1 lemon
1 tablespoon capers, chopped
½ teaspoon salt

½ teaspoon pepper
1 pound fusille or penne
1 pound bay scallops or halved sea scallops
2 tablespoons butter

1. In a medium bowl, combine 2 tablespoons olive oil, lemon juice, lemon zest, capers, ¼ teaspoon salt, and ¼ teaspoon pepper. Blend well and set lemon caper sauce aside.

2. In a large pot of boiling salted water, cook fusille until tender but still firm, 10 to 12 minutes. Drain well.

3. Meanwhile, in a large bowl, toss scallops with remaining 1 tablespoon olive oil and ¼ teaspoon each of salt and pepper. In a large skillet, melt butter over medium heat. Add scallops and cook, turning once, until lightly browned, 2 to 3 minutes. (Do not overcrowd pan. Cook in two batches if necessary, adding additional butter if needed.)

4. Turn pasta into a large warmed bowl. Pour lemon caper sauce over pasta, add scallops, and toss. Serve at once.

208 SHRIMPY MACARONI AND CHEESE
Prep: 5 minutes   Cook: 21 to 38 minutes   Serves: 4 to 6

1 pound elbow macaroni	¼ teaspoon cayenne
2 tablespoons butter	1 pound shrimp, shelled,
3 tablespoons flour	deveined, and cut into
2 cups milk	½-inch pieces
2 cups grated mild Cheddar or	½ red bell pepper, finely diced
colby cheese (½ pound)	1½ cups fresh bread crumbs
½ teaspoon salt	2 tablespoons melted butter

1. Preheat oven to 425°F. In a large saucepan of boiling salted water, cook macaroni until just tender, 6 to 8 minutes. Drain well.

2. Meanwhile, in a medium saucepan, melt butter over medium-high heat. Stir in flour and cook, stirring constantly, 1 to 2 minutes. Gradually whisk in milk and bring to a boil. Cook, stirring frequently, until thickened and smooth, 2 to 3 minutes. Remove from heat, stir in cheese, and season with salt and cayenne.

3. In a large bowl, toss macaroni with cheese sauce, shrimp, and bell pepper. Pour into a lightly buttered 9x13-inch baking dish. Cover with bread crumbs and drizzle melted butter over top. Bake uncovered until golden brown, 15 to 20 minutes.

209 LINGUINE WITH WHITE CLAM SAUCE
Prep: 5 minutes   Cook: 8 to 10 minutes   Serves: 4

This recipe is very good—and easy—made with canned chopped clams. It is incredible made with fresh.

1 pound linguine	¼ cup chopped parsley
24 littleneck or cherrystone	1 teaspoon dried oregano
clams, shucked, liquid	½ cup bottled clam juice or
reserved, or 3 (6½-ounce)	chicken broth
cans chopped clams with	½ teaspoon salt
their liquid	½ teaspoon pepper
¼ cup olive oil	¼ cup grated Parmesan cheese
4 garlic cloves, minced	(optional)

1. In a large pot of boiling salted water, cook linguine until tender but still firm, 8 to 10 minutes.

2. Meanwhile, coarsely chop clams. In a large skillet, heat olive oil over medium-low heat. Add garlic and cook, stirring often, until soft and fragrant, about 2 minutes. Raise heat to high and add clams with their liquid, parsley, oregano, bottled clam juice, salt, and pepper. Cook until clams are slightly firm, 2 to 3 minutes.

3. Drain linguine and divide among 4 large soup plates. Top with clam sauce and sprinkle with Parmesan cheese if desired. Serve at once.

210   TOMATOES STUFFED WITH ORZO, CRAB, AND MUSHROOMS

Prep: 5 minutes   Cook: 19 to 27 minutes   Serves: 4

2 tablespoons butter
3 or 4 medium mushrooms,
   finely diced
¼ cup white wine or chicken
   stock
½ pound fresh or imitation
   crabmeat

½ teaspoon salt
¼ teaspoon pepper
2 cups orzo (rice-shaped pasta)
4 large tomatoes

1. Preheat oven to 375°F. In a medium skillet, melt butter over medium-high heat. Add mushrooms and cook, stirring often, until just giving off liquid, 2 to 3 minutes. Pour in wine, raise heat to high, and boil until only 1 tablespoon of liquid remains, about 2 minutes. Remove from heat, stir in crab, and season with salt and pepper. Set aside.

2. In a large saucepan of boiling salted water, cook orzo until tender but still firm, 5 to 7 minutes. Drain into a sieve, rinse under cold running water, and drain well. Transfer to a bowl and toss with crab and mushroom mixture.

3. Cut tomatoes in half and use a small spoon to scoop out seeds and pulp. Stuff tomatoes with orzo filling and arrange in an oiled baking dish. Cover loosely with foil and bake 10 to 15 minutes, or until tomatoes are tender but still hold their shape.

211   PASTA AND SHRIMP ACAPULCO

Prep: 2 minutes   Cook: 8 to 10 minutes   Serves: 4

1 pound dried fettuccine
3 tablespoons butter
1 pound shrimp, shelled and
   deveined
½ cup dry white wine

2 tablespoons fresh lime juice
½ cup chopped cilantro
½ teaspoon salt
¼ teaspoon pepper
⅛ teaspoon cayenne

1. In a large pot of boiling salted water, cook fettuccine until tender but still firm, 8 to 10 minutes. Drain well.

2. Meanwhile, in a large skillet, melt butter over medium heat. Add shrimp and cook, turning once, until pink and curled, 2 to 3 minutes. Remove to a plate and set aside.

3. Pour wine and lime juice into skillet and boil, scraping up browned bits from bottom of pan, until reduced by half, about 2 minutes. Return shrimp to skillet and add cilantro, salt, pepper, and cayenne. Stir to blend. Cook shrimp sauce until warmed through, 2 to 3 minutes.

4. In a large serving bowl, toss pasta together with shrimp sauce. Serve at once.

212   CURRIED SHRIMP WITH PASTA

Prep: 5 minutes   Cook: 10 to 12 minutes   Serves: 4

1 pound penne or ziti
2 tablespoons butter
1 pound shrimp, shelled and
   deveined
1 small onion, chopped
1 garlic clove, minced
1 (1-inch) piece fresh ginger,
   peeled and minced

1 teaspoon curry powder
1 cup heavy cream
1 tablespoon fresh lime juice
½ teaspoon salt
⅛ teaspoon cayenne

1. In a large pot of boiling salted water, cook pasta until tender but still firm, 10 to 12 minutes. Drain well and keep warm.

2. Meanwhile, in a large skillet, melt 1 tablespoon butter over medium-high heat. Add shrimp and cook, turning, until pink and curled, 2 to 3 minutes. Remove to a plate and set aside.

3. Reduce heat to medium, add remaining 1 tablespoon butter to skillet, and melt. Add onion, garlic, ginger, and curry powder. Cook, stirring often, until onion is softened, about 2 minutes. Pour in cream and increase heat to high. Add lime juice, salt, and cayenne. Boil until reduced by one-third, about 3 minutes.

4. Return shrimp to skillet and cook until heated through, about 1 minute. Toss pasta with shrimp and sauce.

213   SHELLS FILLED WITH SHRIMP MOUSSE

Prep: 2 minutes   Cook: 25 to 32 minutes   Serves: 4

12 ounces jumbo pasta shells
¾ pound medium shrimp,
   shelled and deveined
1 egg
½ cup heavy cream

1 tablespoon minced chives
½ teaspoon salt
¼ teaspoon pepper
2 cups tomato sauce

1. In a large saucepan of boiling salted water, cook pasta until tender but still firm, 10 to 12 minutes. Drain and rinse under cold running water; drain well.

2. Meanwhile, make the shrimp mousse: In a food processor, combine shrimp and egg. Blend until smooth, about 30 seconds. With machine on, slowly pour in cream and process until blended. Add chives, salt, and pepper and pulse briefly to mix.

3. Preheat oven to 375°F. Butter a 9 x 13-inch baking dish.

4. Fill each shell with 1 tablespoon of shrimp mousse and arrange snugly in baking dish. Pour tomato sauce over shells. Cover loosely with aluminum foil and bake 15 to 20 minutes, until sauce is hot and mousse is firm and cooked through. Serve at once.

214 FUSILLE WITH LOBSTER, SCALLOPS, AND SHRIMP

Prep: 5 minutes   Cook: 13 to 15 minutes   Serves: 4 to 6

1 pound spiral-shaped pasta (fusille)
2 tablespoons butter
½ pound large shrimp, shelled, deveined, and cut into ½-inch pieces
½ pound halved sea scallops
3 medium tomatoes, peeled, seeded, and chopped

2 medium zucchini, sliced into thin julienne strips
¼ cup fresh chopped basil
½ teaspoon salt
¼ teaspoon pepper

1. In a large pot of boiling salted water, cook fusille until tender but still firm, about 10 to 12 minutes. Drain well.

2. Meanwhile, melt butter in a large nonreactive skillet or flameproof casserole over medium-high heat. Add shrimp and scallops. Stir until shrimp are pink and scallops are opaque, about 2 minutes. Add tomatoes and zucchini, raise heat to high, and cook rapidly until tomatoes begin to give off juices, about 2 minutes. Remove from heat. Stir in basil and season with salt and pepper.

3. Add pasta to skillet and stir well to blend. Cook until warmed through, about 3 minutes. Serve at once.

215 PASTA WITH TUNA, MINT, AND LIME

Prep: 3 minutes   Cook: 10 to 12 minutes   Serves: 4

1 pound penne or ziti
1 cup heavy cream
1 tablespoon fresh lime juice
  Grated zest of 1 lime
½ teaspoon salt

½ teaspoon pepper
1 pound fresh tuna, cut into 1-inch cubes
1 tablespoon chopped fresh mint

1. In a large pot of boiling salted water, cook pasta until tender but firm, 10 to 12 minutes. Drain well.

2. Meanwhile, in a medium saucepan, combine cream, lime juice, lime zest, salt, and pepper. Bring to a boil over high heat. Boil until reduced by one-third, 2 to 3 minutes. Add tuna chunks and cook, stirring often, until slightly firm, 3 to 5 minutes. Stir in mint and cook, stirring constantly, 1 minute longer.

3. Place pasta in a large serving bowl. Pour tuna and sauce over pasta, toss, and serve.

216   FETTUCCINE WITH CRAB AND LEEKS
Prep: 8 minutes   Cook: 15 to 18 minutes   Serves: 4

3 tablespoons butter
5 medium leeks (white and
    tender green), halved
    lengthwise, well rinsed,
    drained, and thinly sliced

2 cups heavy cream
½ pound fresh crabmeat
½ teaspoon salt
¼ teaspoon pepper
1 pound dried fettuccine

1. In a medium saucepan, melt butter over medium-high heat. Add leeks and cook, stirring often, until softened, 2 to 3 minutes. Pour in cream, raise heat to high, and boil until reduced by half, about 5 minutes. Stir in crab and season with salt and pepper. Remove from heat and set aside, covered to keep warm.

2. In a large pot of boiling salted water, cook fettuccine until tender but still firm, 8 to 10 minutes. Drain pasta and transfer to a large serving bowl. Pour crab and leeks over pasta, toss, and serve.

217   PASTA WITH CLAMS AND BEANS
Prep: 5 minutes   Cook: 8 to 13 minutes   Serves: 4 to 6

Pasta and beans are a classic homey Italian combination. Any long noodle, such as spaghetti or linguine, can be substituted for the fettuccine.

1 pound dried fettuccine
3 tablespoons butter
2 garlic cloves, minced
1 small onion, chopped
1 cup chicken stock or bottled
    clam juice
½ cup heavy cream
2 cups cooked and drained
    navy or Great Northern
    beans

3 (6½-ounce) cans chopped
    clams with their liquid
2 teaspoons minced fresh
    thyme leaves or
    ½ teaspoon dried
½ teaspoon salt
½ teaspoon crushed hot red
    pepper
½ cup grated Parmesan cheese

1. In a large pot of boiling salted water, cook fettuccine until tender but still firm, 8 to 10 minutes. Drain well.

2. Meanwhile, in a medium saucepan, melt butter over medium heat. Add garlic and onion and cook until soft, 2 to 3 minutes. Pour in chicken stock and cream, raise heat to medium-high, and boil until slightly thickened, 3 to 5 minutes.

3. Add beans, clams, thyme, salt, and hot pepper to sauce and cook until heated through, 3 to 5 minutes.

4. Place fettuccine in a large serving bowl. Pour clam and bean sauce over pasta and toss. Sprinkle Parmesan cheese over top and serve.

218 SHRIMP IN GORGONZOLA SAUCE OVER FETTUCCINE

Prep: 2 minutes   Cook: 8 to 10 minutes   Serves: 4

1 pound dried fettuccine
2 tablespoons olive oil
1 pound shrimp, shelled and deveined
2 tablespoons butter
2 garlic cloves, finely minced

½ cup heavy cream
½ cup crumbled gorgonzola cheese (about 2 ounces)
¼ teaspoon salt
½ teaspoon pepper

1. In a large pot of boiling salted water, cook fettuccine until tender but still firm, 8 to 10 minutes. Drain well.

2. Meanwhile, in a large skillet, heat olive oil over medium-high heat. Add shrimp and cook, turning once, until pink and curled, 2 to 3 minutes. Remove to a plate and set aside.

3. Melt butter over low heat in a medium nonstick skillet. Add garlic and cook, stirring occasionally, until soft, 1 to 2 minutes. Add cream and gorgonzola and cook, stirring constantly, until cheese is melted, about 30 seconds. Stir in shrimp and cook until warmed through, about 1 minute. Season with salt and pepper.

4. Divide pasta among 4 serving plates and top with shrimp and gorgonzola. Serve at once.

219 SPAGHETTI WITH TROUT AND HORSERADISH CREAM

Prep: 3 minutes   Cook: 8 to 10 minutes   Serves: 4

¾ cup heavy cream
2 tablespoons prepared white horseradish
½ teaspoon salt

½ teaspoon pepper
1 pound spaghetti
2 trout, 8 to 12 ounces each, boned and butterflied

1. Preheat broiler. In a medium bowl, combine cream, horseradish, ¼ teaspoon salt, and ¼ teaspoon pepper. Stir to blend well, cover, and set sauce aside.

2. In a large pot of salted water, cook pasta, stirring occasionally, until tender but still firm, 8 to 10 minutes. Drain well and transfer to a large bowl.

3. Meanwhile, arrange trout skin side down on a lightly oiled broiling pan and season with remaining ¼ teaspoon each salt and pepper. Broil 4 to 6 inches from heat 6 to 8 minutes, until fish flakes easily with a fork. Cut fish into ½-inch pieces.

4. Pour horseradish sauce over pasta and add fish. Toss to blend and serve at once.

220   PASTA WITH FRESH TUNA AND OLIVE SAUCE

Prep: 5 minutes   Cook: 10 to 12 minutes   Serves: 4

1 pound penne or ziti	½ teaspoon pepper
2 tablespoons butter	2 garlic cloves, minced
2 tablespoons olive oil	1 medium green bell pepper,
1 pound fresh tuna, cut into	finely chopped
1-inch cubes	⅓ cup pitted green olives
¾ teaspoon salt	⅓ cup pitted black olives

1. In a large pot of boiling salted water, cook penne until tender but still firm, 10 to 12 minutes. Measure out and reserve ½ cup pasta cooking water. Drain pasta.

2. Meanwhile, in a large skillet, melt 1 tablespoon butter in 1 tablespoon olive oil over medium-high heat. Add tuna, season with ½ teaspoon salt and ¼ teaspoon pepper, and cook, turning frequently, until lightly browned and firm, 2 to 3 minutes. Remove to a plate and cover to keep warm.

3. Heat remaining butter and oil in skillet over medium-high heat. Add garlic and green pepper and cook, stirring often, until pepper is slightly softened, about 2 minutes. Stir in olives and transfer to a food processor. Add reserved pasta cooking liquid. Blend until finely minced.

4. Transfer pasta to a large serving bowl. Toss with olive sauce, tuna, and remaining salt and pepper. Serve at once.

221   LINGUINE WITH SCALLOPS

Prep: 7 minutes   Cook: 16 to 20 minutes   Serves: 4 to 6

2 tablespoons olive oil	1 teaspoon dried oregano
2 tablespoons butter	½ teaspoon salt
3 garlic cloves, minced	¼ teaspoon crushed hot red
1 medium onion, thinly sliced	pepper
½ medium green bell pepper,	1 cup dry white wine or red
chopped	wine
1 (28-ounce) can Italian peeled	1 pound bay scallops or
tomatoes, drained and	halved sea scallops
chopped	1 pound linguine

1. In a large saucepan, heat olive oil and butter over medium heat. Add garlic, onion, and bell pepper. Cook, stirring occasionally, until tender, about 3 minutes. Stir in tomatoes, oregano, salt, and hot pepper. Cook, stirring often, 5 minutes. Add wine and simmer, stirring frequently, until slightly thickened, 5 to 7 minutes longer. Add scallops to sauce and cook, stirring occasionally, until opaque throughout, 3 to 5 minutes.

2. Meanwhile, cook pasta in a large pot of boiling salted water until tender but still firm, 8 to 10 minutes. Drain. Serve scallops and sauce over linguine.

222   SEAFOOD LASAGNE

Prep: 15 minutes   Cook: 32 to 41 minutes   Serves: 4 to 6

½ pound lasagne noodles
4 tablespoons butter
3 tablespoons flour
2 cups Fish Stock (page 33) or
     bottled clam juice
½ teaspoon salt
¼ teaspoon pepper
1 tablespoon fresh lemon
     juice

1 pound medium shrimp,
     shelled and deveined
1 pound bay scallops or
     halved sea scallops
1 garlic clove, minced
1 teaspoon grated lemon zest
½ cup fresh bread crumbs
1 tablespoon chopped parsley

1. In a large pot of boiling salted water, cook lasagne noodles until tender but still firm, 10 to 12 minutes. Drain and reserve.

2. In a medium saucepan, melt 2 tablespoons butter over medium-high heat. Add flour and cook, stirring constantly, 1 to 2 minutes without allowing flour to color. Gradually whisk in fish stock and raise heat to high. Boil, whisking often, until smooth and thickened, 1 to 2 minutes. Season sauce with salt, pepper, and lemon juice. Remove from heat and let cool slightly.

3. Preheat oven to 375°F. Spread about 2 tablespoons sauce evenly over bottom of an 8x11-inch baking dish. Cover with a single layer of noodles. Add half of shrimp and scallops. Spoon half of sauce over seafood. Top with another layer of noodles, remaining seafood, and sauce.

4. In a small bowl, combine garlic, lemon zest, bread crumbs, and parsley. Stir to blend well. Sprinkle crumbs over lasagne and dot with remaining butter. Bake 20 to 25 minutes, until top is browned and sauce is bubbly.

223   PASTA SHELLS WITH TUNA AND VEGETABLES IN TOMATO SAUCE

Prep: 8 minutes   Cook: 26 to 31 minutes   Serves: 4

2 tablespoons olive oil
1 medium onion, finely
     chopped
1 (28-ounce) can Italian peeled
     tomatoes, drained and
     chopped
1 teaspoon salt
½ teaspoon pepper

½ pound green beans, cut into
     1-inch pieces
3 carrots, cut into ½-inch dice
1 pound small pasta shells
1 (6⅛-ounce) can tuna,
     drained and flaked
¼ cup grated Parmesan cheese

1. In a medium saucepan, heat 2 tablespoons olive oil over medium-high heat. Add onion and cook, stirring often, until softened, about 3 minutes. Add tomatoes, ½ teaspoon salt, and ¼ teaspoon pepper. Cook, stirring occasionally, until thickened, 7 to 10 minutes. Remove from heat, transfer to a food processor or blender, and puree until smooth. Set tomato sauce aside.

2. Bring a large saucepan of salted water to a boil. Add green beans, return to a boil, and cook until tender, about 5 minutes. With a slotted spoon or skimmer, transfer beans to a colander. Rinse under cold running water and drain well. Add carrots to saucepan and cook until just tender, about 3 minutes. Drain.

3. In a large pot of boiling salted water, cook pasta shells until tender but still firm, 8 to 10 minutes. Drain well. Reheat tomato sauce if necessary. Add vegetables to sauce and toss with pasta shells and tuna. Serve warm or at room temperature, with Parmesan cheese sprinkled on top.

---

224 LOBSTER IN GINGER CREAM SAUCE OVER PASTA

Prep: 5 minutes   Cook: 8 to 12 minutes   Serves: 4

2 tablespoons butter	½ teaspoon salt
1 tablespoon olive oil	¼ teaspoon cayenne
1 garlic clove, minced	1 pound spaghettini or angel
2 (1-inch) pieces of fresh	hair pasta
ginger, peeled and	1 pound cooked lobster meat,
minced	cut into ¼-inch pieces
1 cup Fish Stock (page 33) or	½ pound snow peas, stemmed
bottled clam juice	and stringed
1 cup heavy cream	1 tablespoon chopped parsley
½ cup dry white wine	

1. In a large skillet, melt butter in olive oil over medium-low heat. Add garlic and ginger and cook, stirring occasionally, until garlic is soft and fragrant, about 2 minutes. Pour in fish stock, cream, wine, salt, and cayenne. Raise heat to high and boil, stirring often, until sauce is slightly thickened, 3 to 5 minutes.

2. In a large pot of boiling salted water, cook pasta until tender but still firm, 3 to 5 minutes. Drain well. Transfer to a large serving bowl.

3. Meanwhile, add lobster and snow peas to sauce. Cook, stirring occasionally, until lobster is warmed through and snow peas are bright green and crisp-tender, about 3 minutes.

4. Pour lobster sauce over pasta and toss. Sprinkle parsley over top and serve at once.

225   ASIAN SEAFOOD PASTA

Prep: 6 minutes   Cook: 7 minutes   Serves: 4

8 ounces soba noodles (thin
    buckwheat noodles)
1 tablespoon sesame seeds
2 tablespoons vegetable oil
1 small red bell pepper, thinly
    sliced
½ pound snow peas, stemmed
    and stringed
¼ pound medium shrimp,
    shelled, deveined, and
    cut into ½-inch dice

¼ pound bay scallops or
    halved sea scallops
2 teaspoons minced fresh
    ginger
1 tablespoon Asian sesame oil
¼ cup thinly sliced scallions
1 tablespoon soy sauce

1. In a large pot of boiling salted water, cook noodles until tender but still firm, about 7 minutes. Drain well.

2. Meanwhile, in a wok or large dry skillet, cook sesame seeds over medium heat, stirring, until lightly toasted and fragrant, about 2 minutes. Transfer to a small bowl and set aside.

3. Add oil to wok and heat over medium-high heat. Add bell pepper and stir-fry until slightly softened, about 1 minute. Add snow peas, shrimp, and scallops. Cook, stirring and tossing often, until shrimp are bright pink and scallops are firm and opaque throughout, 3 to 4 minutes longer.

4. In a large bowl, combine noodles with seafood and vegetables from wok. Add ginger, sesame oil, sesame seeds, scallions, and soy sauce and toss well to mix. Serve at room temperature.

226   TUNA AND PASTA MEDLEY

Prep: 10 minutes   Marinate: 2 hours   Cook: 10 to 12 minutes
Serves: 4

1   tuna steak cut 1 inch thick,
   about ¾ pound
2   tablespoons soy sauce
1½ tablespoons fresh lemon or
   lime juice
1   pound penne or ziti
20 asparagus spears cut into
   1-inch lengths

3   tablespoons olive oil
2   medium tomatoes, peeled,
   seeded, and chopped
8   to 10 black olives, pitted
2   tablespoons grated
   Parmesan cheese
¼   teaspoon salt
¼   teaspoon pepper

1. Cut tuna steak into ¼-inch strips and arrange flat in a nonreactive baking dish. Pour over soy sauce and lemon juice. Cover and refrigerate for 2 hours, turning once.

2. In a large pot of boiling salted water, cook pasta until tender but still firm, 10 to 12 minutes.

3. Meanwhile, in a large saucepan of boiling salted water, cook asparagus until barely tender, 2 to 3 minutes. Drain into a colander and rinse under cold running water; drain well.

4. Remove tuna from marinade and pat dry with paper towels. Brush bottom of a large skillet with 1 tablespoon of olive oil. Over high heat, cook tuna strips until lightly browned and firm, about 30 seconds per side. Transfer to a platter and cover with aluminum foil to keep warm.

5. Drain pasta well and transfer to a large serving bowl. Add remaining olive oil, tomatoes, asparagus, olives, Parmesan cheese, salt, and pepper and toss. Arrange warm tuna strips on top and serve at once.

Chapter 10

Fish for the Frenzied

Ideas for putting together a quick meal at the end of a busy day are sometimes hard to come up with. Frozen fish, fish sticks, and frozen shrimp are ingredients that can make this task easier.

Frozen fish comes in solid blocks of ice that can be defrosted in no time under cold running water or in the microwave (follow manufacturer's instructions for your particular machine). Breaded fish fillets come ready to pop into the oven just like fish sticks, that modern convenience food active mothers have come to know so well. Frozen shrimp come in various shapes and sizes. Tiny shrimp no larger than a fingernail are good for salads and sandwich fillings. Medium and large shrimp come in boxes or bags to be defrosted and used just like the real thing.

These products need only a sauce, salsa, or accompanying vegetable to be made into a meal in minutes. The following recipes are a few examples of how to make the most of these everyday ingredients.

---

227 QUICK FISH WITH MUSHROOM SAUCE
Prep: 5 minutes   Cook: 22 to 29 minutes   Serves: 4

2 tablespoons butter
½ green bell pepper, chopped
1 onion, finely chopped
5 mushrooms, sliced
½ cup dry white wine
1 (10¾-ounce) can condensed mushroom soup

½ teaspoon salt
¼ teaspoon pepper
1 (1-pound) package frozen fish fillets, thawed

1. Preheat oven to 400°F. In a medium saucepan, melt butter over medium-high heat. Add green pepper, onion, and mushrooms. Cook, stirring often, until lightly browned and tender, 3 to 4 minutes. Pour in wine, raise heat to high, and boil, scraping up brown bits from bottom of pan, until reduced by half, about 2 minutes. Stir in mushroom soup, salt, and pepper. Cook, stirring frequently, until blended and heated through, 2 to 3 minutes.

2. Arrange fish in an 8 x 11-inch baking dish. Pour mushroom sauce over fish. Bake 15 to 20 minutes, until fish flakes easily when tested with a fork. Serve hot.

228   FISH WITH QUICK CLAM SAUCE
Prep: 2 minutes   Cook: 20 to 25 minutes   Serves: 4

1 (10¾-ounce) can cream of
　　potato soup
¼ cup milk
1 (6¾-ounce) can chopped
　　clams with liquid

1 (1-pound) package frozen
　　fish fillets, thawed
½ cup dried bread crumbs
2 tablespoons butter, melted

1. Preheat oven to 400°F. In a small saucepan, combine soup, milk, and clams with liquid. Bring to a simmer over medium-high heat, stirring often.

2. Arrange fish fillets in a single layer in an 8 x 11-inch baking dish. Pour hot potato and clam sauce over fish. Sprinkle bread crumbs on top and drizzle with melted butter. Bake, uncovered, 20 to 25 minutes, until browned on top.

229   QUICK FISH FILLETS WITH MUSTARD-CAPER BUTTER
Prep: 2 minutes   Cook: 15 minutes   Serves: 4

The butter can be made in advance. When blended, place on a small piece of plastic wrap and form into a cylinder about 2 inches long. Twist ends of plastic to seal; store in refrigerator. Top hot fish with thick slices of butter.

1 (1-pound) package frozen
　　fish fillets, thawed
½ teaspoon salt
½ teaspoon pepper

1 stick (4 ounces) butter,
　　softened
1 tablespoon Dijon mustard
2 teaspoons capers, chopped

1. Preheat oven to 400°F. Arrange fish in a single layer on a baking sheet and season with ¼ teaspoon each salt and pepper. Bake about 15 minutes, until fish flakes easily when tested with a fork.

2. Meanwhile, in a small bowl, combine butter, mustard, capers, and remaining ¼ teaspoon each salt and pepper. Blend with a fork until smooth. Cover and let stand at room temperature away from heat.

3. Remove fish from oven and transfer to individual serving plates. Top with a large spoonful of flavored butter and serve at once.

230   CREAMY FISH FLORENTINE

Prep: 1 minute   Cook: 15 minutes   Serves: 4

1 (1-pound) package frozen
   fish fillets, thawed
1 (10-ounce) package frozen
   chopped spinach, thawed
   and drained

½ teaspoon salt
¼ teaspoon pepper
   Pinch of grated nutmeg
1 cup heavy cream

1. Preheat oven to 400°F. Arrange fish fillets in a single layer in an 8 x 11-inch baking dish. Spread spinach over fish and season with salt, pepper, and nutmeg. Pour cream over all. Cover dish loosely with aluminum foil.

2. Bake 15 minutes, or until fish is opaque throughout.

231   EASY FISH BARBECUE

Prep: 2 minutes   Cook: 10 to 12 minutes   Serves: 4

½ cup barbecue sauce
2 tablespoons olive oil
½ teaspoon pepper

1 (1-pound) package frozen
   fish fillets, thawed

1. Preheat broiler. In a small bowl, combine barbecue sauce, olive oil, and pepper. Stir to blend well.

2. Arrange fish fillets in a single layer on a large baking sheet. Brush equal amounts of barbecue sauce over each. Broil about 4 inches from heat 10 to 12 minutes, until lightly browned and fish flakes easily when tested with a fork. Serve hot.

232   QUICK FISH BAKED IN TOMATO CREAM SAUCE

Prep: 2 minutes   Cook: 15 to 20 minutes   Serves: 4

1 (10¾-ounce) can tomato
   soup
1 cup heavy cream
1 tablespoon chopped fresh
   basil or 1 teaspoon dried

1 (1-pound) package frozen
   fish fillets, thawed
¼ teaspoon salt
¼ teaspoon pepper

1. Preheat oven to 400°F. In a small saucepan, combine tomato soup, cream, and basil. Bring sauce to a simmer over medium-high heat, stirring often.

2. Arrange fish fillets in a single layer in an 8 x 11-inch baking dish. Season with salt and pepper. Pour hot sauce over fish and bake 15 to 20 minutes, until fish flakes easily when tested with a fork and top is lightly browned.

233   BAKED FISH AND SALSA
Prep: 3 minutes   Cook: 15 minutes   Serves: 4

1 (1-pound) package frozen
  fish fillets, thawed
½ teaspoon salt
½ teaspoon pepper

1 cup bottled salsa
  Juice of 1 lime
2 tablespoons chopped
  cilantro or parsley

1. Preheat oven to 400°F. Arrange fish fillets in a baking dish large enough to hold them in a single layer. Season with salt and pepper. Pour salsa over fish.

2. Bake 15 minutes, or until fish flakes easily when tested with a fork.

3. Sprinkle lime juice and cilantro over fish and serve.

234   FISH PARMIGIANA
Prep: 3 minutes   Cook: 15 minutes   Serves: 4

This quick recipe is best served with pasta tossed with olive oil and garlic or with plain boiled potatoes.

1 (1-pound) package frozen
  fish fillets, thawed
½ teaspoon salt
¼ teaspoon pepper
1 cup tomato sauce

¼ cup grated Parmesan cheese
¼ cup Italian seasoned bread
  crumbs
2 tablespoons olive oil

1. Preheat oven to 425°F. Arrange fish in a lightly buttered baking dish and season with salt and pepper.

2. Pour tomato sauce over fish. Sprinkle top with cheese and bread crumbs. Drizzle with olive oil and bake about 15 minutes, until fish is opaque throughout.

235   FISH FILLET SANDWICHES
Prep: 3 minutes   Cook: 20 to 25 minutes   Serves: 4

Add strips of crisp cooked bacon for a fish club sandwich.

1 (8-ounce) package frozen
  breaded fish fillets
¼ teaspoon salt
¼ teaspoon pepper
8 slices of white or whole
  wheat bread

¼ cup mayonnaise
1 small red onion, sliced
1 medium tomato, sliced
4 lettuce leaves

1. Preheat oven to 400°F. Arrange fish in a single layer on a baking sheet. Season with salt and pepper and bake 20 to 25 minutes, until crisp.

2. Meanwhile, lightly toast bread, cool, and spread with mayonnaise. Top 4 pieces of toast with slices of onion and tomato. Place a hot fish fillet on each and top with a lettuce leaf. Cover with remaining pieces of toast and cut in half diagonally. Serve warm.

236 CURRIED FISH STICKS

Prep: 2 minutes   Cook: 18 to 22 minutes   Serves: 4

Serve good-quality bottled chutney as an accompaniment.

1 (8-ounce) package frozen breaded fish sticks	1 teaspoon curry powder
2 tablespoons butter	¾ cup sour cream
1 small onion, finely chopped	2 teaspoons fresh lemon juice
	½ teaspoon salt
	¼ teaspoon pepper

1. Preheat oven to 425°F. Arrange fish sticks in a single layer on a large baking sheet and bake 18 to 22 minutes, until crisp.

2. Meanwhile, in a small saucepan, melt butter over medium heat. Add onion and curry and cook, stirring often, until onion is tender, about 3 minutes. Remove from heat and let cool.

3. In a small bowl, combine sour cream, lemon juice, salt, pepper, and cooled onion-curry mixture. Stir to blend well. Serve fish sticks hot, with curry sauce on the side.

237 FISH STICKS MORNAY

Prep: 3 minutes   Cook: 18 to 22 minutes   Serves: 4

1 (8-ounce) package frozen breaded fish sticks	½ cup grated Swiss or Cheddar cheese
2 tablespoons butter	½ teaspoon salt
2 tablespoons flour	¼ teaspoon pepper
1 cup milk	⅛ teaspoon cayenne

1. Preheat oven to 425°F. Arrange fish sticks in a single layer on a large baking sheet. Bake 18 to 22 minutes, until crisp.

2. Meanwhile, in a small saucepan, melt butter over medium-high heat. Add flour and cook, stirring constantly, until lemon colored and bubbly, about 2 minutes. Gradually whisk in milk, raise heat to high, and bring to a boil, whisking until thickened and smooth, 1 to 2 minutes. Reduce heat to low and simmer, stirring often, 3 minutes. Remove from heat, stir in cheese, and season with salt, pepper, and cayenne. Set Mornay sauce aside, covered to keep warm.

3. When fish sticks are done, transfer to serving plate. Reheat Mornay sauce briefly if necessary. Spoon sauce over fish sticks and serve at once.

238   FISH STICKS WITH PICANTE SAUCE
Prep: 5 minutes   Cook: 18 to 22 minutes   Serves: 4

The sauce can be made up to two days ahead. Keep refrigerated until ready to use. Let sauce stand at room temperature for 20 to 30 minutes before serving.

1   (8-ounce) package frozen breaded fish sticks
2   hard-boiled eggs
1   tablespoon chopped fresh herbs (parsley, thyme, chives, rosemary, or oregano) or 1 teaspoon dried

¼   cup chopped sweet or sour pickles
2   tablespoons mayonnaise
½   teaspoon salt
¼   teaspoon pepper

1. Preheat oven to 425°F. Arrange fish sticks in a single layer on a baking sheet. Bake 18 to 22 minutes, until crisp.

2. Meanwhile, finely chop eggs and place in a small bowl. Add herbs, pickles, mayonnaise, salt, and pepper. Stir to blend well.

3. Transfer cooked fish sticks to a platter and serve sauce on the side.

239   FISH STICKS WITH DIPPING SAUCE
Prep: 3 minutes   Cook: 18 to 22 minutes   Serves: 4

1   (8-ounce) package frozen breaded fish sticks
½   cup mayonnaise
¼   cup ketchup
2   tablespoons pickle relish

2   to 4 drops of hot pepper sauce
¼   teaspoon salt
Lemon wedges

1. Preheat oven to 425°F. Arrange fish sticks in a single layer on a baking sheet. Bake 18 to 22 minutes, until crisp.

2. Meanwhile, in a small bowl, combine mayonnaise, ketchup, pickle relish, hot sauce, and salt. Stir to blend well. Cover and refrigerate until ready to use.

3. When fish sticks are done, transfer to serving plates. Garnish with lemon wedges and pass sauce on the side for dipping.

240 FISH STICKS WITH SOUR CREAM AND LUMPFISH CAVIAR

Prep: 3 minutes   Cook: 18 to 22 minutes   Serves: 4

1 (8-ounce) package frozen breaded fish sticks
½ cup sour cream

1 (2-ounce) jar lumpfish caviar
½ teaspoon pepper

1. Preheat oven to 425°F. Arrange fish sticks in a single layer on a baking sheet. Bake 18 to 22 minutes, until crisp.

2. In a small bowl, combine sour cream, caviar, and pepper. Stir gently to combine.

3. Serve fish sticks on individual serving plates and top each with a dollop of sour cream and caviar.

241 SHRIMP CHILI

Prep: 2 minutes   Cook: 13 to 14 minutes   Serves: 4

Use a mild chili powder, if possible. Serve with boiled or steamed rice surrounded by condiments: small bowls of finely chopped onions, grated cheese, sour cream, pickles, and chopped hard-boiled eggs.

2 tablespoons olive oil
1 small onion, finely chopped
1 garlic clove, minced
1 teaspoon chili powder
1 (28-ounce) can Italian peeled tomatoes, drained and chopped

1 (16-ounce) can kidney beans, drained
½ teaspoon salt
½ teaspoon pepper
2 (5-ounce) packages frozen tiny shrimp, thawed

1. In a medium saucepan, heat olive oil over medium heat. Add onion, garlic, and chili powder. Cook, stirring often, until onion is slightly softened, about 2 minutes.

2. Pour tomatoes into saucepan and bring to a simmer. Add kidney beans, salt, and pepper. Cook, stirring often, until slightly thickened, about 10 minutes.

3. Pat shrimp dry with paper towels. Add shrimp to chili mixture and cook until heated through, 1 to 2 minutes.

242   FISH AND SHRIMP STEW

Prep: 2 minutes   Cook: 15 minutes   Serves: 4 to 6

1 tablespoon olive oil
1 small onion, finely chopped
1 garlic clove, minced
2 (16-ounce) cans condensed
   tomato soup
½ cup dry white wine

1 (1-pound) package frozen
   fish fillets, thawed
1 (5-ounce) bag tiny frozen
   shrimp
1 tablespoon chopped parsley

1. In a large nonreactive saucepan, heat oil over medium-high heat. Add onion and garlic. Cook, stirring often, until slightly softened, about 2 minutes. Pour in soup, wine, and ½ cup water. Reduce heat to medium-low and simmer, stirring occasionally, until smooth and bubbly, about 5 minutes.

2. Add fish and shrimp, cover partially, and cook, stirring occasionally to break fish into chunks, until fish is opaque and shrimp are firm, about 10 minutes longer. Stir in chopped parsley and serve at once.

243   SHRIMP AND AVOCADO SANDWICHES

Prep: 3 minutes   Cook: 4 minutes   Serves: 4

2 (5-ounce) packages frozen
   tiny shrimp, thawed
¼ cup mayonnaise
½ cup shredded Swiss or
   Cheddar cheese
¼ teaspoon salt

½ teaspoon pepper
1 avocado, peeled and seeded
2 tablespoons lemon juice
4 English muffins, split
   in half

1. Pat shrimp dry on paper towels and place in a medium bowl. Add mayonnaise, cheese, salt, and pepper. Stir to blend and set aside. Cut avocado into 16 slices, sprinkle with lemon juice, and set aside.

2. Preheat broiler. Lightly toast English muffin halves, about 2 minutes. Let cool slightly; then spread equal amounts of shrimp and cheese mixture over bottom halves. Place on a small baking pan and return to broiler. Broil about 2 minutes, until lightly browned. Place 4 avocado slices on top of each and cover with English muffin tops. Cut in half and serve hot.

Chapter 11

Simply Shrimp

Shrimp is by far the most popular of all shellfish. Most shrimp that finds its way to the market has been frozen at some point in transit. While this may sound off-putting, and nobody denies that the watery, lifeless creature that results is not quite the same as the unadulterated, there is some benefit. Modern technology makes flash freezing on board a modern shrimping boat a far safer system than allowing large catches to sit around in boxes exposed to heat, as was often the case in the past. Trucks equipped with good freezers facilitate handling, making ground transportation easier, too.

Shrimp come in varying sizes. Jumbos come 10 to 15 a pound, large come 16 to 20 a pound, and mediums are 21 to 25 per pound. There are about 31 to 35 small shrimp to a pound. Ready-to-thaw frozen shrimp are easy to find and can be a cost- and time-saving alternative to fresh.

Shelling and deveining are almost always called for in recipes. Peeling shrimp at the table is not a pretty sight. The exception is an old-fashioned shrimp boil, where bowls of the steaming pink crustaceans are set out in an informal setting to be peeled and eaten on-site. In this case, most of us would opt to eat the shrimp with the vein intact. For most recipes, however, the black line or intestinal vein that runs along the back is easily removed with the tip of a sharp knife.

Two pounds of unpeeled, headless shrimp will yield about 1 pound cleaned and trimmed. In most cases, 1 pound will serve four people. This varies, of course, depending on the recipe and particular appetites.

244 BREADED STUFFED SHRIMP

Prep: 10 minutes   Cook: 9 minutes   Serves: 4

4 tablespoons butter
1 small onion, finely chopped
1 celery rib, finely chopped
½ green bell pepper, finely chopped
1 teaspoon fresh thyme leaves or ½ teaspoon dried

½ teaspoon salt
½ teaspoon pepper
1½ cups dried bread crumbs
24 large shrimp, peeled and deveined, with tails intact
Lemon wedges

1. In a medium saucepan, melt butter over medium heat. Add onion, celery, and bell pepper and cook, stirring occasionally, until softened, about 3 minutes. Add thyme, salt, and pepper and cook 1 minute longer. Remove from heat and add bread crumbs and ¼ cup water. Stir well to combine.

2. Preheat oven to 400°F. Split shrimp down back, cutting almost but not quite through to underside, and spread open to butterfly. Fill interiors with about 1 tablespoon of bread mixture. Arrange stuffed shrimp flat on a lightly oiled 9 x 13-inch baking dish. Bake until shrimp are pink and filling is lightly browned, about 5 minutes. Serve immediately with lemon wedges.

245 COOL SHRIMP PESTO

Prep: 5 minutes   Cook: 13 to 15 minutes
Chill: 2 hours plus 30 minutes   Serves: 4

2 pounds medium shrimp
¼ cup pine nuts
2 cups fresh basil, loosely packed
⅓ cup grated Parmesan cheese
1 garlic clove

2 tablespoons lime juice
¼ teaspoon salt
¼ teaspoon pepper
¼ cup olive oil
¼ cup sour cream

1. Bring a large pot of salted water to a boil. Add shrimp and bring back to a boil. Cook rapidly until pink and curled, 3 to 5 minutes. Drain well and cool. Cover and refrigerate until well chilled, at least 2 hours or overnight. Shell and devein.

2. Preheat oven to 325°F. Spread pine nuts evenly on a small baking pan. Toast, stirring occasionally, until golden brown, about 10 minutes. Let cool.

3. In a food processor, combine basil, pine nuts, Parmesan, garlic, lime juice, salt, and pepper. With machine on, slowly drizzle in olive oil and process until mixture becomes a smooth paste, about 30 seconds. Transfer pesto to a medium bowl and stir in sour cream. Cover and refrigerate until thoroughly chilled, about 30 minutes.

4. Place a bowlful of pesto sauce in the center of a large platter. Surround with boiled shrimp and use sauce as a dip.

246   SHRIMP AND BROCCOLI CASSEROLE
Prep: 5 minutes   Cook: 26 minutes   Serves: 4

4 cups broccoli florets,
   about 1 pound
5 tablespoons butter
3 tablespoons flour
2 cups milk
1 cup (about 4 ounces) grated
   Swiss cheese

½ teaspoon salt
¼ teaspoon pepper
¾ pound medium shrimp,
   shelled and deveined
½ cup fresh bread crumbs

1. Bring a large pot of salted water to a boil. Add broccoli and return to a boil over high heat. Cook for 1 minute. Drain and rinse under cold running water to stop cooking. Drain well.

2. In a medium saucepan, melt 2 tablespoons butter over medium-low heat. Add flour and cook, stirring, 2 minutes. Gradually whisk in milk, raise heat to medium-high, and bring to a boil, whisking, until thickened and smooth. Reduce heat to medium and simmer sauce, uncovered, 3 minutes. Remove from heat and stir in cheese, salt, and pepper.

3. Preheat oven to 375°F. Lightly butter a 1-quart baking or soufflé dish. Add broccoli and shrimp to sauce and stir to mix. Pour into baking dish and sprinkle bread crumbs over top. In a microwave oven or small saucepan, melt remaining 2 tablespoons butter. Drizzle over bread crumbs.

4. Bake casserole about 20 minutes, until sauce is bubbly and top is golden brown. Serve hot.

247   SHRIMP COCKTAIL WITH AIOLI SAUCE
Prep: 10 minutes   Cook: 18 to 25 minutes   Serves: 4

1 (3-ounce) box shrimp boil
1¼ teaspoons salt
1½ pounds large shrimp,
   shelled and deveined
   with tails intact

8 garlic cloves, skins on
1 cup mayonnaise
¼ teaspoon salt
¼ teaspoon pepper
¼ teaspoon cumin

1. In a large saucepan, combine the shrimp boil and salt with 3 cups of water. Bring to a boil over high heat. Add shrimp and cook until bright pink and curled, about 3 to 5 minutes. Drain and rinse under cold water to stop cooking. Cover and refrigerate until well chilled.

2. Preheat oven to 425°F. In a small baking dish, roast garlic cloves 15 to 20 minutes, until crisp outside and tender inside.

3. Scrape pulp from garlic cloves into a medium bowl. Add mayonnaise, salt, pepper, and cumin. Whisk vigorously to blend well. Cover and refrigerate until chilled. Serve cold shrimp with roasted garlic mayonnaise on the side for dipping.

248   SHRIMP CROQUETTES

Prep: 15 minutes   Chill: 1 hour   Cook: 6 minutes   Serves: 4

1 pound medium shrimp,
   shelled and deveined
2 tablespoons butter
1 small onion, finely chopped
1 large all-purpose potato
   (about 4 ounces), peeled,
   boiled, and mashed
½ teaspoon salt

¼ teaspoon pepper
1 tablespoon chopped parsley
2 tablespoons milk
1 cup fresh bread crumbs
2 eggs
   Vegetable oil, for deep-
   frying

1. Cut shrimp into ¼-inch dice and set aside. In a small saucepan, melt butter over medium-high heat. Add onion and cook, stirring frequently, until softened, about 2 minutes. Transfer to a medium bowl.

2. Add mashed potato, shrimp, salt, pepper, and parsley to onion. Stir in milk and blend well. Cover and refrigerate until well chilled, about 1 hour.

3. Place bread crumbs in a small shallow bowl. In a separate small bowl, beat eggs with a fork until frothy. Pour oil to measure 3 inches deep into a wok or large, heavy saucepan, and heat to 365°F on a deep-frying thermometer.

4. Shape chilled shrimp mixture into cylindrical croquettes that measure about 2½ inches long and 1 inch thick. Roll in bread crumbs to coat. Dip in egg, then dredge again in bread crumbs to coat. Add to hot fat and fry until browned and crisp, about 4 minutes. Drain on paper towels and serve hot.

249   SHRIMP FRIED RICE

Prep: 5 minutes   Cook: 6 minutes   Serves: 4

3 cups cooked white rice,
   thoroughly chilled
1 egg, lightly beaten
½ teaspoon salt
¼ cup vegetable oil
2 scallions, thinly sliced

1½ pounds medium shrimp,
   shelled and deveined
1 cup frozen peas, thawed
2 tablespoons soy sauce
½ teaspoon pepper

1. Using wet hands, rub cooked rice to separate grains. Beat egg with ¼ teaspoon salt. In a wok or large skillet, heat 1 tablespoon oil over medium heat. Add scallions and stir-fry 30 seconds. Add egg and cook until barely firm, about 15 seconds. Transfer scallions and egg to a small bowl and set aside.

2. Raise heat to medium-high and add 1 tablespoon oil to wok or skillet. Add shrimp and peas and stir-fry, tossing frequently, until shrimp are pink and curled, about 2 minutes. Remove to a plate or platter and set aside.

3. Heat remaining 2 tablespoons oil, add rice, and stir-fry until heated through, about 2 minutes. Stir in soy sauce, shrimp, and peas. Add egg and gently stir until egg is in small pieces, about 1 minute. Season with pepper and remaining salt. Serve hot.

250   JACKSONVILLE'S SHRIMP SPREAD

Prep: 8 minutes   Cook: none   Chill: 1 hour   Serves: 4

Serve this flavorful dip with an assortment of breads and crackers. Use as a spread for appetizers.

8 ounces cream cheese,
  softened
1 celery rib, finely chopped
2 scallions (green part only),
  thinly sliced
½ teaspoon Worcestershire
  sauce

½ teaspoon salt
¼ teaspoon garlic powder
4 to 5 dashes of bottled hot
  pepper sauce, or to taste
1 pound boiled shrimp,
  peeled, deveined, and
  thoroughly chilled

1. In a medium bowl, combine cream cheese, celery, scallions, Worcestershire sauce, salt, garlic powder, and hot sauce.

2. Cut shrimp into ½-inch pieces. Add to cream cheese mixture and blend well. Cover and refrigerate at least 1 hour before serving or up to overnight.

251   STIR-FRIED SHRIMP WITH SNOW PEAS

*Prep: 10 minutes   Marinate: 15 minutes   Cook: 6 minutes
Serves: 4*

2 teaspoons soy sauce
2 teaspoons dry sherry
2 teaspoons cornstarch
3 tablespoons vegetable oil
½ teaspoon pepper
1½ pounds medium shrimp,
  shelled and deveined
1 (1-inch) piece of fresh
  ginger, peeled and
  minced

2 garlic cloves, minced
¼ pound snow peas, stemmed
  and stringed
1 (8-ounce) can sliced water
  chestnuts, drained

1. In a large bowl, combine soy sauce, sherry, cornstarch, 1 tablespoon oil, pepper, and 3 tablespoons water. Stir to blend well. Add shrimp and toss to coat. Marinate at room temperature for 15 minutes.

2. In a wok or large skillet, heat remaining 2 tablespoons oil over high heat. Add ginger and garlic and cook, stirring once, for 30 seconds. Add shrimp with marinade and stir-fry until pink and curled, about 2 minutes. Use a slotted spoon to transfer shrimp to a plate. Set aside.

3. Add snow peas, water chestnuts, and 2 tablespoons water to wok. Stir-fry over medium-high heat until snow peas are bright green and slightly tender, about 1½ minutes. Return shrimp to pan and cook, stirring occasionally, until warmed through, about 2 minutes. Serve immediately.

252 STIR-FRIED SHRIMP WITH BLACK BEAN SAUCE

Prep: 3 minutes   Cook: 8 minutes   Serves: 4

3 tablespoons vegetable oil
1 pound medium shrimp, unpeeled
2 tablespoons Chinese fermented black beans, rinsed and drained
1 (1-inch) piece of fresh ginger, peeled and finely chopped

1 garlic clove, minced
2 scallions (white and 1 inch of greens), thinly sliced
½ cup fish stock, chicken stock, or water
2 tablespoons dry sherry
2 tablespoons soy sauce
1 teaspoon cornstarch

1. In a wok or large skillet, heat oil until hot but not smoking. Add shrimp and cook over medium-high heat, stirring, until pink and loosely curled, about 2 minutes. Add black beans, ginger, and garlic.

2. Raise heat to high and cook rapidly for about 30 seconds. Add scallions and cook about 10 seconds longer. Pour in stock or water and bring to a boil. Reduce heat to medium-low, cover loosely, and simmer for about 3 minutes.

3. In a small bowl, combine sherry, soy sauce, and cornstarch. Stir to dissolve cornstarch. Add to shrimp and raise heat to medium-high. Cook, stirring constantly, until sauce boils and thickens, about 2 minutes. Serve at once.

253 POTTED SHRIMP

Prep: 8 minutes   Cook: 1 hour   Chill: 2 hours   Serves: 8

This is a favorite recipe from noted cookbook author and teacher Anne Willan. The essential element is clarified butter, which will not burn during the lengthy cooking process.

3 sticks (12 ounces) butter
2 pounds medium shrimp, shelled and deveined
½ teaspoon salt

¼ teaspoon pepper
¼ teaspoon grated nutmeg
Pinch of cayenne

1. Place butter in a heavy saucepan. Melt over medium heat, about 3 minutes. Skim off foam that rises to surface. Let stand 2 to 3 minutes to settle. Carefully pour thick yellow layer into a bowl and discard remaining milky white residue at bottom.

2. Preheat oven to 300°F. Place shrimp in an ovenproof baking dish and season with salt, pepper, nutmeg, and cayenne. Pour three-fourths of clarified butter over shrimp. Cover and bake about 1 hour, or until butter is golden. Let cool in pan.

3. Transfer butter and shrimp to a food processor. Pulse several times to coarsely chop. Pack into four 1-cup ramekins or small crocks, filling each about three-fourths full. Pour remaining clarified butter over top and spread evenly to seal. Refrigerate for at least 2 hours or up to 2 weeks before serving.

254 LOW-COUNTRY SHRIMP
Prep: 12 minutes   Cook: 27 minutes   Serves: 4

Shrimp are especially popular in the coastal areas of Georgia, close to Florida and not too far from the rice-loving Carolinas. The following recipe is Southernly inspired. I served it with black-eyed peas on the side during a recent visit down yonder. Yankees might prefer green beans, broccoli, or fresh green peas as an accompaniment.

To prepare rice in advance, follow the instructions below. Set cooked rice in a colander over a large pot containing an inch or two of barely simmering water. Cover loosely and stir frequently. Do not hold for more than 30 to 45 minutes, or the rice will dry out.

¼ cup olive oil	2 medium tomatoes, peeled, seeded, and diced
1 cup rice	
2 cups boiling water	1 pound medium shrimp, shelled, deveined, and cut into ½-inch dice
1 teaspoon salt	
1 medium onion, coarsely chopped	
1 carrot, peeled and coarsely chopped	1 pound okra, trimmed and cut into ¼-inch-thick slices
1 celery rib, coarsely chopped	¼ teaspoon pepper

1. In a small saucepan, heat 2 tablespoons of olive oil over medium heat. Add rice and cook, stirring frequently, until translucent, about 2 minutes. Carefully pour boiling water into saucepan. Add ½ teaspoon salt and bring to a boil over high heat. Reduce heat to medium-low, cover, and cook until rice is tender and water is absorbed, about 20 minutes. Stir rice gently with a spoon and let stand, covered, 5 minutes longer.

2. Meanwhile, in a large skillet, cook onion, carrot, and celery in 1 tablespoon olive oil over medium heat, stirring occasionally, until softened, about 5 minutes. Add tomatoes and cook, stirring occasionally, until thick and pulpy, about 10 minutes. Transfer mixture in skillet to a food processor or blender and puree until smooth. Set aside.

3. Wipe out skillet and add remaining 1 tablespoon of olive oil to pan. Set over medium heat and add shrimp and okra. Cook, stirring occasionally, until shrimp are pink and okra is slightly softened, about 2 minutes. Pour in tomato puree and cook 3 minutes longer. Season with pepper and remaining ½ teaspoon salt.

255   SHRIMP FRITTERS
Prep: 10 minutes   Cook: 2 minutes per batch   Serves: 4

½ pound medium shrimp,
      shelled and deveined
2 garlic cloves, minced
2 scallions, thinly sliced
1 (1-inch) piece of fresh
      ginger, peeled and
      minced
1 egg

3 tablespoons flour
1 tablespoon olive oil
½ teaspoon salt
¼ teaspoon pepper
   Vegetable oil, for frying
   Chinese Dipping Sauce
      (recipe follows)

1. In a food processor, pulse shrimp to a creamy paste. Transfer to a medium bowl and mix in garlic, scallions, ginger, egg, flour, olive oil, salt, and pepper.

2. In an electric frying pan or large skillet, pour in enough oil to measure 2 inches deep. Heat to 375°F. Add shrimp mixture by tablespoonfuls and cook, turning once, until golden brown on both sides, about 2 minutes. (Work in batches if necessary, so as not to crowd pan.) Drain on paper towels and serve immediately with Chinese Dipping Sauce.

CHINESE DIPPING SAUCE
Makes: about ½ cup

3 tablespoons soy sauce
2 tablespoons red wine
      vinegar

1 scallion, thinly sliced
¼ teaspoon pepper

In a small bowl, combine soy sauce, vinegar, scallion, pepper, and 3 tablespoons of water. Stir well to blend.

256   SHRIMP IN BEER
Prep: 2 minutes   Cook: 3 minutes   Serves: 4

Place a bowlful of these shrimp in the center of the table and let guests peel their own. Serve shrimp with a spicy tomato cocktail sauce and lemon wedges accompanied by a green salad and a fresh loaf of French bread.

2 cups beer
2 tablespoons fresh lemon
      juice
2 bay leaves

1 teaspoon salt
½ teaspoon cayenne
1½ pounds medium shrimp, in
      their shells

1. In a large saucepan, combine beer, lemon juice, bay leaves, salt, cayenne, and 1 cup water. Bring to a boil.

2. Add shrimp and cook until shrimp are pink and curled, about 3 minutes. Drain and rinse under cold water to stop cooking. Cover and refrigerate until chilled. Serve cold.

257   SHRIMP IN MUSHROOM CREAM
Prep: 8 minutes   Cook: 6 to 9 minutes   Serves: 4

Plain white rice is the best accompaniment for this dish. Hot buttered Brussels sprouts, halved and well seasoned with salt and pepper, make a welcome and colorful addition.

2 tablespoons butter
2 tablespoons vegetable oil
½ pound mushrooms, thinly sliced
2 pounds medium shrimp, shelled and deveined

1 cup heavy cream
½ teaspoon salt
¼ teaspoon pepper

1. In a large skillet, melt butter and oil over medium-high heat. Add mushrooms, raise heat to high, and cook, tossing often, until lightly browned, 2 to 4 minutes. Add shrimp and cook over high heat, tossing, until bright pink, about 1 minute.

2. Pour in cream and bring to a boil. Cook, stirring occasionally, over high heat until cream is reduced and thickened and shrimp are cooked through, 3 to 4 minutes. Season with salt and pepper and serve hot.

258   SHRIMP IN SATAY SAUCE
Prep: 15 minutes   Cook: 8 to 11 minutes   Serves: 4

For an exotic touch, replace milk with canned unsweetened coconut milk. Serve with steamed white rice.

1 medium onion, finely chopped
1 (1-inch) piece fresh ginger, peeled and minced
2 garlic cloves, minced
1 teaspoon curry powder
3 tablespoons vegetable oil
½ cup smooth peanut butter
1 cup milk
1 tablespoon soy sauce

3 tablespoons fresh lemon juice
1 scant teaspoon grated lemon zest
1 cinnamon stick
2 bay leaves
½ teaspoon salt
½ teaspoon chili powder
2 pounds medium shrimp, shelled and deveined

1. In a large saucepan, cook onion, ginger, garlic, and curry powder in oil over medium-low heat, stirring occasionally, until onion is softened, about 3 minutes. Add peanut butter, milk, soy sauce, lemon juice, lemon zest, cinnamon stick, bay leaves, salt, and chili powder. Cook over medium heat, stirring occasionally, until sauce is blended and thick, 3 to 5 minutes.

2. Add shrimp to sauce and stir to coat. Cook until shrimp are opaque throughout, 2 to 3 minutes. Remove and discard cinnamon stick and bay leaves. Serve shrimp in satay sauce at once.

259 SHRIMP IN RED WINE

Prep: 8 minutes   Cook: 12 to 13 minutes   Serves: 4

2 tablespoons butter
2 tablespoons vegetable oil
2 pounds medium shrimp,
   shelled and deveined
2 or 3 large shallots, minced
   (about ¼ cup)

1 cup dry red wine
½ cup heavy cream
½ teaspoon salt
¼ teaspoon pepper
1 tablespoon chopped parsley

1. In a large skillet, melt butter in oil over medium heat. Add shrimp and cook, stirring, until just pink, about 1 to 2 minutes.

2. Remove shrimp to a plate and set aside. Pour off all but 1 tablespoon fat. Add shallots, reduce heat to low, and cook, stirring, until softened, about 30 seconds.

3. Pour in wine, raise heat to high, and boil until reduced by half, about 3 minutes. Add cream and boil until reduced by half, about 4 minutes. Return shrimp to sauce, reduce heat to medium, and cook, stirring occasionally, until shrimp are opaque throughout and sauce is thick enough to coat back of a spoon, about 3 minutes. Season with salt and pepper. Sprinkle with parsley and serve at once.

260 SHRIMP-STUFFED AVOCADO BOATS

Prep: 10 minutes   Cook: none   Serves: 4

½ cup mayonnaise
½ cup sour cream
2 tablespoons olive oil
3 tablespoons fresh lime juice
2 tablespoons minced fresh
   chives
3 tablespoons chopped
   cilantro
1 teaspoon salt

½ teaspoon pepper
1½ pounds boiled shrimp,
   shelled, deveined, and
   thoroughly chilled
2 avocados, halved, pitted,
   and sprinkled with
   lemon juice
Lemon or lime wedges

1. In a large bowl, combine mayonnaise, sour cream, olive oil, lime juice, chives, cilantro, salt, and pepper. Stir to blend.

2. Cut shrimp into ½-inch pieces. Add to sauce and blend well.

3. Spoon even amounts of shrimp salad into avocado halves and serve cold, with lemon or lime wedges on the side.

261 SHRIMP WITH A CREAMY MUSTARD SAUCE

Prep: 8 minutes   Cook: 8 minutes   Serves: 4

2 tablespoons butter	¼ cup dry white wine
2 tablespoons olive oil	1 cup heavy cream
2 pounds medium shrimp, shelled and deveined	2 tablespoons Dijon mustard
	2 teaspoons chopped capers

1. In a large skillet, melt butter in olive oil over medium-high heat. Add shrimp and cook, stirring, until bright pink, about 1 minute. Remove shrimp to a plate.

2. Pour off fat from skillet. Raise heat to high, slowly pour in wine, and stir constantly until reduced by half, about 1 minute. Pour in cream and boil until reduced by half, about 4 minutes.

3. Remove from heat and stir in mustard and capers. Return shrimp to skillet, partially cover, and cook over low heat until shrimp are opaque throughout, about 2 minutes. Serve at once.

262 SHRIMP BOIL

Prep: 5 minutes   Cook: 3 to 5 minutes   Serves: 4

Place a bowl of cooked shrimp in the center of the table and let guests peel their own. Serve with a spicy marinara or cocktail sauce and lemon wedges.

6 sprigs of parsley	1 teaspoon black peppercorns
3 bay leaves	1 cup dry white wine
3 garlic cloves, peeled and halved	1 teaspoon salt
3 strips of lemon peel	2 pounds medium shrimp in the shell

1. In a 6 x 6-inch piece of cheesecloth, combine parsley, bay leaves, garlic, lemon peel, and peppercorns. Bring up corners to meet and tie securely closed with white kitchen string.

2. In a large saucepan, combine wine, seasoning bag, salt, and 2 cups of water. Bring to a boil over high heat. Add shrimp and cook until bright pink and curled, 3 to 5 minutes. Drain well, discard seasoning bag, and serve warm.

263   SHRIMP WITH ORANGE

Prep: 8 minutes   Cook: 8 minutes   Serves: 4

For a flavorful and attractive garnish, remove the peel and white pith from 2 oranges. Cut the oranges into sections and stir into the sauce just before serving.

1 small onion, thinly sliced	2 teaspoons grated orange zest
2 tablespoons olive oil	½ teaspoon salt
2 pounds medium shrimp,	¼ teaspoon pepper
shelled and deveined	2 tablespoons butter, softened
½ cup fresh orange juice	

1. In a large nonstick skillet, cook onion in olive oil over medium-low heat until slightly softened, about 2 minutes. Add shrimp and increase heat to medium. Cook, stirring and tossing, until onion is lightly browned and shrimp are bright pink and cooked through, about 5 minutes. Remove shrimp with a slotted spoon to a serving platter. Cover with aluminum foil and keep warm.

2. Add orange juice and orange zest to skillet. Raise heat to high and boil until reduced by half, about 1 minute. Season with salt and pepper. Swirl in butter and pour sauce over shrimp.

264   TEQUILA SHRIMP

Prep: 8 minutes   Cook: 5 minutes   Serves: 4

Serve this dish over creamed corn with thin red pepper strips.

2 tablespoons olive oil	3 tablespoons fresh lime juice
2 pounds medium shrimp,	½ cup chopped cilantro
shelled and deveined	½ teaspoon salt
½ cup tequila	½ teaspoon pepper

1. In a large skillet, heat olive oil over medium-high heat. Add shrimp and cook, tossing, until pink and slightly curled, about 2 minutes. Pour in tequila, raise heat to high, and boil, stirring to scrape bits from bottom of pan, until liquid is reduced by half, about 2 minutes longer.

2. Add lime juice, cilantro, salt, and pepper and cook, stirring occasionally, until shrimp are firm and flavors have blended, about 1 minute.

265   SPINACH-STUFFED SHRIMP
Prep: 7 minutes   Cook: 5 minutes   Serves: 4

1 (10-ounce) package frozen
   chopped spinach, thawed
¼ cup fresh bread crumbs
⅓ cup grated Parmesan cheese
1 teaspoon fresh lemon juice
	¼ teaspoon salt
	¼ teaspoon pepper
	   Pinch of grated nutmeg
	24 large shrimp, shelled and
	   deveined, with tails intact

1. Preheat oven to 400°F. Use hands to squeeze out excess water from spinach. In a medium bowl, combine spinach, bread crumbs, Parmesan cheese, lemon juice, salt, pepper, and nutmeg. Stir well to blend.

2. Split shrimp down back, cutting almost through to underside, and spread open to butterfly. Fill each cavity with about 1 tablespoon spinach mixture. Arrange flat on a lightly oiled 9 x 13-inch baking dish. Bake until shrimp are bright pink and filling is lightly browned, about 5 minutes.

266   QUICK AND ZESTY SHRIMP
Prep: 5 minutes   Marinate: 30 minutes   Cook: 4 minutes   Serves: 4

24 large shrimp, shelled and
   deveined
	1 (8-ounce) bottle Italian
	   dressing

1. Place shrimp in a 9 x 13-inch baking dish. Pour enough dressing over shrimp to cover. Marinate for 30 minutes at room temperature.

2. Prepare a medium-hot fire in a charcoal grill or preheat broiler. Remove shrimp from marinade and thread securely on 4 long metal skewers. Brush lightly with marinade. On a well-oiled grill over a medium-hot fire or on a lightly oiled broiling pan, cook shrimp about 2 minutes per side, until lightly browned outside and opaque in center. Serve immediately.

267   PIGGYBACK SHRIMP
Prep: 8 minutes   Cook: 6 to 8 minutes   Serves: 4

Serve these appetizers on a platter decorated with lots of parsley or watercress. Alternatively, remove toothpicks and place on individual serving plates mounded with dressed greens for a great salad.

24 medium shrimp, shelled
   and deveined, tails intact
	8 slices of bacon, each cut into
	   3 pieces

1. Preheat broiler. Wrap each shrimp in a piece of bacon, secure with a toothpick, and place seam side down on a large baking sheet.

2. Broil about 4 inches from source of heat 6 to 8 minutes, turning once, until bacon is browned and crisp and shrimp are opaque throughout. Drain on paper towels and serve hot.

268   SIMPLE SHRIMP CURRY

Prep: 6 minutes   Cook: 12 minutes   Serves: 4

3 tablespoons butter
2 pounds medium shrimp,
  shelled and deveined
1 small onion, thinly sliced

1 to 2 teaspoons curry powder,
  or to taste
1 cup heavy cream
¼ teaspoon salt

1. In a large skillet, melt 1½ tablespoons butter. Add shrimp and cook over medium-high heat, stirring, until pink, about 3 minutes. With a slotted spoon, transfer shrimp to a plate.

2. Add remaining butter to skillet and melt over medium heat. Add onion and curry powder. Cook, stirring occasionally, until onion is softened, about 3 minutes. Pour in cream, raise heat to high, and boil until reduced by half, about 4 minutes.

3. Return shrimp to skillet, reduce heat to medium, and cook until shrimp are opaque throughout, about 2 minutes. Season with salt.

269   SHRIMP WITH TOMATOES AND THYME

Prep: 10 minutes   Cook: 7 to 9 minutes   Serves: 4

1 small onion, finely chopped
1 garlic clove, minced
2 tablespoons olive oil
2 pounds medium shrimp,
  shelled and deveined
2 medium tomatoes, peeled,
  seeded, and chopped

½ teaspoon salt
¼ teaspoon pepper
1 tablespoon chopped thyme
  leaves or 1 teaspoon dried

1. In a large skillet, cook onion and garlic in olive oil over medium heat, stirring occasionally, until softened, about 2 minutes.

2. Add shrimp, tomatoes, salt, pepper, and thyme. Raise heat to medium-high. Simmer, stirring frequently, until shrimp are curled and pink and juices are thickened to a pulpy sauce, 5 to 7 minutes.

270   TOMATOES STUFFED WITH SHRIMP AND COUSCOUS

Prep: 10 minutes   Stand: 5 minutes   Cook: 28 to 30 minutes
Serves: 4

4 large tomatoes	½ pound medium shrimp,
¾ teaspoon salt	shelled, deveined, and
¼ teaspoon pepper	cut into ¼-inch dice
2 tablespoons olive oil	¼ cup dry white wine
1 tablespoon butter	½ cup tomato juice
½ cup couscous	1 tablespoon chopped parsley

1. Preheat oven to 325°F. Slice about ¼ inch off tops of tomatoes and scoop out pulp and seeds, leaving a ¼-inch-thick shell. Season insides with ¼ teaspoon salt and pepper. Drizzle 1 tablespoon olive oil equally among tomato shells and gently swirl to coat interiors. Place in a lightly oiled 9 x 13-inch baking dish and bake 15 minutes, or until tomatoes are slightly softened but still hold their shape. Invert onto a wire rack to drain.

2. In a small saucepan, bring ¾ cup water to a boil with butter and ¼ teaspoon salt. Remove from heat, stir in couscous, cover, and let stand for 5 minutes.

3. Heat remaining 1 tablespoon olive oil in a large skillet over medium-high heat. Add shrimp and cook, stirring, until opaque throughout, about 1 minute. Remove to a plate with a slotted spoon. Pour off fat from skillet and pour in wine. Raise heat to high and boil, stirring to scrape bits from bottom of pan, until reduced by half, about 1 minute. Pour in tomato juice and boil until slightly thickened, about 1 minute. Remove from heat, stir in couscous, shrimp, parsley, and remaining ¼ teaspoon salt.

4. Raise oven temperature to 350°F. Fill tomatoes with equal amounts of stuffing, mounding high in center. Place tomatoes on a lightly oiled baking sheet and bake until lightly browned on top, 10 to 12 minutes. Serve hot.

Chapter 12

From Humble Beginnings

From oh-so-humble beginnings come some pretty good endings. The purpose of this chapter is to provide interesting ideas for making use of the kinds of less expensive fish products found on most grocery-store shelves. Anchovies, salt cod, lumpfish caviar, canned tuna, canned crab, canned salmon, sardines, canned smoked oysters, and increasingly, surimi, or imitation crab, are used herein to make both classic and new dishes.

Tuna Noodle Casserole, Salmon Croquettes, and Salmon Mousse are a part of many a home cook's repertoire. But what about new ideas like a Crab Surimi Stir-Fry, Salmon Quesadillas, or Smoked Oyster Pita Pizzas, a quick pizza made with pita bread and smoked oysters?

While not as convenient as the others listed above, salt cod is included in this section because it falls under the category of humble. Fishermen used to salt fish to preserve large catches for future use. It soon became a staple in many ethnic communities, where today it is considered a delicacy. Salt cod needs to be soaked overnight in several changes of cold water before preparing. Once this step is done, however, it cooks rapidly with surprisingly good results. Try the recipe for Brandade de Morue on page 180, for example, and you'll agree that great things can indeed come from this sort of humble beginning.

Canned and preserved fish have been around for a long time. Economical and versatile, these products continue to be popular choices when planning meals. Hopefully the recipes included in this section will inspire cooks to try new and innovative ways of treating fish of humble origins.

271   TUNA AND CHICK-PEA SALAD
Prep: 4 minutes   Cook: none   Chill: 1 hour   Serves: 4

1 (6⅛-ounce) can tuna,
  drained and flaked
1 (15-ounce) can chick-peas
  (garbanzo beans),
  drained
½ cup pitted black olives,
  sliced or chopped
1 shallot or small onion,
  minced
2 tablespoons fresh lemon
  juice

2 tablespoons red wine
  vinegar
½ cup olive oil
1 tablespoon fresh thyme
  leaves or ½ teaspoon
  dried
¾ teaspoon salt
½ teaspoon pepper
4 cups loosely packed salad
  greens

1. In a medium bowl, combine tuna, chick-peas, olives, shallot, 1 table-spoon lemon juice, 1 tablespoon vinegar, ¼ cup olive oil, thyme, ½ tea-spoon salt, and ¼ teaspoon pepper. Gently stir to blend, cover, and chill at least 1 hour for flavors to blend.

2. In a large bowl, combine remaining 1 tablespoon lemon juice, 1 table-spoon vinegar, ¼ cup olive oil, ¼ teaspoon salt, and ¼ teaspoon pepper. Stir well, add salad greens, and toss to coat. Divide greens evenly among 4 serv-ing plates and top each with a mound of tuna and chick-pea salad.

272   TUNA À LA KING
Prep: 5 minutes   Cook: 13 to 15 minutes   Serves: 4

Serve over buttered toasts, in pastry shells, or over a bed of hot buttered noodles or rice.

3 tablespoons butter
1 small onion, finely chopped
1 celery rib, thinly sliced
½ green bell pepper, finely
  chopped
3 tablespoons flour
2 cups chicken stock or
  canned broth

1 (6⅛-ounce) can tuna,
  drained and flaked
1 tablespoon fresh lemon
  juice
½ teaspoon salt
¼ teaspoon pepper
1 tablespoon chopped parsley

1. In a medium saucepan, melt butter over medium-high heat. Add onion, celery, and green pepper. Cook, stirring frequently, until softened, about 3 minutes. Sprinkle on flour and cook, stirring, 2 minutes. Gradually whisk in chicken stock, raise heat to high, and bring to a boil. Cook, stirring often, until thickened and smooth, about 2 minutes. Reduce heat to low and sim-mer, stirring often, 3 minutes longer.

2. Just before serving, stir in tuna, lemon juice, salt, pepper, and chopped parsley. Bring to a simmer over medium-high heat and cook until heated through, 3 to 5 minutes. Serve hot.

273   TUNA NOODLE CASSEROLE
Prep: 3 minutes   Cook: 25 to 32 minutes   Serves: 4

Tuna casserole is an American institution. This recipe can be dressed up with all sorts of embellishments like strips of red or yellow bell pepper, sautéed mushrooms, chopped tomatoes, fried onion rings, or fresh herbs. Crushed potato chips or cracker crumbs can be used in place of the bread crumbs on top.

8 ounces penne or ziti
1 (6⅛-ounce) can tuna,
    drained and flaked
1 (10¾-ounce) can cream of
    mushroom soup

½ teaspoon salt
½ teaspoon pepper
¼ cup dry bread crumbs
2 tablespoons butter, melted

1. In a large pot of boiling salted water, cook pasta until tender but still firm, 10 to 12 minutes. Drain well.

2. Preheat oven to 375°F. In a large bowl, combine pasta, tuna, mushroom soup, salt, and pepper. Pour into a 1½-quart casserole. Top with bread crumbs and drizzle with butter.

3. Bake 15 to 20 minutes, until casserole is heated through and crumbs are golden brown on top. Serve hot.

274   TUNA PIZZAS WITH GOAT CHEESE AND OLIVES
Prep: 2 minutes   Cook: 12 to 15 minutes   Serves: 4

When tomatoes are in season, a homemade tomato sauce makes these easy pizzas even better.

4 pita breads
½ cup tomato sauce
1 (6⅛-ounce) can tuna,
    drained and flaked
12 oil-cured black olives, pitted
    and sliced

4 ounces goat cheese,
    crumbled (about 1 cup)
1 teaspoon dried oregano
½ teaspoon pepper

1. Preheat oven to 375°F. Place pita breads flat on 2 large cookie sheets. Spread 2 tablespoons of tomato sauce over each pita. Sprinkle with equal amounts of tuna, olives, goat cheese, oregano, and pepper.

2. Bake pizzas until bread is lightly browned around edges and cheese is melted, 12 to 15 minutes. Cut into wedges and serve at once.

275   TUNA TETRAZZINI
Prep: 5 minutes   Cook: 30 to 33 minutes   Serves: 4

½ pound egg noodles
6 tablespoons butter, melted
2 tablespoons flour
2 cups milk
1 (6⅛-ounce) can tuna, drained and flaked
1 teaspoon salt
½ teaspoon pepper

5 medium mushrooms, quartered
¼ cup dry white wine
1 tablespoon chopped parsley
1 tablespoon fresh lemon juice
¼ cup grated Parmesan cheese
¼ cup dry bread crumbs

1. In a large pot of boiling salted water, cook noodles until tender but still firm, about 5 to 7 minutes. Drain and set aside.

2. Combine 2 tablespoons butter and flour in a medium saucepan. Cook over medium heat, stirring constantly, 1 to 2 minutes. Gradually whisk in milk, raise heat to medium-high, and bring to a boil, whisking until thickened and smooth, about 2 minutes. Reduce heat to low and simmer, whisking often, 3 minutes. Add tuna, ½ teaspoon salt, and ¼ teaspoon pepper. Stir well to mix. Remove from heat.

3. In a medium skillet, melt remaining 2 tablespoons butter. Add mushrooms and cook over medium heat, stirring and tossing until lightly browned, about 3 minutes. Pour in wine, add parsley, lemon juice, remaining ½ teaspoon salt, and ¼ teaspoon pepper. Cook 1 minute longer and remove from heat.

4. Preheat oven to 425°F. In a large bowl, combine cooked noodles, tuna with sauce, and mushrooms. Toss to mix well. Turn into a medium buttered baking dish. Sprinkle Parmesan cheese and bread crumbs over top. Drizzle on remaining 2 tablespoons butter. Bake uncovered 15 minutes, or until nicely browned on top.

276   TUNA LENTIL CASSEROLE
Prep: 5 minutes   Cook: 48 to 55 minutes   Serves: 4

1 cup lentils
½ teaspoon salt
3 tablespoons olive oil
1 small onion, finely chopped
1 medium green bell pepper, finely chopped
1 garlic clove, minced

3 medium tomatoes, peeled, seeded, and chopped
⅛ teaspoon pepper
1 (6⅛-ounce) can tuna, drained and flaked
¼ cup grated Parmesan cheese

1. Place lentils in a medium saucepan and add cold water to cover by 1 inch. Add ¼ teaspoon salt and bring to a boil over high heat. Reduce heat to medium and simmer until tender, 25 to 30 minutes. Drain well.

2. In a medium saucepan, heat 2 tablespoons olive oil over medium-high heat. Add onion, bell pepper, and garlic. Cook, stirring often, until softened, 3 to 5 minutes. Stir in tomatoes and cook until thick and pulpy, about 5 minutes. Remove from heat and season with remaining ¼ teaspoon salt and pepper.

3. Preheat oven to 375°F. In a large bowl, combine cooked lentils with tomato mixture and tuna. Stir to mix well. Pour into a 1-quart casserole and sprinkle Parmesan cheese over top. Drizzle remaining 1 tablespoon olive oil over cheese. Bake casserole 15 minutes, or until lightly browned on top.

---

277 TUNA MOUSSE WITH CUCUMBER YOGURT SAUCE

Prep: 10 minutes   Chill: 4 hours   Cook: none   Serves: 8 to 10

3 **envelopes unflavored gelatin**
2 **cups mayonnaise**
2 **tablespoons fresh lemon juice**
1 **teaspoon salt**
3 **(6⅛-ounce) cans tuna packed in water, drained and flaked**

1 **small onion, finely chopped**
2 **celery ribs, thinly sliced**
2 **tablespoons capers, chopped**
   Cucumber Yogurt Sauce (recipe follows)

1. In a double boiler, sprinkle gelatin over ¾ cup cold water and let soften for 3 minutes. Place over simmering water and stir until dissolved. Remove from heat and let cool slightly.

2. In a large bowl, combine dissolved gelatin with mayonnaise, lemon juice, and salt. Blend well. Stir in tuna, onion, celery, and capers. Blend well and transfer to an oiled 2-quart mold. Cover and refrigerate until set, at least 4 hours or overnight. Unmold and serve with a bowl of cucumber yogurt sauce on the side.

CUCUMBER YOGURT SAUCE

Makes: about 2½ cups

2 **medium cucumbers, peeled, seeded, and finely chopped**
1 **small onion, minced**
1 **cup plain yogurt**

½ **cup sour cream**
1 **tablespoon chopped fresh dill or ¾ teaspoon dried**
½ **teaspoon salt**
¼ **teaspoon pepper**

In a medium bowl, combine cucumbers, onion, yogurt, sour cream, dill, salt, and pepper. Stir until well blended. Cover and refrigerate until well chilled, about 2 hours before serving.

278 CHARLIE'S TUNA AND RICE
Prep: 3 minutes   Cook: 26 minutes   Stand: 5 minutes   Serves: 4

2 tablespoons butter
1 small onion, chopped
1 garlic clove, minced
1 cup long-grain white rice
½ cup sliced water chestnuts
1 cup chicken broth

1 tablespoon soy sauce
¼ teaspoon salt
½ teaspoon pepper
1 (6⅛-ounce) can tuna,
    drained and flaked
1 tablespoon sesame seeds

1. In a medium saucepan, melt butter over medium heat. Add onion and garlic and cook, stirring often, until tender, 3 minutes. Add rice and cook, stirring, 1 minute longer. Add water chestnuts, chicken broth, soy sauce, salt, pepper, and 1 cup water. Raise heat to high and bring to a boil. Cover, reduce heat to low, and cook until liquid is absorbed, about 20 minutes. Remove from heat, stir to fluff, cover again and let stand 5 minutes longer.

2. Just before serving, stir tuna and sesame seeds into rice. Warm over medium heat, stirring once, until tuna is heated through, about 2 minutes longer. Serve hot.

279 TUNA FISH SANDWICH SUPREME
Prep: 5 minutes   Cook: none   Chill: 1 hour   Serves: 4

1 (6⅛-ounce) can tuna,
    drained and flaked
2 hard-boiled eggs, chopped
1 celery rib, finely chopped
1 small onion, finely chopped
½ cup walnut pieces, finely
    chopped
2 small sweet gherkin pickles,
    halved lengthwise and
    thinly sliced

1 tablespoon capers, chopped
1 cup mayonnaise
2 tablespoons fresh lemon
    juice
2 tablespoons chopped
    parsley
½ teaspoon salt
½ teaspoon pepper
8 slices of white or whole
    wheat bread

1. In a medium mixing bowl, combine tuna, eggs, celery, onion, walnuts, pickles, capers, mayonnaise, lemon juice, parsley, salt, and pepper. Stir to blend well. Cover and refrigerate for at least an hour to allow flavors to blend.

2. Lightly toast bread. Divide tuna mixture among 4 pieces, spread evenly, and top with remaining toasts. Cut in half diagonally and serve at once.

280   TUNA BURGERS

Prep: 5 minutes   Cook: 5 minutes   Serves: 4

Tuna burgers are best served on toasted buns with your favorite condiments, such as slices of ripe tomato and sweet onion, relish, mustard, and ketchup. This recipe will please even the most ardent red meat lovers.

2 **(6⅛-ounce) cans tuna,**	¾ **teaspoon salt**
drained	½ **teaspoon pepper**
2 **garlic cloves, minced**	½ **cup dry bread crumbs**
1 **small onion, finely chopped**	1 **tablespoon butter**
1 **egg**	1 **tablespoon olive oil**

1. In a medium bowl, combine tuna, garlic, onion, egg, salt, and pepper. Blend well. With your hands, shape tuna mixture into 4 round patties 3 to 4 inches in diameter. Pour bread crumbs into a shallow bowl and coat each tuna patty on both sides.

2. In a large skillet, preferably nonstick, melt butter with olive oil over medium-high heat. Add tuna burgers and cook, turning once, until golden brown outside and egg is set in center, about 5 minutes. Serve hot.

281   TUNA AND WHITE BEAN CASSEROLE

Prep: 2 minutes   Cook: 25 minutes   Serves: 4

2 **cups cooked or canned**	1 **teaspoon dried thyme leaves**
white beans, drained	½ **teaspoon salt**
1 **(28-ounce) can Italian seeded**	¼ **teaspoon pepper**
tomatoes, drained and	½ **cup bread crumbs**
chopped	2 **tablespoons olive oil**
2 **(6⅛-ounce) cans tuna,**	
drained and flaked	

1. Preheat oven to 350°F. In a large bowl, combine beans, tomatoes, tuna, thyme, salt, and pepper. Stir well to blend. Turn into an oiled 8 x 11-inch baking dish and sprinkle bread crumbs over top. Drizzle olive oil over crumbs.

2. Bake casserole about 25 minutes, until browned on top and bubbly. Serve hot.

282   TUNA ON TOAST
Prep: 4 minutes   Chill: 1 hour   Cook: none   Serves: 4

1   (6⅛-ounce) can tuna,
    drained and flaked
1   celery rib, finely chopped
2   scallions, thinly sliced
½   cup mayonnaise
2   teaspoons Dijon mustard

1   tablespoon fresh lime juice
¼   teaspoon garlic powder
½   teaspoon salt
½   teaspoon pepper
8   slices of white or whole
    wheat bread, toasted

1. In a medium bowl, combine tuna, celery, scallions, mayonnaise, mustard, lime juice, garlic powder, salt, and pepper. Blend well. Cover and refrigerate until thoroughly chilled and flavors are well blended, at least 1 hour.

2. Divide tuna salad evenly among 4 pieces of toast, spreading to cover slices. Top with remaining toasts. Cut in half diagonally and serve at once.

283   BRANDADE DE MORUE
Prep: 5 minutes   Soak: 24 hours   Cook: 20 to 25 minutes
Serves: 6 to 8

This salt cod puree is a French classic, especially in the southern part of the country, where it abounds in colorful markets. The preserved fish can be found in many American supermarkets, especially in areas with a large Portuguese or Spanish population. Serve the *brandade* with toasted slices of hearty country bread.

2   pounds salt cod
1½   cups olive oil
1¼   cups milk

1   teaspoon fresh lemon juice
½   teaspoon pepper
1   garlic clove, crushed

1. Soak salt cod in a large quantity of cold water for 1 to 2 days in refrigerator. Change water frequently, always keeping fish submerged.

2. Drain cod and place it in a large covered pot or saucepan. Pour in enough cold water to cover. Bring to a boil over high heat. Reduce heat to medium-low, cover, and simmer until tender, 10 to 15 minutes. Drain and cool. When cool enough to handle, flake with a fork, discarding any skin and bones.

3. Gently heat olive oil and milk over low heat in separate saucepans. Place cod in a food processor. With machine on, gradually pour in olive oil and milk, alternating with small amounts of each. Puree until smooth. Season with lemon juice and pepper.

4. Preheat oven to 350°F. Rub bottom and sides of a 2-quart baking dish with crushed garlic; discard garlic. Pour pureed cod into dish and place in oven. Bake, uncovered, until lightly browned on top and heated through, about 10 minutes.

284 SALMON CROQUETTES

Prep: 15 minutes   Chill: 3 hours   Cook: 3 to 4 minutes per batch
Makes: 12

Leftover mashed potatoes are perfect for this dish. If you make them from scratch, you'll want to use about 3 medium potatoes to yield 2 cups mashed.

1 (7½-ounce) can salmon, drained	1 small onion, minced
2 cups mashed potatoes	2 teaspoons fresh lemon juice
1 teaspoon salt	½ cup flour
½ teaspoon pepper	½ cup cornmeal
3 eggs	Vegetable oil, for frying

1. In a large bowl, combine salmon, mashed potatoes, ½ teaspoon salt, ¼ teaspoon pepper, 1 egg, onion, and lemon juice. Blend well with a wooden spoon. Cover and refrigerate for at least 2 hours.

2. Shape chilled salmon mixture into cylinders about 2 inches long and 1½ inches in diameter.

3. In a shallow dish, beat remaining 2 eggs with remaining ½ teaspoon salt and ¼ teaspoon pepper. Place flour and cornmeal on 2 separate plates.

4. Working with one croquette at a time, roll in flour to coat thoroughly, then dip in egg mixture. Drain off excess and transfer to cornmeal. Roll to coat all over. Transfer to a plate and refrigerate, uncovered, for 1 to 2 hours.

5. In an electric skillet or large frying pan, pour in enough oil to measure 2 inches deep and heat to 370°F. Fry croquettes in hot oil in batches without crowding, turning once, until golden brown, 3 to 4 minutes. Drain on paper towels and serve hot.

285 SALMON SALAD SANDWICHES

Prep: 5 minutes   Chill: 1 hour   Cook: none   Serves: 4

1 (7½-ounce) can salmon, drained and flaked	⅓ cup mayonnaise
½ green or red bell pepper, finely chopped	1 teaspoon Dijon mustard
	½ teaspoon salt
2 scallions, thinly sliced	½ teaspoon pepper
2 tablespoons chopped fresh basil or parsley	8 slices of white or whole wheat bread

1. In a medium bowl, combine salmon, bell pepper, scallions, basil, mayonnaise, mustard, salt, and pepper. Stir to blend well. Cover and refrigerate until thoroughly chilled, at least 1 hour.

2. Lightly toast bread. Divide salmon salad evenly among 4 pieces and spread out to cover. Top with remaining toasts. Cut in half diagonally and serve at once.

286 SALMON LOAF

Prep: 6 minutes   Cook: 23 minutes   Serves: 4 to 6

Tomato sauce flavored with fresh herbs or a lemony mayonnaise makes a flavorful accompaniment to this simple recipe.

3 tablespoons butter	¼ cup bread crumbs
1 small onion, chopped	½ teaspoon dried thyme leaves
1 celery rib, chopped	2 tablespoons fresh lemon
½ green bell pepper, chopped	juice
2 garlic cloves, minced	½ teaspoon salt
2 (7½-ounce) cans salmon,	¼ teaspoon pepper
drained and flaked	¼ teaspoon cayenne
2 eggs	

1. In a medium skillet, melt butter over medium-high heat. Add onion, celery, bell pepper, and garlic. Cook, stirring often, until softened, about 3 minutes. Set aside.

2. Preheat oven to 350°F and lightly oil an 8 x 4 x 2½-inch loaf pan. In a large bowl, combine salmon, eggs, bread crumbs, thyme, lemon juice, salt, pepper, and cayenne. Blend well. Stir in cooked onion mixture and mix well. Transfer to loaf pan and spread top evenly.

3. Bake loaf 20 minutes, or until lightly browned on top and cooked through. Let cool slightly, pour off any accumulated juices, and turn out onto a platter. Cut into thick slices and serve warm.

287 SALMON QUESADILLAS

Prep: 6 minutes   Cook: 5 to 7 minutes   Serves: 4

1 (7½-ounce) can salmon,	½ teaspoon salt
drained and flaked	½ teaspoon pepper
1 cup shredded Monterey Jack	12 flour tortillas (6 to 7 inches in
cheese (4 ounces)	diameter)
1 small red onion, finely	Salsa and sour cream, as
chopped	accompaniments
1 jalapeño pepper or other	
fresh green chile, seeded	
and minced	

1. Preheat oven to 400°F. In a medium bowl, combine salmon, cheese, onion, jalapeño, salt, and pepper. Gently stir to combine. Lay 4 tortillas flat on a work surface. Spread 2 tablespoons of salmon mixture over each and cover with another tortilla. Sprinkle an additional 2 tablespoons salmon mixture on top and cover with remaining tortillas. Transfer with a spatula to a large baking sheet.

2. Bake quesadillas 5 to 7 minutes, or until crisp on top and heated through. Remove from oven, cut into wedges, and transfer to 4 individual serving plates. Pass bowls of salsa and sour cream separately.

288 SALMON COUSCOUS CASSEROLE
Prep: 5 minutes   Cook: 15 minutes   Serves: 4

1 tablespoon butter	1 (7½-ounce) can salmon,
1 teaspoon salt	drained and flaked
1 cup couscous	¼ teaspoon pepper
1 (28-ounce) can Italian peeled	1 tablespoon chopped parsley
tomatoes, drained and	½ cup grated Parmesan cheese
coarsely chopped	

1. Preheat oven to 375°F. In a small saucepan, bring 1½ cups water to a boil with butter and ½ teaspoon salt. Remove from heat, stir in couscous, cover, and set aside for 5 minutes.

2. Transfer couscous to a large bowl. Stir in tomatoes and salmon. Add pepper, parsley, and remaining ½ teaspoon salt. Blend well.

3. Spread tuna and couscous mixture evenly in an 8 x 11-inch baking dish. Sprinkle cheese evenly over top. Bake casserole about 15 minutes, until lightly browned on top. Serve hot.

289 SALMON MOUSSE
Prep: 5 minutes   Chill: 4½ hours   Cook: none   Serves: 6 to 8

This is an all-time favorite adapted from the original *New York Times Cook Book*. Serve with a doubled recipe of Cucumber Yogurt Sauce (page 177).

1 envelope unflavored gelatin	2 (7½-ounce) cans salmon,
½ cup boiling water	drained and finely
½ cup mayonnaise	chopped
2 tablespoons fresh lemon	2 tablespoons chopped fresh
juice	dill or parsley
1 small onion, minced	½ cup heavy cream
½ teaspoon salt	3 cups cottage cheese
¼ teaspoon pepper	

1. In a small bowl, sprinkle gelatin over ¼ cup cold water. Pour on boiling water and stir to dissolve. Set aside to cool.

2. Add mayonnaise, lemon juice, onion, salt, and pepper to gelatin. Stir well, cover, and refrigerate until texture resembles that of an unbeaten egg white, about 30 minutes. Stir in salmon and dill.

3. Whip cream in a medium bowl until stiff. Fold into salmon mixture and turn into an oiled 2-quart mold. Top with cottage cheese to fill mold. Cover and refrigerate until set, 4 to 6 hours or overnight. Unmold onto a chilled platter.

290   SASSY SARDINE SANDWICHES

Prep: 35 minutes   Stand: 10 minutes   Cook: 5 to 7 minutes
Serves: 4

1   large red bell pepper
2   tablespoons butter, softened
4   English muffins, split in
      half
8   leaves of fresh basil
      (optional)
2   hard-boiled eggs, sliced

½   cup sliced black olives
2   (4⅜-ounce) cans sardines,
      drained and coarsely
      chopped
½   teaspoon salt
¼   teaspoon pepper

1. Preheat broiler. Place bell pepper on a broiling pan set about 4 inches from source of heat. Roast pepper, turning frequently, until charred all over, 5 to 7 minutes. Transfer to a plastic bag. Seal and set aside until skin is loosened, 10 to 15 minutes. Remove skin, core, and seeds and cut pepper into long, thin strips.

2. Toast English muffin halves and spread with butter. Let cool.

3. Place 2 basil leaves each on bottoms of English muffins. Top with egg and olive slices, red pepper strips, and sardines. Season with salt and pepper, top with remaining English muffin halves, and serve at once.

291   SARDINE-STUFFED TOMATOES

Prep: 5 minutes   Cook: 15 minutes   Serves: 4

4   medium tomatoes
¾   teaspoon salt
½   teaspoon pepper
1   tablespoon olive oil
2   (4⅜-ounce) cans sardines,
      drained and chopped

½   medium onion, chopped
½   teaspoon dried thyme leaves
1   tablespoon fresh lemon
      juice
¼   cup soda cracker crumbs
2   tablespoons melted butter

1. Cut ¼ inch off top of tomatoes and gently hollow out with a small spoon. Sprinkle cavities evenly with ½ teaspoon salt, ¼ teaspoon pepper, and olive oil.

2. Preheat oven to 350°F. In a small bowl, combine sardines, onion, thyme, lemon juice, and remaining ¼ teaspoon each salt and pepper. Fill tomatoes with equal amounts of sardine mixture, sprinkle with cracker crumbs, and drizzle top with butter.

3. Transfer stuffed tomatoes to a small baking dish. Bake 15 minutes, or until heated through and golden brown on top. Serve hot.

292 SMOKED OYSTER PITA PIZZAS
Prep: 4 minutes   Cook: 18 to 22 minutes   Serves: 4

2 tablespoons butter
4 onions, very thinly sliced
1 teaspoon sugar
4 pita breads
¼ cup olive oil
2 (3¾-ounce) cans smoked
  oysters, drained

12 oil-cured black olives, pitted
   and sliced
1 teaspoon dried thyme leaves
¼ teaspoon crushed hot red
   pepper

1. In a large skillet, melt butter over medium-high heat. Add onions and cook, stirring often, until slightly tender, about 3 minutes. Sprinkle on sugar and cook, stirring constantly, until browned, 3 to 4 minutes longer. Remove from heat and set aside.

2. Preheat oven to 375°F. Arrange pita bread on 2 large cookie sheets. Brush 1 tablespoon of olive oil over each pita. Cover with equal amounts of caramelized onions. Top with smoked oysters and olives and season with thyme and hot pepper.

3. Bake 12 to 15 minutes, until lightly browned around edges and heated through. Cut into wedges and serve at once.

293 THREE-SEAFOOD CASSEROLE
Prep: 5 minutes   Cook: 26 to 28 minutes   Serves: 4 to 6

8 ounces elbow macaroni
1 (6⅛-ounce) can tuna,
  drained and flaked
1 (7½-ounce) can salmon,
  drained and flaked
1 (6-ounce) can crabmeat,
  drained and flaked
1 small onion, chopped
1 small green bell pepper,
  finely chopped

2 garlic cloves, minced
½ cup mayonnaise
½ cup grated Parmesan cheese
1 tablespoon Worcestershire
  sauce
1 teaspoon salt
½ teaspoon pepper
½ cup soda cracker crumbs
2 tablespoons melted butter

1. In a large pot of boiling salted water, cook macaroni until tender but still firm, 6 to 8 minutes. Drain well.

2. Preheat oven to 350°F. In a large bowl, combine cooked macaroni with tuna, salmon, crab, onion, bell pepper, garlic, mayonnaise, Parmesan cheese, Worcestershire, salt, and pepper. Stir to blend well. Turn into a 9 x 13-inch baking dish and spread out evenly. Sprinkle cracker crumbs over top. Drizzle on butter.

3. Bake casserole about 20 minutes, until heated through and crumbs are golden brown. Serve hot.

294   SCALLOPED POTATOES WITH CRAB
Prep: 5 minutes   Cook: 54 to 70 minutes   Serves: 4

6 tablespoons butter
1 onion, thinly sliced
2 tablespoons flour
2 cups milk
¾ teaspoon salt
½ teaspoon pepper
1 cup grated Swiss cheese

3 medium all-purpose
potatoes, peeled and
thinly sliced
2 (6-ounce) cans crabmeat,
drained
¼ cup fresh bread crumbs

1. In a small skillet, melt 2 tablespoons butter over medium-high heat. Add onion and cook, stirring often, until soft, about 3 minutes.

2. In a medium saucepan, melt remaining butter over medium heat. Add flour and cook, stirring constantly, until blended and bubbling, about 2 minutes. Gradually whisk in milk, raise heat to high, and bring to a boil, whisking until thickened and smooth, 1 to 2 minutes. Reduce heat to low and simmer, whisking often, 3 minutes. Remove from heat, season with salt and pepper, and stir in cheese.

3. Preheat oven to 400°F. Spread one-third of cheese sauce over bottom of a lightly buttered 1½-quart casserole. Arrange half of potatoes and onions over cheese sauce. Sprinkle on crab and top with half of remaining sauce. Cover with remaining potatoes, onions, and sauce. Sprinkle bread crumbs over top. Bake uncovered, 45 minutes to 1 hour, until potatoes are tender and top is browned.

295   QUICK CRAB AU GRATIN
Prep: 2 minutes   Cook: 15 to 22 minutes   Serves: 4

2 tablespoons butter
3 tablespoons flour
2 cups milk
½ cup grated Swiss cheese
½ teaspoon salt

¼ teaspoon pepper
1 (8-ounce) package crab
surimi (imitation crab)
¼ cup dry bread crumbs
¼ cup grated Parmesan cheese

1. Melt butter in a medium saucepan over medium heat. Add flour and cook, stirring often, 1 to 2 minutes without allowing flour to color. Whisk milk in gradually. Bring to a boil, whisking often, until sauce is creamy and smooth, 1 to 2 minutes. Reduce heat and simmer 3 minutes longer. Remove from heat, stir in cheese, and season with salt and pepper. Set aside to cool slightly.

2. Preheat oven to 425°F. Stir surimi into cheese sauce and transfer to an 8 x 11-inch baking dish. Sprinkle bread crumbs and Parmesan cheese over top. Bake 10 to 15 minutes, until browned on top.

296 CRAB SURIMI STIR-FRY

Prep: 7 minutes   Cook: 6 to 7 minutes   Serves: 4

Sprinkle on chopped peanuts or toasted coconut for embellishment. And don't forget plenty of rice.

2 tablespoons olive oil
2 garlic cloves, minced
1 (1-inch) piece of fresh ginger, peeled and minced
1 small red bell pepper, thinly sliced
1 carrot, peeled and thinly sliced
2 tablespoons soy sauce

1 (3-ounce) can sliced water chestnuts
1 (10-ounce) package frozen peas, thawed
1 (8-ounce) package crab surimi (imitation crab)
2 scallions, thinly sliced
¼ teaspoon salt
½ teaspoon pepper

1. In a wok or large skillet, heat olive oil over medium-high heat until hot. Add garlic, ginger, bell pepper, and carrot. Stir-fry until slightly tender, about 3 minutes. Stir in soy sauce, water chestnuts, and peas and stir-fry until heated through, 1 to 2 minutes.

2. Add surimi, scallions, salt, and pepper to wok. Toss and stir over medium-high heat until scallions are slightly wilted and all ingredients are heated through, about 2 minutes. Serve hot.

297 SURIMI THAI

Prep: 5 minutes   Cook: 6 to 7 minutes   Serves: 4

Serve this spicy dish with steamed white rice or hot buttered noodles.

2 tablespoons olive oil
1 small onion, chopped
1 garlic clove, minced
1 cup unsweetened coconut milk
1 teaspoon lime zest
2 tablespoons fresh lime juice

¼ teaspoon salt
½ teaspoon crushed hot red pepper
1 tablespoon peanut butter
1 (8-ounce) package lobster or crab surimi
1 tablespoon chopped cilantro

1. In a large skillet, heat olive oil over medium-high heat until hot. Add onion and garlic and cook, stirring often, until softened, about 3 minutes. Pour in coconut milk, lime zest, lime juice, salt, and hot pepper. Raise heat to high and boil, stirring constantly, until reduced slightly, about 1 minute.

2. Add peanut butter, reduce heat to low, and cook, stirring until thickened, about 1 minute. Stir in surimi and cook, stirring constantly, until warmed through, 1 to 2 minutes. Serve hot, garnished with chopped cilantro.

298 CODFISH BALLS

Prep: 20 minutes   Soak: 24 hours   Cook: 31 to 42 minutes
Serves: 6

Serve these old-fashioned favorites with tomato sauce or tartar sauce.

1½ pounds salt cod, cut into
      1-inch pieces
3 to 4 medium all-purpose
      potatoes
½ teaspoon salt
2 tablespoons butter

1 small onion, finely chopped
½ teaspoon pepper
1 egg
2 tablespoons milk
1 cup flour
   Vegetable oil for frying

1. Place salt cod in a large bowl and cover with cold water. Soak 1 to 2 days in refrigerator, changing water often to remove saltiness. Transfer soaked and drained cod to a large saucepan and cover with cold water. Bring to a boil over medium-high heat. Reduce heat to medium and simmer, covered, until tender, 10 to 15 minutes. Drain well and set aside to cool. When cool enough to handle, squeeze well to remove excess moisture. Use fingers to flake finely, discarding any bones and skin. Set aside.

2. Peel potatoes, cut into 1½- to 2-inch chunks, and place in a large saucepan. Cover with cold water, add salt, and bring to a boil over high heat. Reduce heat to medium and simmer until tender, 20 to 25 minutes. Drain well.

3. Meanwhile, melt butter in a small skillet over medium-high heat. Add onion and cook, stirring often, until tender, about 3 minutes.

4. Add onion and butter to potatoes, season with pepper, and mash until pureed. In a small bowl, beat egg with milk and add to potatoes. Stir well to blend. Add flaked salt cod and mix well. Use hands to form into balls that measure about 1½ inches in diameter.

5. Pour enough oil into a large skillet or electric frying pan to measure about 2 inches deep; heat to 375°F. Place flour in a shallow bowl. Roll each ball in flour to coat, shaking off excess. Fry in hot oil, in batches without crowding, until browned, 1 to 2 minutes. Drain on paper towels and serve warm.

299   CAVIAR AND POTATO SALAD

Prep: 3 minutes   Cook: 12 minutes   Stand: 30 minutes   Serves: 4

Lumpfish caviar is a flavorful bargain found on supermarket shelves. Line a large platter with lettuce leaves and mound this salad in the center. Garnish with sprigs of fresh dill or parsley. Surround with halved hard-boiled eggs and tomatoes for color.

2 pounds small red or new potatoes, scrubbed	½ cup mayonnaise
2 tablespoons olive oil	½ cup sour cream
1 small onion, chopped	½ teaspoon salt
¼ cup dry white wine	½ teaspoon pepper
	1 (2-ounce) jar lumpfish caviar

1. Place potatoes in a large saucepan, pour in enough cold salted water to cover, and bring to a boil over high heat. Reduce heat to medium and cook until potatoes are tender, about 12 minutes. Drain and set aside.

2. Meanwhile, in a small skillet, heat olive oil over medium-high heat. Add onion and cook, stirring often, until tender, about 2 minutes. Pour in wine and remove skillet from heat.

3. Cut warm potatoes in half or in quarters and place in a large bowl. Pour in contents of skillet and toss and stir until liquid is absorbed. Add mayonnaise, sour cream, salt, and pepper. Blend well. Gently stir in caviar, cover, and let stand for at least 30 minutes but not more than 1 hour before serving.

Chapter 13

Best of the Bivalves

Oysters, clams, scallops, and mussels are indeed the best of the bivalves. Briny fresh, scrubbed clean, and handled with the respect they are due, these are the greatest of the sea's delicacies.

Oysters are the most popular of the bivalves. Apalachicola, Blue Point, Chesapeake Bay, Cape Cod, Pacific, Olympia, and aquacultured species like Belon are the best known of the American oysters. They must be as fresh as possible for best results. Know your fishmonger and trust his advice. Make sure that he keeps his oysters on ice and well chilled. It saves an enormous amount of time and energy if the fishmonger will shuck them for you. (Preparation times for the recipes below do not include time for shucking.) Be sure that you ask him to save the flavorful "liquor," the briny liquid that comes from opening the oyster, used to flavor soups, sauces, or in cooking of oysters. Oysters also come shucked in pints or quarts right from the processing facility.

To open oysters yourself, hold each flat against a towel on the table, large side down. Insert a sturdy, blunt-shaped oyster knife between the two shells, forcing the bivalve open by firmly twisting. Hold over a small bowl to catch liquor while severing the muscle that attaches the meat to the top and bottom shells. Place shucked oysters in a bowl and pick over to remove any stray pieces of shell. If to be served on the half shell, discard the top shell of each opened oyster, sever the muscle, and simply leave the oyster on the bottom shell. Keep well chilled until ready to serve.

Baked oysters are often cooked on a bed of rock or coarse salt. This allows heat to rise up from the bottom of the pan while holding the shell upright. The same effect can be had by loosely crumpling several pieces of aluminum foil in the bottom of a baking dish. The malleable foil will hold the oysters firmly in place.

Littleneck, cherrystone, and quahog clams are sold in their shell and should be alive and tightly shut. Clams also come shucked in pints or quarts with their liquid, like oysters, and they are available frozen, canned (either minced or whole), and smoked. Open clams as you would an oyster, saving the liquor as described above. Bottled clam juice is a good substitute for fish stock; it is sometimes diluted with equal amounts of cold water for less fishy results.

The bivalve mollusk known as the scallop is a true nugget of pure white delight for the seafood enthusiast. Small, tender bay scallops come from bays and inlets near the shore from October to March. Larger and much more abundant sea scallops come from deep waters and are available year round. Sea scallops can be halved or even quartered and cooked like bay scallops. Purists like to cut away the tough connective tissue known as the foot before preparing scallops. Pencil-eraser-tough scallops are the result of too much cooking, so be careful to follow times indicated in the recipes below.

Mussels have long been popular in Europe and are now finding increasing acceptance on this side of the Atlantic. Most of our mussels are of the blue variety, even though the green New Zealand mussels are appearing in more and more fish stores due to a successful marketing campaign. Mussels are best in the fall, winter, and spring. Be sure to discard any mussels with open shells before cooking. Scrub thoroughly with a stiff brush and remove the beard, the stringy connective fiber that protrudes from the side. To do this, simply grab the center mass of string and cut off or gently pull away from the shell. The mussels are then ready to prepare, usually steamed in their own juices with flavorings of a subtle nature. Discard any mussels that do not open after cooking.

---

300   CLAM-STUFFED POTATOES
Prep: 10 minutes   Cook: 55 to 60 minutes   Serves: 4

Here's a stuffed baked potato that's a meal in a spud. Serve with buttered broccoli and a nice tossed salad.

4 medium baking potatoes, about 8 ounces each	½ cup milk
	½ cup shredded Swiss cheese
1 pint shucked fresh clams, or 1 (8-ounce) can whole clams, drained and coarsely chopped	2 tablespoons butter
	¼ cup minced fresh chives
	1 teaspoon salt
	½ teaspoon pepper

1. Preheat oven to 425°F. Place potatoes in oven and bake until tender when pierced with a fork, 45 to 50 minutes. Let cool slightly, then cut a ¼-inch-thick lengthwise slice off top of each potato. Without tearing skin, scoop potato out into a medium bowl, leaving a ¼-inch shell, and mash with a fork. Reserve potato shells. Add clams, milk, cheese, butter, chives, salt, and pepper to mashed potatoes. Stir to blend well.

2. Spoon mixture into reserved potato shells, place on a lightly oiled 9 x 13-inch baking dish, and bake until heated through and lightly browned on top, about 10 minutes. Garnish with additional chopped chives and serve hot.

301 CLAMS WITH HERB BUTTER
Prep: 15 minutes   Cook: 6 to 8 minutes   Serves: 4

36 littleneck clams on the half
   shell
6 tablespoons butter, melted
3 tablespoons dry white wine
2 tablespoons fresh lemon
   juice
2 medium shallots, minced

1 tablespoon fresh chopped
   tarragon or 1 teaspoon
   dried
1 tablespoon chopped parsley
½ teaspoon salt
½ teaspoon pepper

1. Preheat oven to 425°F. Arrange clams on a large baking sheet filled ¼ inch deep with rock salt or coarse salt or sheets of crumpled aluminum foil. Push shells down slightly to prevent tipping.

2. In a medium bowl, combine butter, wine, lemon juice, shallots, tarragon, parsley, salt, and pepper. Drizzle 1 teaspoon herb butter over each clam.

3. Bake until clams are slightly firm and juices are bubbly, 6 to 8 minutes. Serve immediately.

302 GRILLED CLAMS WITH RED PEPPER PUREE
Prep: 2 minutes   Cook: 4 to 7 minutes   Serves: 8 to 10 as an appetizer

1 large red bell pepper, cored,
   seeded, and cut into
   chunks
1 small onion, halved
1 garlic clove
2 tablespoons olive oil
1 tablespoon red wine vinegar

1 teaspoon Dijon mustard
½ teaspoon salt
¼ teaspoon pepper
4 pounds hard-shell clams,
   such as littlenecks or
   cherrystones, scrubbed

1. In a food processor or blender, combine bell pepper, onion, garlic, olive oil, vinegar, mustard, salt, and pepper. Puree until very smooth. Set puree aside at room temperature.

2. Prepare a medium-hot fire in your barbecue grill. Set grill about 6 inches from source of heat. Place clams directly on grill and cook until opened, 4 to 7 minutes. Discard any clams that do not open.

3. To serve, break off top shell and loosen meat with a small knife. Spoon about 1 teaspoon of puree over each clam and serve at once.

303   CLAMS OREGANATA

Prep: 15 minutes   Cook: 7 to 10 minutes   Serves: 4

Rock salt or coarse salt
36 littleneck clams, on the half
    shell
1 cup fresh bread crumbs
1½ teaspoons dried oregano
¼ cup grated Parmesan cheese

2 garlic cloves, crushed
    through a press
½ teaspoon salt
¼ teaspoon pepper
¼ cup olive oil
Lemon wedges

1. Preheat oven to 425°F. Make a bed of rock salt or coarse salt on a large baking sheet (or use crumpled aluminum foil) and arrange clams on it securely, pushing them down slightly to prevent tipping.

2. In a medium bowl, combine bread crumbs, oregano, Parmesan cheese, garlic, salt, and pepper. Stir to blend well. Top each clam with 1 teaspoon of crumb mixture and drizzle ¼ to ½ teaspoon olive oil over each.

3. Bake until clams are lightly browned on top and bubbly, 7 to 10 minutes. Serve hot with lemon wedges.

304   CLAMS TERIYAKI

Prep: 10 minutes   Cook: 5 minutes   Serves: 4

36 littleneck clams, on the half
    shell
½ cup soy sauce
½ cup sake or dry white wine

¼ cup sugar
2 garlic cloves, crushed
    through a press
½ teaspoon pepper

1. Pour a ½-inch layer of rock salt or coarse salt into bottom of a large baking sheet. Place clams snugly on sheet and set aside.

2. Preheat broiler. In a small saucepan, combine soy sauce, sake, sugar, garlic, and pepper. Bring to a boil over medium-high heat, stirring until sugar dissolves. Remove from heat. Baste each clam with sauce.

3. Broil clams 4 inches from source of heat until slightly firm and lightly browned, about 5 minutes. Serve hot with remaining teriyaki sauce on the side.

305 MUSSELS MARINIÈRE

Prep: 10 minutes   Cook: 7 to 9 minutes   Serves: 4

This is a classic French recipe that serves up the mussels plump and moist along with plenty of flavorful liquid. Serve in soup plates with a fork and a soup spoon and a basket of crusty bread to soak up every last drop of those juices.

3 quarts mussels	2 tablespoons butter
1 cup white wine	½ teaspoon pepper
1 small onion, thinly sliced	Salt
2 tablespoons chopped parsley	

1. Pull or cut off hairy brown beard from each mussel; scrub mussels. In a large nonreactive saucepan or flameproof casserole, combine wine, onion, parsley, and butter. Bring to a boil over high heat. Reduce heat to medium and simmer for 2 minutes.

2. Add mussels, cover, and raise heat to high. Cook, tossing and stirring once or twice, until mussels have opened and are cooked through, 5 to 7 minutes. Discard any mussels that do not open. Remove mussels to a large serving bowl.

3. Strain liquid from pot through a sieve lined with a double layer of cheese-cloth. Season with pepper and salt to taste. Pour over mussels and serve at once.

306 MUSSELS MADRAS

Prep: 15 minutes   Cook: 10 to 12 minutes   Serves: 4

3 dozen mussels	¼ cup dry white wine

2 medium shallots, finely
     chopped
	2 large tomatoes, seeded and
	     chopped

2 garlic cloves, minced	2 teaspoons fresh lemon juice
1 tablespoon curry powder	½ teaspoon salt
2 tablespoons olive oil	½ teaspoon pepper

1. Scrub mussels well. Pull or cut off hairy brown beard from each mussel.

2. In a large saucepan, cook shallots, garlic, and curry powder in olive oil over medium heat, stirring often, until shallots and garlic soften slightly, about 2 minutes. Add wine, tomatoes, lemon juice, salt, and pepper. Cook until thick and pulpy, 3 to 5 minutes.

3. Add mussels, cover, and cook until mussels open and flesh separates from one side of shell, about 5 minutes. Spoon mussels with sauce into individual serving bowls and serve at once.

307   MUSSELS MARINARA
Prep: 5 minutes   Cook: 27 to 32 minutes   Serves: 4

Serve this dish as a main course with a green salad and a loaf of Italian garlic bread.

3 dozen fresh mussels	1 cup dry red wine
1 medium onion, thinly sliced	2 bay leaves
4 garlic cloves, minced	1 teaspoon dried basil
3 tablespoons olive oil	½ teaspoon salt
2 (28-ounce) cans Italian	½ teaspoon crushed hot red
peeled tomatoes, drained	pepper
and chopped	¼ cup grated Parmesan cheese

1. Scrub mussels well. Pull or cut off hairy brown beard from each mussel.

2. In a large saucepan, cook onion and garlic in olive oil over medium heat, stirring frequently, until softened, about 2 minutes. Add tomatoes, wine, bay leaves, basil, salt, and hot pepper. Stir to mix. Partially cover and cook, stirring occasionally, until sauce thickens, about 20 minutes.

3. Add mussels, raise heat to medium-high, cover, and cook, stirring occasionally, until mussels open, 5 to 10 minutes. Discard any that do not open. Spoon out servings of mussels and sauce into individual bowls and sprinkle Parmesan on top. Serve immediately.

308   RISOTTO WITH MUSSELS
Prep: 10 minutes   Cook: 25 to 27 minutes   Serves: 4

If you can find them, small, bite-size mussels are best for this risotto. Arborio rice, the traditional ingredient for risotto, is available in specialty food shops and in some supermarkets. Ordinary short-grain rice can be substituted, but the texture will not be the same.

4 tablespoons butter	1 cup Arborio or short-grain
1 small onion, finely chopped	rice
2 pounds small mussels,	½ teaspoon salt
scrubbed and debearded	¼ teaspoon pepper
1½ cups Fish Stock (page 33)	
or bottled clam juice	

1. In a large soup pot or kettle, melt 2 tablespoons butter. Add onion and cook over medium-high heat, stirring often, until softened, about 2 minutes. Add mussels, pour on fish stock, and cover. Cook until mussels are barely open, 3 to 5 minutes. Remove mussels to a large bowl to cool. Strain liquid through a sieve lined with several layers of dampened cheesecloth. There should be at least 2 cups. Add additional stock if amount is less; if there is more than 2 cups, reserve excess for another use.

2. When mussels are cool enough to handle, remove meat from shells and set aside. Discard shells.

3. In a small saucepan, bring strained cooking liquid to a boil over high heat. Reduce heat to medium and maintain a steady simmer.

4. Melt remaining 2 tablespoons butter in a medium saucepan over low heat. Add rice and stir to coat. Raise heat to medium-high and add ½ cup of simmering liquid. Cook, stirring constantly, until liquid is completely absorbed. Add another ½ cup liquid and stir until absorbed. Repeat procedure until rice is tender but still firm in the center and bound with a creamy sauce, about 20 minutes. Season with salt and pepper. Stir in mussels and serve at once.

309 STEAMED MUSSELS
Prep: 15 minutes   Cook: 5 minutes   Serves: 4

3 **dozen mussels**	1 **tablespoon fresh thyme**
2 **cups dry white wine**	**leaves or 1 teaspoon dried**
2 **tablespoons olive oil**	1 **teaspoon salt**
3 **medium shallots, minced**	½ **teaspoon pepper**
2 **garlic cloves, minced**	

1. Scrub mussels with a stiff brush. Pull or cut off beards.

2. In a large saucepan, combine wine, olive oil, shallots, garlic, thyme, salt, and pepper. Bring to a boil over medium-high heat. Add mussels, cover, and steam until mussels have opened and flesh separates from one side of shell, about 5 minutes. Discard any that do not open.

3. Spoon out mussels with broth into individual serving bowls and serve at once.

310 BARBECUED OYSTERS
Prep: 10 minutes   Cook: 5 to 8 minutes   Serves: 4

½ **cup barbecue sauce**	24 **oysters on the half shell**
1 **garlic clove, minced**	**Rock salt or coarse salt**
2 **tablespoons butter, melted**	

1. Prepare a medium-hot fire in your barbecue grill or preheat oven to 400°F.

2. In a small bowl, combine barbecue sauce, garlic, and butter. Stir until sauce is smooth and blended.

3. Arrange oysters on a grill over hot coals or place on top of a ¼-inch-thick bed of rock salt or coarse salt in a large baking dish. Top each oyster with about 1 teaspoon of sauce. Grill or bake until oysters are plump and edges begin to curl, 5 to 8 minutes. Serve hot.

311 SCALLOPED OYSTERS
Prep: 5 minutes   Cook: 32 to 33 minutes   Serves: 4 to 6

Where I'm from in Georgia, this dish was always served alongside the roast turkey on our Thanksgiving table.

1 quart shucked oysters	½ cup milk
½ teaspoon salt	1 egg
¼ teaspoon pepper	½ cup dried bread crumbs
3 tablespoons butter, cut into thin slivers	2 tablespoons butter, melted
2 cups crushed saltine crackers	

1. In a medium saucepan, warm oysters over low heat until edges curl, 2 to 3 minutes. Drain in a colander. Set aside.

2. Butter a 9 x 13-inch baking dish. Layer bottom with one-third of oysters. Season with one-third of salt and pepper. Dot with slivers of butter. Sprinkle one-third cracker crumbs over oysters. Repeat with 2 more layers, using remaining oysters and crackers, seasoning with salt and pepper, and dotting with butter.

3. Preheat oven to 350°F. In a small bowl, beat together milk and egg. Pour over oysters and crackers. Top with bread crumbs. Drizzle melted butter evenly over top.

4. Bake until bubbly and lightly browned on top, about 30 minutes. Serve at once.

312 OYSTER OMELET
Prep: 1 minute   Cook: 4 minutes   Serves: 2

4 tablespoons butter	4 eggs
½ pint shucked oysters, drained	½ teaspoon salt
	¼ teaspoon pepper

1. In a small saucepan, melt 2 tablespoons butter over medium-high heat. Add oysters, reduce heat to low, cover, and simmer gently until oysters are plump and firm, about 3 minutes. Set aside, covered to keep warm.

2. In a medium bowl, beat eggs with salt and pepper until frothy. Melt remaining butter in a large nonstick skillet or omelet pan over medium-high heat. When butter ceases to bubble, add eggs. Using flat part of a fork, stir eggs quickly until almost set, about 15 seconds. Lift egg and tilt pan to allow uncooked egg to settle on bottom. Cook, shaking pan and lifting egg to dislodge omelet, until set, about 15 seconds longer.

3. Spoon oysters over eggs, fold top edge over bottom, and turn out onto a small serving platter, seam side down. Brush top with additional butter, if desired. Serve at once.

313   OYSTERS IN CHAMPAGNE BUTTER SAUCE
Prep: 3 minutes   Cook: 18 to 19 minutes
Serves: 4 as a first course, 8 as an hors d'oeuvre

This is an extravagantly rich dish, perfect as a first course at your fanciest dinner party or as a hot hors d'oeuvre (served on small plates with cocktail forks) at an elegant celebration, like New Year's Eve. If you order the oysters on the half shell, be sure to ask the fish market to reserve the liquor for you. It adds oyster essence to the sauce.

2 dozen medium oysters on the half shell, liquor reserved	4 egg yolks
	2 sticks (8 ounces) butter, melted
1½ cups brut champagne or sparkling wine	½ teaspoon salt
1 small onion, minced	¼ teaspoon pepper
	¼ teaspoon fresh lemon juice

1. Arrange oysters on a 1-inch-thick layer of coarse salt in bottom of a broiling pan. Place shells snugly in salt and set an oyster in each one. Strain liquor through a fine sieve and reserve.

2. In a medium nonreactive saucepan, boil champagne with onion over high heat until reduced to about 2 tablespoons, about 10 minutes. Remove from heat and let cool slightly. Whisk egg yolks and strained oyster liquid into reduced champagne. Cook over medium heat, whisking constantly, until frothy and thickened, 3 to 4 minutes; do not let boil.

3. Remove pan from heat and slowly whisk in a few drops of melted butter. Continue adding butter in droplets, whisking constantly, until sauce is thick and emulsified. Season with salt, pepper, and lemon juice.

4. Preheat broiler. Spoon a small amount of sauce over each oyster. Broil about 4 inches from heat until bubbly and browned, about 5 minutes. Serve immediately.

314   OYSTER SHOOTERS
Prep: 2 minutes   Cook: none   Serves: 6 to 8

Serve these shooters as an appetizer at a cocktail party or before dinner. They are a real conversation piece. They are best if made with a premium vodka.

24 fresh oysters, shucked	¾ cup vodka
1½ cups cocktail sauce (page 13 or bottled)	Juice of 1 lemon
	Freshly ground pepper

Place an oyster in a shot glass or small cup. Top with 2 tablespoons cocktail sauce, 2 teaspoons vodka, a sprinkling of lemon juice, and a dash of pepper. Drink in one quick gulp.

315   OYSTERS WITH CILANTRO PESTO

Prep: 15 minutes   Cook: 12 to 13 minutes   Serves: 6

¼ cup pine nuts
½ cup chopped cilantro
¼ cup chopped parsley
¼ cup grated Parmesan cheese
1 garlic clove, smashed
¼ teaspoon salt
½ teaspoon pepper

Coarse salt or rock salt
¼ cup olive oil
36 oysters on the half shell,
   liquor reserved
½ cup dry white wine
2 medium shallots, minced

1. Preheat oven to 325°F. Spread out pine nuts in a small baking dish and bake, stirring once or twice, until toasted and fragrant, about 5 minutes. Watch carefully to avoid burning nuts.

2. In a food processor, combine cilantro, parsley, pine nuts, Parmesan cheese, and garlic. Process until finely chopped. With machine on, drizzle in olive oil and process until mixture resembles a smooth paste. Season with salt and pepper. Set pesto aside.

3. Raise oven temperature to 425°F. Arrange oysters on a large baking sheet filled with ¼ inch of coarse salt or rock salt or with pieces of loosely crinkled aluminum foil to hold shells in place.

4. Strain oyster liquor into a small nonreactive saucepan. Add wine and shallots and boil over high heat until liquid has reduced to 2 tablespoons, 2 to 3 minutes. Add to pesto and stir to blend well. Spoon about ½ teaspoon pesto on each oyster and bake until slightly browned, about 5 minutes. Serve immediately.

316   CHILLED OYSTERS WITH CUCUMBER YOGURT SAUCE

Prep: 5 minutes   Cook: none   Serves: 4

2 dozen raw oysters on the
   half shell, chilled
1 medium cucumber, peeled,
   seeded, and very thinly
   sliced

1 cup plain yogurt
½ teaspoon salt
¼ teaspoon pepper
   Sprigs of fresh dill

1. Fill a large shallow serving dish with cracked ice and arrange oysters on top.

2. In a small bowl, combine cucumber, yogurt, salt, and pepper. Stir well to blend.

3. Spoon a small amount of sauce over top of each oyster. Garnish with sprigs of dill and serve at once.

317 DOWN-HOME OYSTER STUFFING
Prep: 5 minutes   Cook: 18 to 23 minutes   Serves: 4

This stuffing makes enough for a large roasting chicken. Double or triple ingredients for a turkey, depending on size.

1 medium onion, chopped	3 cups crumbled cornbread
1 celery rib, chopped	2 tablespoons chopped
6 tablespoons butter	parsley
1 cup chicken stock or canned	½ teaspoon salt
broth	½ teaspoon pepper
1 small (12-ounce) loaf of	1 pint shucked oysters
French or Italian bread,	
crust removed, bread	
cubed	

1. Preheat oven to 350°F. In a large skillet, cook onion and celery in butter over medium heat, stirring occasionally, until softened, about 3 minutes. Remove from heat and stir in chicken stock, bread cubes, cornbread, parsley, salt, and pepper. Stir to combine well but do not overmix.

2. Add oysters and their liquor and fold into bread mixture. Use to stuff a 5- to 6-pound roasting chicken, or place in a lightly oiled 9 x 13-inch baking dish and bake until lightly browned and heated through, 15 to 20 minutes.

318 OYSTERS BUBBLY
Prep: 3 minutes   Cook: 7 minutes   Serves: 4

Elegant yet simple to put together, these oysters make an excellent first course for a formal dinner.

1 small onion, minced	1 pint shucked oysters, with
4 tablespoons butter	their liquor reserved
1 cup brut champagne or	2 tablespoons flour
sparkling wine	2 tablespoons heavy cream
½ teaspoon salt	Lemon slices
½ teaspoon pepper	

1. In a large saucepan, cook onion in 2 tablespoons butter over medium heat until softened, about 2 minutes. Pour in champagne, season with salt and pepper, and reduce heat to low. Add oysters with their liquor, cover, and simmer until oysters are slightly firm, about 2 minutes.

2. In a small bowl, combine remaining 2 tablespoons butter and flour. Use fingertips or a fork to work mixture into a smooth paste. Add pea-size amounts of flour paste to champagne and oysters, stirring constantly until sauce thickens, about 2 minutes. Stir in cream and cook 1 minute longer. Serve in individual ramekins and garnish with lemon slices.

319   OYSTERS WITH BLACK BEAN AND GARLIC SAUCE

Prep: 15 minutes   Cook: 20 to 21 minutes   Serves: 4

Chinese fermented black beans are available in packages and bottles in the Asian cooking departments of many large supermarkets, in specialty food stores, and in Chinese markets throughout the country.

4 garlic cloves, minced	2 tablespoons dry sherry
1 (1-inch) piece of fresh ginger, peeled and finely chopped	1 cup chicken stock or canned broth
2 tablespoons olive oil	1 tablespoon soy sauce
2 scallions, thinly sliced	1 teaspoon sugar
2 tablespoons Chinese fermented black beans, rinsed and mashed slightly	¼ teaspoon chili powder
	¼ teaspoon salt
	2 teaspoons cornstarch
36 oysters on the half shell, liquor reserved	Rock salt or coarse salt

1. Preheat oven to 425°F. In a medium skillet, cook garlic and ginger in olive oil over medium heat, stirring occasionally, until softened, about 2 minutes. Add scallions and black beans and cook, stirring often, until scallions are softened, about 2 minutes. Add reserved oyster liquor, sherry, chicken stock, soy sauce, sugar, chili power, and salt. Cook sauce, stirring occasionally, until flavors are well blended, about 10 minutes.

2. In a small bowl, dissolve cornstarch in 1 tablespoon water. Stir cornstarch mixture into sauce and bring to a boil, stirring until sauce is smooth and slightly thickened, 1 to 2 minutes. Remove from heat.

3. Arrange oysters securely on a large baking sheet filled with ¼ inch of rock salt or coarse salt or crumpled pieces of loosely arranged aluminum foil.

4. Spoon 1 teaspoon of sauce over each oyster. Set baking sheet in oven and bake until lightly browned, about 5 minutes. Serve hot.

320   SCALLOPS IN SAFFRON CREAM SAUCE

Prep: 2 minutes   Cook: 4 minutes   Serves: 4

1½ pounds bay scallops or halved sea scallops	½ teaspoon salt
1 cup heavy cream	¼ teaspoon pepper
½ teaspoon saffron threads	1 tablespoon chopped parsley

Pat scallops dry on paper towels. In a large skillet, combine scallops, cream, saffron, salt, and pepper. Cook over high heat, stirring constantly, until cream has reduced and thickened and scallops are firm and opaque, about 4 minutes. Stir in parsley and serve at once.

321 SCALLOPS ON CAESAR SALAD

Prep: 10 minutes   Chill: 1 hour   Cook: 2 to 3 minutes   Serves: 4

Golden brown scallops make a visual and flavorful addition to a classic Caesar salad. Serve as a first course at dinner or a main-course salad at lunch.

1 garlic clove, crushed
½ tablespoon fresh lemon
   juice
½ tablespoon red wine vinegar
1 teaspoon Dijon mustard
3 anchovy fillets, finely
   chopped
½ cup olive oil
⅓ cup grated Parmesan cheese

½ teaspoon salt
½ teaspoon pepper
1½ pounds bay scallops or
   halved sea scallops
1 large head of romaine
   lettuce, rinsed and
   thoroughly dried
1 cup bread croutons,
   homemade or prepared

1. In a large bowl, combine garlic, lemon juice, vinegar, mustard, and anchovies. Mash with a fork to blend. Add ½ cup olive oil, drop by drop, whisking constantly, until thick and emulsified. Stir in Parmesan cheese, salt, and pepper. Cover with plastic wrap and refrigerate until well chilled, at least 1 hour. (This dressing can be made 1 day in advance.)

2. Pat scallops dry on paper towels. In a large lightly oiled nonstick skillet, cook scallops over medium-high heat, turning, until golden brown and firm, 2 to 3 minutes. Remove to a plate and cover to keep warm.

3. Coarsely tear romaine leaves. In a large bowl, toss romaine with croutons and Caesar dressing. Divide among 4 plates and top each with several scallops. Serve at once.

322 SCALLOPS PROVENÇAL

Prep: 5 minutes   Cook: 3½ to 4½ minutes   Serves: 4

Try substituting oregano, rosemary, chervil, parsley, or tarragon for the thyme called for below. Any fresh herb will add a subtle flavor.

1½ pounds bay scallops or
   halved sea scallops
½ teaspoon salt
½ teaspoon pepper
2 tablespoons olive oil

2 medium tomatoes, peeled,
   seeded, and chopped
1 garlic clove, minced
1 tablespoon fresh thyme
   leaves or 1 teaspoon dried

1. Pat scallops dry on paper towels. Season with ¼ teaspoon salt and ¼ teaspoon pepper. In a large skillet, heat olive oil over medium-high heat until hot but not smoking. Add scallops and cook, turning, until opaque and firm, about 1½ minutes.

2. Add tomatoes, garlic, thyme, and remaining salt and pepper to skillet. Raise heat to high and boil rapidly until tomatoes are softened and scallops are cooked through, 2 to 3 minutes. Serve at once.

323   SCALLOPS WITH ENDIVE AND GINGER
Prep: 7 minutes   Cook: 34 to 35 minutes   Serves: 4

Belgian endive is slightly bitter. Substitute 4 or 5 sliced large leeks if the bitterness does not appeal to you. Serve over hot buttered noodles.

2 tablespoons butter
1 medium onion, finely
     chopped
8 to 10 Belgian endives (about
     2½ pounds), cut into
     ¼-inch rounds
1 teaspoon salt
½ teaspoon pepper
1 cup heavy cream

1 teaspoon fresh lemon juice
1 (1-inch) piece of fresh
     ginger, peeled and finely
     chopped
1½ pounds bay scallops or
     halved sea scallops
2 tablespoons chopped
     parsley

1. In a large skillet, melt butter over medium heat. Add onion and cook, stirring often, until softened, about 2 minutes.

2. Add endives to skillet and season with salt and pepper. Stir in cream, lemon juice, and ginger. Cover and cook over very low heat, stirring occasionally, until endives are tender, about 30 minutes.

3. Remove cover, raise heat to medium-low, add scallops, and cook until firm and white throughout, 2 to 3 minutes. Remove from heat, stir in parsley, and serve at once.

324   SCALLOPS IN COGNAC CREAM SAUCE
Prep: 1 minute   Cook: 4½ minutes   Serves: 4

1½ pounds bay scallops or
     halved sea scallops
½ cup Cognac or brandy

1 cup heavy cream
½ teaspoon salt
¼ teaspoon pepper

1. Pat scallops dry on paper towels. In a large lightly oiled nonstick skillet, cook scallops over medium-high heat until lightly browned on one side, about 2 minutes. Do not overcrowd pan. If necessary, cook in 2 batches. Remove to a plate and set aside.

2. Raise heat to high, carefully pour Cognac into skillet, and stir, scraping up browned bits from bottom of pan. Boil until reduced by half. Add cream, salt, and pepper and continue boiling until sauce is thick enough to coat back of a spoon, about 2 minutes. Return scallops to skillet to heat through, about 30 seconds. Serve hot.

325   SCALLOPS WITH GRAPEFRUIT BUTTER SAUCE ON SPINACH

Prep: 3 minutes   Cook: 12 to 14 minutes   Serves: 4

2 **bunches of fresh spinach**	2 **shallots, minced**
1½ **pounds bay scallops or**	½ **teaspoon salt**
halved sea scallops	¼ **teaspoon pepper**
3 **tablespoons olive oil**	6 **tablespoons cold butter, cut**
½ **cup dry white wine**	**into bits**
½ **cup fresh grapefruit juice**	1½ **tablespoons minced chives**

1. Wash spinach well to remove sand; remove and discard coarse stems. Place in a large pot with no additional water. Cover and steam until slightly wilted, 3 to 5 minutes. Drain, then transfer to a bowl and cover to keep warm.

2. Pat scallops dry on paper towels. In a large lightly oiled nonstick skillet, cook half of scallops over medium-high heat, tossing, until lightly browned and firm, about 2 minutes. Transfer to a plate. Repeat with remaining scallops.

3. Add wine, grapefruit juice, shallots, salt, and pepper to skillet. Raise heat to high and cook, scraping up brown bits from bottom of pan, until liquid is reduced to ⅓ cup, about 3 minutes. Reduce heat to low. Whisk in butter, a few pieces at a time, until sauce is thick and emulsified. Do not allow to boil.

4. Return scallops to pan along with juices that have collected on plate. Cook until just heated through, about 2 minutes. Place a small amount of warm spinach on individual serving plates, top with a generous amount of scallops and about 2 tablespoons sauce. Sprinkle with chives.

---

326   STEAMED CLAMS WITH WINE AND HERBS

Prep: 1 minute   Cook: 10 minutes   Serves 4

4 **quarts soft-shell clams,**	1 **tablespoon chopped fresh**
scrubbed	**rosemary or 1 teaspoon**
1 **cup dry white wine**	**dried**
1 **tablespoon chopped fresh**	1 **garlic clove, minced**
thyme leaves or	
1 teaspoon dried	

1. Place clams in a clam steamer or a large pot or kettle fitted with a colander. Pour in wine and 1 cup water. Sprinkle thyme, rosemary, and garlic over clams. Cover pot tightly and steam over medium-high heat until opened, about 10 minutes.

2. Place clams in a large bowl, discarding any that have not opened. Spoon out individual servings with broth, leaving any sand or grit at bottom of pan. Serve at once.

327   SCALLOPS ALMONDINE
Prep: 2 minutes   Cook: 4 minutes   Serves: 4

In this easy but elegant dish, scallops and almonds are enhanced with the nutty flavor of sherry. Serve with plain boiled potatoes or steamed white rice.

1½ **pounds bay scallops or**	3 **tablespoons dry sherry**
halved sea scallops	½ **teaspoon salt**
2 **tablespoons butter**	¼ **teaspoon pepper**
½ **cup sliced almonds**	

1. Pat scallops dry on paper towels. In a large skillet, melt butter over medium heat. Add almonds and cook, stirring constantly, until golden brown, about 1 minute. Remove almonds with a slotted spoon and set aside.

2. Add scallops to skillet, raise heat to medium-high, and cook, tossing, until firm and opaque in center, about 2 minutes. Add sherry, raise heat to high, and cook 1 minute. Stir in browned almonds, season with salt and pepper, and serve at once.

328   SKEWERED SCALLOPS WITH MUSHROOMS AND CHERRY TOMATOES
Prep: 5 minutes   Marinate: 1 hour   Cook: 8 to 12 minutes
Serves: 4

12 **large sea scallops**	½ **teaspoon salt**
½ **cup olive oil**	¼ **teaspoon pepper**
1 **garlic clove, minced**	6 **medium mushrooms,**
2 **tablespoons fresh lemon**	**halved**
juice	12 **cherry tomatoes**

1. Pat scallops dry on paper towels. In a medium bowl, combine scallops, olive oil, garlic, lemon juice, salt, and pepper. Stir to blend, cover with plastic wrap, and marinate at room temperature for 1 hour.

2. Prepare a medium-hot fire in your barbecue grill, or preheat broiler. Drain scallops and reserve marinade. On 4 long (12-inch) metal skewers, alternate scallops, mushroom halves, and tomatoes. Brush skewered ingredients with marinade and grill or broil about 6 inches from heat, turning often, until scallops are lightly browned and firm, 8 to 12 minutes.

329   PESTO SCALLOPS
Prep: 2 minutes   Cook: 3 to 4 minutes   Serves: 4

1½ pounds bay scallops or
    halved sea scallops
½ cup pesto

¼ teaspoon salt
¼ teaspoon pepper

1. Pat scallops dry on paper towels. In a large lightly oiled nonstick skillet, cook scallops over medium-high heat, turning occasionally, until opaque in center, 1 to 2 minutes.

2. Add pesto to skillet. Reduce heat to medium and cook, stirring, until heated through, about 2 minutes. Season with salt and pepper and serve at once.

330   HERB-BREADED SCALLOPS
Prep: 3 minutes   Cook: 2 to 3 minutes   Serves: 4

Use any mixture of fresh herbs that are available—thyme, rosemary, chives, oregano, and/or parsley.

2 cups fresh bread crumbs
2 tablespoons minced fresh
    herbs
1 teaspoon salt
½ teaspoon pepper

1½ pounds bay scallops or
    halved sea scallops
2 tablespoons butter
2 tablespoons vegetable oil

1. In a large bowl, combine bread crumbs, herbs, salt, and pepper. Mix well. Add scallops and toss to coat.

2. In a large nonstick skillet, melt butter in oil over medium-high heat. Add scallops and cook, tossing occasionally, until lightly browned and firm, 2 to 3 minutes. (Do not overcrowd pan. If necessary, cook in 2 batches.) Serve immediately.

331   SCALLOPS WITH WINE AND CAPERS
Prep: 1 minute   Cook: 3 to 4 minutes   Serves: 4

1½ pounds bay scallops or
    halved sea scallops
2 tablespoons butter
1 cup dry white wine

½ teaspoon salt
¼ teaspoon pepper
2 tablespoons capers

1. Pat scallops dry on paper towels. In a large skillet, melt butter over medium-high heat. Add scallops and cook, turning occasionally, until firm and opaque, about 1 to 2 minutes.

2. Pour in wine, raise heat to high, and boil until liquid is reduced by half, about 2 minutes. Season with salt and pepper, stir in capers, and serve hot.

Chapter 14

Luxury from the Sea

Crab, lobster, and crayfish are some of the best eating in the world. We in America are blessed with a large quantity of deep and shallow waters that provide an infinite variety of these majestic crustaceans.

Most abundant from summer through fall, the blue crab is found from Cape Cod to Florida around the Gulf Coast to Texas. The popular Dungeness crab is found in lesser numbers on the West Coast from California to Alaska. The flesh of the two can be used interchangeably. Most ready-to-eat and cooked crab is bought in its lump form—that is to say large chunks of white meat extracted from the body. To remove the meat from cooked crab yourself, twist off claws and legs. Turn crab on its back, pull off the bottom shell, then lift off top to remove the spongy gills and intestines. Snap remaining body in half and remove body meat with a small-tined fork or fingers. Crack claws with a mallet or handle of a large knife and remove claw meat.

Soft-shell crabs are simply blue crabs that have just molted or backed out of their hard shells. The season runs from mid-May to late September. The soft-shell crab is a very clean seafood because the crab will stop eating about three days before it molts. Its digestive system is cleaned and it is just like a cleaned fish. They are either sold live or dressed and cleaned, ready to cook. Soft-shell crabs are relatively easy to clean yourself. Lift the pointed edge on each side of the crab and cut out the spongy gills, using small scissors. Cut away the eyes and lift the shell between the eye sockets to remove the translucent sand sack. Cut off the apron. Rinse to remove traces of yellow; dry on paper towels.

King crabs come from Alaska, usually frozen and consisting of leg meat. The time and trouble it takes to pick out crabmeat for commercial selling makes real lump crabmeat an expensive product. Increasingly popular is the imitation product known as surimi seafood. Introduced from Japan in the early 1970s, surimi is usually made from a lean white fish like pollack. Raw fish is mixed with salt, water, and binders like egg whites to produce a thick paste. This paste is flavored, molded, cooked, and cut into desired shapes, ready to be used just like crab where it is called for in any recipe. Sold loose or in small packages, this economical and convenient food is a product with some merit. Nothing will replace the rich creamy flavor of fresh lump crabmeat. Surimi, however, may be the answer for those who don't mind the tradeoff. The same is true for canned crab. While plentiful and certainly an acceptable substitute in most recipes, canned crab doesn't have the depth of character of the real thing. But neither does it have the same price tag!

Lobsters are a special breed of seafood. Exotic to look at, extremely pleasing to eat, this most noble of all crustaceans is a treat in any form. The American lobster is found from New England to North Carolina but most famously so in Maine and eastern Canada. Available year round, lobsters are abundant in October and November as they molt in June and July.

Many lobster lovers are partial to the tender flesh of the female species. To distinguish between him and her, look closely at the abdomen. The male has a narrow abdomen with bony appendages. The female has a broader abdomen with soft, feathery or hairy-looking feelers. And of course, the female carries the roe or coral, which is delicious when added to sauces. Both sexes have the green tomalley or liver, also full of flavor when used for making sauces.

The spiny or rock lobster is similar to the American lobster but has no claws. It favors the warmer coastal waters of the world and is the variety that usually comes to us frozen. Rock lobster tails from South Africa and the far Pacific are exported frozen, ready to thaw and use.

Many fish stores will boil lobsters for a nominal fee. This saves some trouble and mess for the busy cook. The meat can be extracted and used in many of the recipes herein. Some of the recipes call for lobsters that are split in half lengthwise, then stuffed and baked. Most fish stores will be happy to do this in house, relieving the home cook of the mess that such a procedure can make. For a detailed description of how to clean and eat a lobster, see the recipe for Boiled Lobster on page 212.

Lobster-flavored surimi is available in the same form as crabmeat surimi described above. A money-saving alternative, it can be used in most recipes where fresh lobster is called for—but at a price. Nothing can take the place of sweet, succulent lobster.

Crayfish are small fresh-water crustaceans native to Louisiana (where they're known as crawfish) but increasingly being farmed in other states, notably South Carolina. They may be cooked and eaten from the shell or parboiled and used in dishes like the Étouffée found on page 227. Five to six pounds of live crayfish yield about one pound of peeled tails. Frozen tails are often available in fine seafood shops.

332   BAKED STUFFED LOBSTER
Prep: 15 minutes   Cook: 14 to 18 minutes   Serves: 4

4 tablespoons butter
1 small onion, finely chopped
1 celery rib, finely chopped
2 cups fresh bread crumbs
1 teaspoon grated lemon zest
  (optional)
2 tablespoons fresh lemon
  juice
1 tablespoon chopped fresh
  thyme leaves or 1
  teaspoon dried

1 tablespoon chopped fresh
  oregano or 1 teaspoon
  dried
½ teaspoon salt
½ teaspoon pepper
4 live lobsters, 1¼ to 1½
  pounds each, split
  lengthwise in half

1. Melt butter in a medium saucepan. Add onions and celery and cook over medium heat, stirring frequently, until soft, 2 to 3 minutes. Remove from heat. Stir in bread crumbs, lemon zest, lemon juice, thyme, oregano, salt, and pepper.

2. Lay split lobsters on their backs and press down lightly to flatten. Remove and discard center vein that runs along tail and hard sac near head. Crack claws gently with a heavy mallet or handle.

3. Preheat oven to 450°F. Arrange lobsters in a large roasting pan. Spoon equal amounts of bread mixture into upper body cavity and along split tail. Bake until lobster meat is firm and opaque, 12 to 15 minutes.

333   DEVILED LOBSTER
Prep: 5 minutes   Cook: 10 to 13 minutes   Serves: 4

4 tablespoons butter
1 small onion, finely chopped
1 celery rib, finely chopped
1 small red bell pepper, finely
  chopped
1 pound cooked lobster meat,
  cut into ½-inch pieces

1 cup fresh bread crumbs
2 tablespoons fresh lemon
  juice
2 teaspoons Worcestershire
  sauce
½ teaspoon salt
½ teaspoon pepper

1. Preheat oven to 400°F. In a large skillet, melt 3 tablespoons butter over medium heat. Add onion, celery, and bell pepper. Cook, stirring occasionally, until softened, about 3 minutes. Remove from heat.

2. Stir in lobster, bread crumbs, lemon juice, Worcestershire sauce, salt, and pepper. Divide mixture evenly among either 4 lobster tail shells, scallop shells, or individual ramekins. Melt remaining 1 tablespoon butter and drizzle over deviled lobster. Bake until warmed through and lightly browned on top, 7 to 10 minutes. Serve hot.

334 BOILED LOBSTER
Prep: 1 minute   Cook: 17 minutes   Serves: 4

Eating a boiled lobster can be lots of fun, but it is messy. Have plenty of napkins on hand and bowls for the empty shells.

To begin eating, break off tail from body and let liquid drain. Split tail in half lengthwise and remove the intestine, which is gray or green in color. Pull the tail meat out with a fork. Break off large claws and, with a nut-cracker, crack each large claw in the middle to remove the large piece of meat. Crack knuckles and remove meat with a tiny fork. The upper body contains a small quantity of meat, as well as the tomalley or liver and coral or eggs, if it is a female. All are sweet and delicious, so give them a try. The feelers also contain little morsels of delicate flesh and juices to be sucked or picked out by the enthusiast.

2 tablespoons salt	1 stick (8 ounces) butter
1 teaspoon pepper	1 garlic clove, minced
4 (1½-pound) live lobsters, preferably female	

1. Bring a large stockpot of water to a boil. Add salt and pepper. Plunge lobsters in headfirst, cover, and cook for 15 minutes after water has returned to a boil. (The general rule for boiling lobsters is 7 minutes per pound.) Drain and remove lobsters to individual serving plates.

2. In a small saucepan, heat butter with garlic over very low heat until bubbly, about 2 minutes. Serve hot in individual dipping bowls alongside cooked lobsters.

335 BAKED LOBSTER WITH SAGE STUFFING
Prep: 15 minutes   Cook: 15 to 18 minutes   Serves: 4

The blackish-green tomalley (or liver) located in the abdomen of the lobster, which turns light green when cooked, is considered a delicacy. The black roe in females turns red when cooked and is very tasty. To add extra flavor to the stuffing below, lift out and reserve both after splitting lobster in half and blend into bread crumb mixture in step 2.

4 live lobsters, 1¼ to 1½ pounds each, split lengthwise	1 tablespoon chopped fresh sage leaves or ¾ teaspoon dried
4 tablespoons butter	¼ cup cream
1 small onion, finely chopped	½ teaspoon salt
2 cups fresh bread crumbs	½ teaspoon pepper

1. Preheat oven to 450°F. If fish market has not done so (or if you've split lobsters yourself), remove and discard center vein that runs along tail and hard sac near head. Press down lightly to flatten body. Crack claws gently with a heavy mallet or handle.

2. In a medium saucepan, melt butter over medium heat. Add onion and cook until soft, about 3 minutes. Remove from heat. Stir in bread crumbs, sage, cream, salt, and pepper. Mix well to combine.

3. Arrange lobsters in a large roasting pan. Spoon equal amounts of bread crumb mixture into upper body cavity and along split tail. Bake until lobster meat is firm and opaque, 12 to 15 minutes.

---

336 LOBSTER À L'AMÉRICANE
Prep: 15 minutes   Cook: 18 to 19 minutes   Serves: 2

1 live lobster, 1½ to 2 pounds, split completely in half lengthwise
¼ cup olive oil
¼ teaspoon salt
¼ teaspoon pepper
1 large onion, finely chopped
2 medium tomatoes, peeled, seeded, and chopped
1 tablespoon tomato paste
1 teaspoon grated lemon zest

1 garlic clove, crushed through a press
1 tablespoon chopped fresh thyme leaves or 1 teaspoon dried
½ cup white wine
½ cup fish stock, chicken broth, or water
2 tablespoons dry sherry
4 tablespoons butter, cut into small pieces

1. If fish market has not done so, remove intestinal vein and hard sac in head from lobster. Remove and reserve dark liver (tomalley) and coral, if there is any, for sauce. Twist off claws; crack large claws. With a large knife or cleaver, cut lobster in shell into 2-inch pieces.

2. In a heavy flameproof casserole fitted with a lid, heat olive oil over medium-high heat. Add lobster pieces and season with salt and pepper. Cook, turning to sear all sides, about 3 minutes. Remove and set aside.

3. Add onion to pan and cook, stirring occasionally, until soft, 2 to 3 minutes. Stir in tomatoes, tomato paste, lemon zest, garlic, and thyme. Return lobster to pan and add wine, fish stock, and sherry. Bring to a boil, partially cover, and reduce heat to medium-low. Simmer until lobster is cooked through, about 10 minutes. Remove lobster pieces to a serving platter and keep warm.

4. Raise heat to high. Bring pan juices to a boil and boil until reduced by half, about 2 minutes. Whisk in reserved liver and coral and cook, whisking, 1 minute longer. Reduce heat to low and whisk in butter, bit by bit until smooth and just emulsified. Pour sauce over lobster and serve at once.

337   LOBSTER SOUFFLÉ

Prep: 2 minutes   Cook: 23 to 28 minutes   Serves: 4

1 cup milk	¼ teaspoon pepper
1½ tablespoons butter	2 cups cooked lobster, cut into
1½ tablespoons flour	small dice
5 eggs, separated	2 tablespoons heavy cream
½ teaspoon salt	

1. In a small saucepan, bring milk to a simmer over medium-high heat. Meanwhile, in a medium saucepan, melt butter over medium-high heat. Add flour and stir to blend. Cook, stirring, 1 minute. Remove from heat and whisk in hot milk. Return sauce to heat and bring to a boil over medium-high heat, stirring constantly, until thickened and smooth, about 2 minutes. Reduce heat to low, add egg yolks, one at a time, beating well after each addition. Season with salt and pepper. Stir in lobster and cream, remove from heat, and let cool slightly.

2. Preheat oven to 375°F. Butter a 1½-quart soufflé dish. In a large bowl, beat egg whites until stiff but not dry. Stir one-quarter of beaten egg whites into lobster sauce, then fold this mixture into remaining beaten whites in bowl. Then pour into prepared soufflé dish.

3. Bake until soufflé is puffed and lightly browned on top and just set in center, 20 to 25 minutes. Serve immediately.

338   LOBSTER IN ROASTED TOMATOES

Prep: 10 minutes   Cook: 1 hour and 3 minutes   Serves: 2

This dish is best in summer when tomatoes are at their best. Long, slow cooking renders the tomato halves tender and sweet, perfect for succulent lobster. This is a loose adaptation of a recipe from one of France's most famous chefs, Michel Guérard.

1 (1- to 1¼-pound) boiled	½ cup mayonnaise
lobster	½ teaspoon Dijon mustard
2 medium tomatoes	1 teaspoon fresh lemon juice
2 tablespoons olive oil	1 tablespoon chopped parsley
2 garlic cloves, minced	½ pound green beans,
½ teaspoon salt	trimmed
¼ teaspoon pepper	6 large lettuce leaves

1. Preheat oven to 250°F. Cut tomatoes in half crosswise. Gently squeeze to remove seeds. Place cut sides up in a small, lightly oiled baking dish. Sprinkle with olive oil, garlic, salt, and pepper. Bake until very soft and slightly dried out, about 1 hour. Remove and let cool completely. Do not refrigerate.

2. In a small bowl, combine mayonnaise, mustard, lemon juice, and parsley. Stir to blend, cover, and refrigerate until ready to serve.

3. Crack lobster claws and remove meat. Cut along middle of tail, spread open, and remove meat in 1 piece. Slice into 6 thick slices. Remove claw meat and cut into small dice.

4. Bring a medium saucepan of salted water to a boil. Add green beans and cook until just tender, about 3 minutes. Drain and rinse under cold running water. Drain on paper towels.

5. Line 2 dinner plates with 3 lettuce leaves each. Place 2 tomato halves in center of each plate. Surround with green beans. Place 1 slice of lobster tail in center of each tomato half. Cover with diced claw meat. Top with chilled, flavored mayonnaise. Garnish each plate with 1 of remaining tail slices.

---

339   LOBSTER À L'ORANGE
Prep: 15 minutes   Cook: 9 to 10 minutes   Serves: 2

1 large lobster, 2 to 2½ pounds, split in half lengthwise
3 tablespoons olive oil
2 shallots, minced
1 medium onion, finely chopped
1 garlic clove, minced
1 juice orange, seeded and cut with peel into ½-inch dice

1 tablespoon chopped thyme leaves or 1 teaspoon dried
½ cup fresh orange juice
2 tablespoons heavy cream
1 tablespoon Cognac or brandy
½ teaspoon salt
¼ teaspoon pepper

1. Press split lobster halves down lightly to flatten. If fish market has not done so, remove and discard center vein that runs along tail and hard sac near head. Remove green tomalley and coral and reserve. Cut off claws and crack gently.

2. In a large skillet or flameproof casserole, heat olive oil over medium-high heat. Add shallots, onion, and garlic. Cook, stirring occasionally, until softened but not browned, 2 to 3 minutes. Add orange pieces and thyme. Stir briefly to blend. Push mixture to one side of pan. Place lobster, cracked claws and halves, meaty side down, in skillet and cook for 3 minutes. Pour in orange juice, turn lobster over onto shell side, and cook 1 minute longer. Remove lobster and reserve orange mixture for garnish.

3. In a blender or food processor, combine reserved coral and tomalley, cream, Cognac, salt, and pepper. Puree until smooth.

4. Preheat broiler. Place lobster halves, meaty side up, on a broiling pan. Spread puree over body and tail. Place cracked claws on side. Broil until body is lightly browned on top and claws are bright red, about 3 minutes. Serve at once, garnished with reserved orange mixture.

340   BAKED LOBSTER WITH TOMATO AND COUSCOUS

Prep: 15 minutes   Stand: 5 minutes   Cook: 12 to 15 minutes
Serves: 4

¾   teaspoon salt
5   tablespoons butter
1   cup couscous
3   medium tomatoes, peeled, seeded, and chopped
½   teaspoon pepper

1   garlic clove, minced
1   tablespoon chopped parsley
4   live lobsters, 1¼ to 1½ pounds each, split lengthwise in half

1. In a small saucepan, bring 1½ cups water to a boil with ¼ teaspoon salt and 1 tablespoon butter. Remove from heat, stir in couscous, and cover. Let stand 5 minutes.

2. In a medium bowl, combine cooked couscous with tomatoes, remaining ½ teaspoon salt, pepper, garlic, and parsley. Stir to blend well.

3. Lay split lobsters on their backs and press down lightly to flatten. Remove and discard center vein that runs along tail and hard sac near head. Crack claws gently with a heavy mallet or handle.

4. Preheat oven to 450°F. Arrange lobsters in a large roasting pan. Spoon equal amounts of couscous mixture into upper body cavity and along split tail. Bake until lobster is firm and opaque, 12 to 15 minutes.

341   LOBSTER TERIYAKI

Prep: 3 minutes   Marinate: 30 minutes   Cook: 7 to 10 minutes
Serves: 4

Lobster has a surprising natural affinity for soy sauce. Serve this luxurious version of the Japanese classic with sautéed snow peas and steamed white rice.

½   cup soy sauce
½   cup sake
3   tablespoons Asian sesame oil or vegetable oil
2   tablespoons fresh lemon juice

2   garlic cloves, minced
1   teaspoon pepper
4   rock lobster tails, 4 to 6 ounces each

1. In a medium bowl, combine soy sauce, sake, sesame oil, lemon juice, garlic, and pepper. Mix well. Cut underside cartilage of lobster tails through length of center and press on sides to slightly open. Add lobster tails to soy mixture and turn to coat. Cover and marinate, meaty side down, for 30 minutes to 1 hour at room temperature.

2. Preheat broiler. Transfer lobster tails to a large broiling pan, arranging them shell side down; reserve marinade. Broil, basting occasionally with marinade, until firm and opaque, 7 to 10 minutes.

342   LOBSTER CANTONESE

Prep: 5 minutes   Cook: 7 minutes   Serves: 4 to 6

1 tablespoon cornstarch
2 tablespoons soy sauce
2 tablespoons dry sherry
½ cup chicken broth
½ teaspoon pepper
3 tablespoons vegetable oil
2 garlic cloves, minced
1 (1-inch) piece of fresh
    ginger, peeled and
    minced

4 rock lobster tails, 4 to 6
    ounces each, cut
    lengthwise in half
2 scallions, thinly sliced
1 egg, lightly beaten

1. In a small bowl, combine cornstarch, soy sauce, sherry, broth, and pepper. Stir to dissolve cornstarch. Set sauce aside.

2. In a wok or large skillet, heat oil until hot but not smoking over high heat. Add garlic and ginger and cook, stirring constantly, until softened and fragrant, about 30 seconds. Add lobster and cook, stirring occasionally, until shells turn red and meat is opaque throughout, about 4 minutes. Stir in reserved sauce and cook, stirring, until thickened, about 2 minutes. Stir in scallions and egg. Cook until egg begins to firm slightly, about 30 seconds. Remove from heat and serve lobster in shell with sauce.

343   LOBSTER STUFFED WITH CRABMEAT

Prep: 15 minutes   Cook: 14 to 18 minutes   Serves: 4

4 tablespoons butter
1 small onion, finely chopped
1 celery rib, thinly sliced
½ pound fresh crabmeat
1 cup fresh bread crumbs
1 tablespoon Dijon mustard
1 teaspoon grated lemon zest
    (optional)
2 tablespoons fresh lemon
    juice

1 tablespoon chopped fresh
    thyme leaves or
    1 teaspoon dried
½ teaspoon salt
½ teaspoon pepper
4 live lobsters, 1¼ to 1½
    pounds each, split
    lengthwise in half
Lemon wedges

1. Preheat oven to 450°F. Melt butter in a medium saucepan. Add onion and celery and cook over medium heat, stirring often, until softened, 2 to 3 minutes. Remove from heat. Stir in crabmeat, bread crumbs, mustard, lemon zest, lemon juice, thyme, salt, and pepper.

2. Press split lobsters down lightly to flatten. Remove and discard center vein that runs along tail and hard sac near head. Crack claws gently.

3. Arrange lobsters on their backs in a large roasting pan. Spoon equal amounts of crab stuffing into upper body cavities and along split tails. Bake until lobster meat is firm and opaque throughout and stuffing is lightly browned on top, 12 to 15 minutes. Serve hot with lemon wedges.

344   LOBSTER NEWBURG

Prep: 12 minutes   Cook: 8 to 10 minutes   Serves: 4

This is an American classic. While the egg and cream enrichment may seem old-fashioned, it is a wonderful dish for special occasions. Serve with rice, in pastry shells, or over buttered toasts. This dish can be made with 1 pound shelled and deveined cooked shrimp or 1 pound lump crabmeat in place of lobster.

1 **boiled lobster, 1½ to 2 pounds**	⅛ **teaspoon grated nutmeg**
2 **tablespoons butter**	¼ **cup dry sherry**
½ **teaspoon salt**	1 **cup heavy cream**
¼ **teaspoon cayenne**	2 **egg yolks**

1. Lay lobster on its back. Place tip of sharp knife at center of head and split in half lengthwise, leaving shell intact. Crack claws. With a fork pull out meat from tail and claws; cut into ½-inch chunks.

2. In a medium saucepan, melt butter over low heat. Add lobster meat and season with salt, cayenne, nutmeg, and sherry. Cook gently until warmed through, about 5 minutes.

3. In a small bowl, beat together cream and egg yolks. Pour into pan with lobster and cook over low heat, stirring constantly, until mixture starts to thicken, 3 to 5 minutes. Do not boil. Serve at once.

345   NEW ENGLAND LOBSTER ROLLS

Prep: 7 minutes   Cook: none   Serves: 4

1½ **pounds cooked lobster meat, cut into ¼-inch chunks**	1 **tablespoon capers, chopped**
	½ **teaspoon salt**
¾ **cup mayonnaise**	½ **teaspoon pepper**
2 **celery ribs, finely chopped**	2 **tablespoons butter, softened**
2 **scallions, thinly sliced**	4 **small Italian rolls, cut in half lengthwise**
2 **tablespoons fresh lemon juice**	

1. In a medium bowl, combine lobster, mayonnaise, celery, scallions, lemon juice, capers, salt, and pepper. Stir well to blend.

2. Spread butter evenly over each roll half and toast lightly. Divide lobster mixture evenly among bottom halves of rolls. Cover with tops and serve at once.

346   PEPPERED LEMON ROCK LOBSTER TAILS
Prep: 5 minutes   Cook: 7 to 10 minutes   Serves: 4

4 rock lobster tails, 4 to 6
   ounces each
¼ cup olive oil
2 tablespoons fresh lemon
   juice

½ teaspoon salt
1 tablespoon black
   peppercorns, crushed

1. Cut cartilage of lobster tails through length of center and press on sides to open slightly. Place lobsters, shell sides down, on a large broiling pan.

2. Preheat broiler. In a small bowl, combine olive oil, lemon juice, and salt. Drizzle evenly over lobster tails. Sprinkle equal amounts of cracked peppercorns over each.

3. Broil until shells are pink and lobster meat is lightly browned, 7 to 10 minutes.

347   LOBSTER THERMIDOR
Prep: 5 minutes   Cook: 8 to 13 minutes   Serves: 2

1 (1½- to 2-pound) boiled
   lobster
2 tablespoons butter
1 small onion, finely chopped
1 tablespoon flour
½ cup dry white wine
½ cup fish stock or bottled
   clam juice

1 tablespoon dry sherry
1 tablespoon heavy cream
¼ cup grated Parmesan cheese
¼ teaspoon salt
¼ teaspoon pepper
1 tablespoon chopped parsley

1. Cut lobster lengthwise in half, cutting completely through shell to make 2 pieces. Remove lobster meat from tail and claws and cut into 1-inch pieces. Scoop out shell, rinse well, drain, and reserve.

2. In a small saucepan, melt butter over medium heat. Add onion and cook, stirring often, until softened, 2 to 3 minutes. Add flour and blend well. Cook, stirring, 1 minute. Whisk in wine, fish stock, and sherry. Raise heat to medium-high and cook, stirring often, until thickened and smooth, 2 to 4 minutes. Add cream and half of Parmesan cheese. Remove from heat and add lobster pieces. Season with salt and pepper.

3. Preheat broiler. Fill lobster shells with lobster and sauce. Sprinkle remaining Parmesan cheese on top. Broil about 6 inches from heat until lightly browned, 3 to 5 minutes. Garnish with parsley and serve at once.

348 ARTICHOKE AND CRABMEAT CASSEROLE

Prep: 3 minutes   Cook: 25 minutes   Serves: 4

1 (14-ounce) can artichoke
  hearts, drained
1 pound fresh crabmeat or
  2 (6-ounce) cans, drained
3 or 4 medium mushrooms,
  thinly sliced
3 tablespoons butter

3 tablespoons flour
1 cup half-and-half
1 cup milk
2 tablespoons dry sherry
½ teaspoon salt
¼ teaspoon pepper
¼ cup grated Parmesan cheese

1. Preheat oven to 375°F. Cut artichokes into quarters and place in bottom of a buttered 1-quart casserole. Cover with crab and mushrooms. Set aside.

2. In a medium saucepan, melt butter over medium-high heat. Add flour and cook, stirring, 1 minute. Gradually whisk in half-and-half and milk. Bring to a boil, whisking constantly until thick and smooth. Stir in sherry. Season with salt and pepper.

3. Pour sauce over contents of casserole. Sprinkle Parmesan cheese over all. Bake until bubbly and lightly browned on top, about 20 minutes.

349 CRAB AU GRATIN

Prep: 3 minutes   Cook: 16 minutes   Serves: 4

Serve hot as a first course. If you have individual 6-ounce ramekins or small gratin dishes, divide the crab mixture among them and offer them as individual portions.

3 tablespoons butter
3 tablespoons flour
2 cups milk
½ cup shredded Swiss cheese
⅛ teaspoon grated nutmeg

¼ teaspoon salt
¼ teaspoon pepper
1 pound fresh crabmeat or
  2 (6-ounce) cans, drained
¼ cup grated Parmesan cheese

1. Preheat oven to 425°F.

2. In a small saucepan, melt butter over medium-high heat. Stir in flour to blend. Cook until foaming, about 1 minute. Pour in milk and bring to a boil, stirring constantly until thick and smooth. Remove from heat and add Swiss cheese, nutmeg, salt, and pepper. Stir until cheese has melted.

3. Place crab in a small gratin or baking dish. Spoon cheese sauce over crab and sprinkle Parmesan cheese on top. Bake until lightly browned on top and bubbly, about 10 minutes.

350 SPICY CRAB BOIL

Prep: 2 minutes   Cook: 5 minutes   Stand: 15 minutes   Serves: 4

Crab boils are messy eating. The best way to partake of such a feast is to eat outside on a picnic table covered with newspaper, preferably in the shade of a big tree. Otherwise, cover inside table with lots of newspaper and pretend you can feel the gentle breezes. Serve with garlic-flavored melted butter and lemon wedges, and provide diners with nutcrackers and picks.

2 teaspoons cayenne
6 garlic cloves, peeled and cut
   in half
4 sprigs of fresh thyme or
   1 teaspoon dried

3 bay leaves
Juice of 1 lemon
16 to 20 live blue crabs

1. In a large pot, bring 2 quarts (8 cups) of heavily salted water to a boil. Add cayenne, garlic, thyme, bay leaves, and lemon juice. Discard any crabs that show no sign of life. Add live crabs, cover, return to a boil, and boil for 5 minutes.

2. Remove from heat and let crabs sit in seasoned water for at least 15 minutes. Drain and serve warm or let come to room temperature, cover, and refrigerate until thoroughly chilled.

351 DEVILED CRAB

Prep: 5 minutes   Cook: 23 minutes   Serves: 4

4 tablespoons butter
½ green bell pepper, finely
   chopped
1 celery rib, finely chopped
¾ cup fresh bread crumbs
1 scallion (white part only),
   thinly sliced

1 teaspoon Dijon mustard
1 teaspoon Worcestershire
   sauce
½ teaspoon salt
¼ teaspoon cayenne
2 (6-ounce) cans crabmeat,
   drained, or 1 pound fresh

1. Preheat oven to 400°F. In a large skillet, melt 3 tablespoons butter over low heat. Add green pepper and celery and cook, stirring occasionally, until softened, about 3 minutes. Remove from heat and stir in bread crumbs, scallion, mustard, Worcestershire sauce, salt, and cayenne. Mix well to combine. Gently stir in crabmeat.

2. Divide mixture evenly among 4 cleaned crab shells or small ramekins. Dot with remaining butter and bake until cooked through and lightly browned on top, about 20 minutes.

352 SAUTÉED KING CRAB
Prep: 3 minutes   Cook: 4 to 6 minutes   Serves: 4

This is a recipe for lazy crab eaters who don't like to get their fingers messy. Count on 3½ pounds of king crab legs to yield about 1½ pounds of crabmeat. Serve with rice and grilled zucchini.

3½ pounds Alaskan king crab	1 tablespoon chopped parsley
4 tablespoons butter	¼ teaspoon salt
2 garlic cloves, minced	¼ teaspoon cayenne
½ cup dry white wine	Lemon or lime wedges

1. Remove crabmeat from shells. In a large skillet, melt butter over low heat. Add garlic and cook, stirring often, until soft and fragrant, about 1 minute. Add wine, parsley, salt, and cayenne. Raise heat to high and boil until reduced by half, 1 to 2 minutes.

2. Stir in crabmeat. Reduce heat to medium and cook, stirring occasionally, until warmed through, 2 to 3 minutes. Serve hot with lemon or lime wedges.

353 RAGTIME'S CRAB WONTONS
Prep: 15 minutes   Cook: 1 minute per batch   Serves: 8

Ragtime, a popular restaurant in Atlantic Beach, Florida, is known for excellent seafood and its buzzing atmosphere. A house favorite follows. Serve warm on a large platter with or without your favorite dipping sauce, such as the Chinese Dipping Sauce on page 164.

½ pound fresh crabmeat	½ teaspoon paprika
1 pound cream cheese, softened	¼ teaspoon cayenne
¼ teaspoon dried thyme	¼ teaspoon black pepper
1 teaspoon hot pepper sauce	¼ teaspoon garlic powder
2 teaspoons Worcestershire sauce	1 (8-ounce) package wonton wrappers
1 teaspoon white pepper	Vegetable oil, for deep-frying
½ teaspoon salt	

1. In a medium bowl, combine crabmeat, cream cheese, thyme, hot sauce, Worcestershire, white pepper, salt, paprika, cayenne, black pepper, and garlic powder. Stir to blend crab filling.

2. Working with 1 wonton at a time, lay wrapper flat on a large work surface. Place 1 teaspoon of crab mixture in center and fold one corner of wrapper diagonally over filling to meet opposite corner. Moisten edges with water and press down slightly to seal. Moisten two side corners with water and bring together in center, overlapping slightly. Press with fingertips to seal tightly. Place on a large baking sheet and cover with a damp cloth to prevent drying out. Continue until all wontons are filled.

3. In an electric skillet or deep fryer, pour in enough oil to measure 3 inches. Preheat oil to 350°F. Fry wontons 4 to 6 at a time, turning occasionally, until brown on both sides, about 1 minute. Remove with a slotted spoon and drain on paper towels. Serve hot.

---

354 KING CRAB FONDUE
Prep: 5 minutes   Cook: 8 to 10 minutes   Serves: 4

Alaskan king crab claws are perfect for fondue. Serve individual bowls of cracked claws for each guest to remove the crabmeat and dip it into the bubbling sauce.

3 tablespoons butter	3 tablespoons dry sherry
1 small onion, finely chopped	½ teaspoon salt
2 garlic cloves, minced	¼ teaspoon cayenne
1 cup heavy cream	2 pounds king crab legs,
1½ cups Swiss cheese, finely diced	cracked and warmed

1. In a large saucepan, melt butter over low heat. Add onion and garlic and cook, stirring frequently, until softened, about 2 minutes. Add cream, raise heat to medium, and cook until warmed through, 2 to 3 minutes. Do not boil.

2. Stir cheese into hot cream, a few pieces at a time, and cook, stirring constantly, until melted and smooth, 2 to 3 minutes. Add sherry, salt, and cayenne. Cook, stirring frequently, 2 minutes longer.

3. To serve, set a fondue pot or chafing dish in middle of table. Let each guest remove meat from crab legs with long forks and dip into hot fondue.

---

355 SOFT-SHELL CRABS MARINATED IN BUTTERMILK
Prep: 5 minutes   Marinate: 30 minutes   Cook: 6 minutes   Serves: 4

12 soft-shell crabs, cleaned	1 teaspoon salt
1½ cups buttermilk	½ teaspoon pepper
1 cup flour	½ teaspoon cayenne
1 tablespoon chopped fresh thyme leaves or 1 teaspoon dried	2 tablespoons butter
	2 tablespoons vegetable oil
	Lemon wedges

1. In a large bowl, marinate crabs in buttermilk for 30 minutes at room temperature or up to 2 hours covered and refrigerated. In a shallow bowl, combine flour, thyme, salt, pepper, and cayenne. Remove crabs from buttermilk, drain off excess, and dredge in seasoned flour to coat both sides lightly.

2. In a large skillet, melt butter with oil over medium-high heat. Add crabs and cook, turning once until lightly browned, about 3 minutes per side. Cook in 2 batches if necessary, using additional butter and oil if needed. Serve hot with lemon wedges.

356   BROILED SOFT-SHELL CRABS WITH TOMATOES AND WHITE BEANS

Prep: 5 minutes   Cook: 16 minutes   Serves: 4

6 tablespoons butter
2 tablespoons olive oil
1 medium onion, finely chopped
2 cloves garlic, minced
2 medium tomatoes, peeled, seeded, and finely chopped

2 cups cooked or canned white beans, drained
¾ teaspoon salt
¾ teaspoon pepper
3 tablespoons fresh lime juice
12 soft-shell crabs, cleaned

1. In a large skillet, melt 2 tablespoons butter with olive oil over medium heat. Add onion and garlic and cook, stirring occasionally, until softened, about 3 minutes. Raise heat to medium, add tomatoes, and cook, stirring frequently, until thick and pulpy, about 5 minutes. Stir in beans, ½ teaspoon salt, and ½ teaspoon pepper and cook until warmed through, about 2 minutes. Remove from heat and cover to keep warm.

2. Preheat broiler. In a small saucepan, melt remaining butter over low heat. Remove from heat and stir in lime juice and remaining ¼ teaspoon each salt and pepper. Place crabs on their backs on a broiling pan and brush lightly with some of butter mixture.

3. Broil crabs about 4 inches from heat until lightly browned, about 3 minutes. Turn, brush with remaining butter mixture, and broil until lightly browned, about 3 minutes longer.

4. Divide tomato and bean mixture evenly among 4 individual serving plates. Arrange crabs attractively on top of each and serve hot.

357   GARLICKY BROILED SOFT-SHELL CRABS

Prep: 3 minutes   Cook: 6 minutes   Serves: 4

12 soft-shell crabs, cleaned
½ teaspoon salt
¼ teaspoon pepper
1 stick (8 ounces) butter, melted

1 tablespoon fresh lemon juice
2 garlic cloves, crushed through a press
1 tablespoon chopped parsley

1. Preheat broiler. Place crabs on their backs on a broiling pan and season with salt and pepper.

2. In a small bowl, combine butter, lemon juice, garlic, and parsley. Stir well to blend. Brush crabs liberally with garlic butter. Broil about 4 inches from heat until golden brown on top, about 3 minutes. Turn crabs over, brush with remaining garlic butter, and continue broiling until nicely browned and cooked through, about 3 minutes longer. Serve hot.

358 SOFT-SHELL CRABS WITH LIME AND CILANTRO

Prep: 5 minutes   Cook: 6 minutes   Serves: 4

12 soft-shell crabs, cleaned	2 tablespoons butter
1 cup flour	2 tablespoons olive oil
½ teaspoon salt	3 tablespoons fresh lime juice
¼ teaspoon pepper	½ cup chopped fresh cilantro

1. Dry crabs thoroughly on paper towels. Place flour in a shallow bowl. Dredge crabs lightly in flour, place on a large platter, and season with salt and pepper.

2. In a large skillet, melt butter in oil over high heat. Add crabs and cook, turning once, until lightly browned, 3 minutes per side. (Do not overcrowd pan. Do in two batches if necessary, using additional butter and oil if needed.)

3. Squeeze lime juice to taste over cooked crabs and garnish with chopped cilantro. Serve hot.

359 NUTTY SOFT-SHELL CRABS

Prep: 5 minutes   Cook: 6 minutes   Serves: 4

Serve warm, drizzled with vinaigrette dressing and garnished with toasted sliced almonds.

1 cup sliced almonds	12 soft-shell crabs, cleaned
1 cup flour	1 cup milk
½ teaspoon salt	3 tablespoons butter
¼ teaspoon pepper	3 tablespoons vegetable oil
⅛ teaspoon cayenne	

1. Preheat oven to 325°F. Spread out almonds on a small baking sheet and bake, stirring once or twice, until lightly browned, about 5 minutes. Immediately transfer to a plate to cool.

2. In a food processor, combine toasted almonds, flour, salt, pepper, and cayenne. Process until almonds are finely ground, about 30 seconds. Place almond flour in a large bowl.

3. One at a time, dip half the crabs into milk, then dredge lightly in almond flour. In a large skillet, heat 1½ tablespoons each butter and oil over medium-high heat until hot but not smoking. Add coated crabs and cook, turning once, until golden brown, about 3 minutes per side. Drain on paper towels. Repeat with remaining ingredients. Serve at once.

360   CRISPY SAUTÉED SOFT-SHELL CRABS

Prep: 5 minutes   Cook: 6 minutes per batch   Serves: 4

1 cup flour
1 teaspoon salt
1 teaspoon pepper
1 teaspoon paprika

6 tablespoons butter
12 soft-shell crabs, cleaned
Lemon or lime wedges

1. In a shallow bowl, combine flour, salt, pepper, and paprika. Dry crabs thoroughly on paper towels and dredge lightly in seasoned flour.

2. In a large nonstick skillet, melt 3 tablespoons butter over medium-high heat, add half the crabs, and sauté until lightly browned, 3 minutes per side. Melt remaining butter and continue with remaining crabs. Serve hot with lemon or lime wedges.

361   OPEN-FACED CRAB SANDWICHES

Prep: 5 minutes   Cook: 2 to 3 minutes   Serves: 4

Great for brunch, lunch, or a light supper. Serve right out of the oven for best results.

1 pound fresh crabmeat
1 cup grated Swiss cheese
1 tablespoon minced chives
¼ cup mayonnaise
1 tablespoon lime juice
½ teaspoon salt

½ teaspoon pepper
2 to 3 dashes of hot pepper
   sauce
2 tablespoons butter, softened
4 English muffins, split in
   half

1. In a medium bowl, mix crabmeat with Swiss cheese and chives. Stir in mayonnaise, lime juice, salt, pepper, and hot sauce.

2. Preheat broiler. Butter English muffin halves and spread crab mixture evenly over each half. Place on a baking sheet or broiling pan and broil until lightly browned, 2 to 3 minutes. Serve hot.

362   CRAB-STUFFED ZUCCHINI
Prep: 5 minutes   Cook: 15 to 17 minutes   Serves: 4

4 zucchini, cut lengthwise in half
1 teaspoon salt
1 teaspoon pepper
2 (6-ounce) cans crabmeat, drained

¼ cup dried bread crumbs
¼ cup grated Parmesan cheese
4 tablespoons butter, melted

1. Preheat oven to 400°F. Use a small spoon to scrape out and discard pulp from zucchini halves, leaving a shell about ¼ inch thick. Season shells with ½ teaspoon each of salt and pepper. Fill zucchini halves with equal amounts of crabmeat and season with remaining salt and pepper.

2. In a small bowl, combine bread crumbs and Parmesan. Sprinkle about 1 tablespoon over each zucchini half. Drizzle with melted butter. Place on an oiled baking dish and bake until lightly browned, 15 to 17 minutes. Serve hot.

363   CRAWFISH ÉTOUFFÉE
Prep: 10 minutes   Cook: 11 to 13 minutes   Serves: 4

This Cajun specialty without lots of steaming hot rice is like New Orleans without Mardi Gras. Also offer garlic bread and a green salad.

1 pound peeled crawfish tails
½ teaspoon salt
½ teaspoon pepper
2 tablespoons butter
1 onion, finely chopped
2 garlic cloves, minced
1 celery rib, finely chopped
½ green bell pepper, finely chopped

2 tablespoons flour
2 medium tomatoes, peeled, seeded, and chopped
½ cup dry white wine, chicken broth, or water
2 tablespoons chopped parsley

1. Season crawfish tails with ¼ teaspoon each salt and pepper. Set aside.

2. In a heavy medium saucepan, melt butter over medium-high heat. Add onion, garlic, celery, and green pepper. Reduce heat to medium and cook, stirring occasionally, until softened, 3 to 5 minutes. Add crawfish tails and cook until firm, about 5 minutes.

3. Stir in flour to blend. Add tomatoes and wine, raise heat to high, and bring to a boil. Season with remaining ¼ teaspoon each salt and pepper. Cook, stirring occasionally, until thickened, about 3 minutes. Serve hot, garnished with chopped parsley.

364   CRAWFISH BOIL
Prep: 1 minute   Cook: 17 to 20 minutes   Serves: 4

Crawfish take well to heavy seasoning. Pile them in a large bowl and let guests peel their own. Serve with melted butter for dipping, along with boiled potatoes and tender ears of sweet corn.

8 pounds live crawfish
3 tablespoons salt
2 lemons, halved
1 onion, halved
2 garlic cloves, crushed

1 teaspoon mustard seeds
2 small dried hot red peppers
1 (3-ounce) box commercial
   crab boil seasoning

1. Place crawfish in a large bowl and cover with cold water. Rinse well and discard those that show no signs of life.

2. In a large stockpot or soup kettle, combine salt, lemons, onion, garlic, mustard seeds, hot peppers, and crab boil. Pour in 2 gallons (8 quarts) of water and bring to a boil over high heat. Boil rapidly for 10 minutes to develop flavors.

3. Add crawfish to pot, return to a boil, and cook until firm and bright red, 7 to 10 minutes. Drain and serve hot.

365   CRAWFISH SAUTÉ
Prep: 3 minutes   Cook: 7 minutes   Serves: 4

Serve over rice or hot buttered noodles with okra and stewed tomatoes.

1 pound crawfish tails,
   shelled and deveined
½ teaspoon salt
½ teaspoon pepper
4 tablespoons butter
2 scallions, thinly sliced

1 garlic clove, minced
⅛ teaspoon cayenne
Several drops of hot pepper
   sauce
½ cup dry white wine

1. Pat crawfish tails dry with paper towels. Season with ¼ teaspoon each salt and pepper. In a medium skillet, melt butter over medium-high heat. Add scallions and garlic and cook, stirring frequently, until just wilted, about 1 minute. Add crawfish tails and cook, stirring constantly, about 2 minutes. Season with remaining salt, pepper, cayenne, and hot sauce.

2. Pour in wine, raise heat to high, and cook, stirring constantly, until crawfish are firm and liquid is slightly reduced, about 4 minutes.

Index